THE OVERSTREET GUIDE TO COLLECTING MOVIE POSTERS

BY AMANDA SHERIFF
WITH ROBERT M. OVERSTREET

ERIC BRADLEY, ROB HUGHES,
LEONARD MALTIN, MICHAEL SOLOF
AND J.C. VAUGHN
CONTRIBUTING WRITERS

MARK HUESMAN
LAYOUT & DESIGN

MARK HUESMAN
AMANDA SHERIFF
J.C. VAUGHN
CARRIE WOOD
EDITORS

TOM GAREY, KATHY WEAVER, BRETT CANBY, ANGELA PHILLIPS-MILLS
ACCOUNTING SERVICES

SPECIAL THANKS TO
ALL POSTER FORUM, MIKE BOLLINGER, ERIC BRADLEY, CGC,
RALPH DELUCA, DIAMOND INTERNATIONAL GALLERIES, EMOVIEPOSTER.COM,
JOSH GEPPI, STEVE GEPPI, GEPPI'S ENTERTAINMENT MUSEUM,
HAKE'S AMERICANA & COLLECTIBLES, HERITAGE AUCTIONS,
BRUCE HERSHENSON, ROB HUGHES, TERENCE KEAN, DAVE LIEBERMAN,
LEONARD MALTIN, JEFF POTOKAR, ANDREW RAWLS, GREY SMITH,
MICHAEL SOLOF, CHARLIE STEVENS, PHIL WAGES,
ALEX WINTER AND PHIL WOOD

GEMSTONE PUBLISHING • TIMONIUM, MARYLAND
WWW.GEMSTONEPUB.COM

Iconic Moments and More

From *Casablanca* to *Vertigo*, from *Chinatown* to *Apocalypse Now*, from *Blade Runner* to *Scarface*, and from *Snow White* to *Frankenstein*, the best movie posters have almost always had the ability to project us into the world that the movie depicts before we actually see the film.

Sometimes they carve out brief, pivotal moments in the story, ones that compel us to see the movie or get us even more excited about a film we already planned to attend. At other times they capture more of the feeling or the tone of a movie rather than a specific element. And in yet other instances they focus on the stars or the characters...

Like so many great collectibles, there is no *one* answer about what makes movie posters iconic, but perhaps there is a way to describe their effect.

Writing on the Creative Bloq website in 2013, Cavan Scott said, "An iconic movie poster is one that has been burned onto the public consciousness, something that has become so recognizable that you feel that you've always known it. It should spring to mind as soon as you hear the film's name, be easily described and trigger excitement and intrigue, no matter how many times you see it."

Take a moment to consider the posters you love. Once we get beyond nostalgia – always a powerful force – it frequently boils down to the images that grab us and hold our attention, sometimes even if the film itself isn't all that good.

In this book, Amanda Sheriff and our team of contributors cover the basics, get insights from serious collectors and two premiere-level auctioneers, and shine the spotlight on some of the great artists in the field. They take a look at different ways to collect and some closely related collectibles, as well. It's a fun ride!

I hope you'll enjoy our effort.

Bob

Robert M. Overstreet
Publisher

GEMSTONE PUBLISHING

STEPHEN A. GEPPI
PRESIDENT AND
CHIEF EXECUTIVE OFFICER

ROBERT M. OVERSTREET
PUBLISHER

J.C. VAUGHN
VICE-PRESIDENT
OF PUBLISHING

MARK HUESMAN
CREATIVE DIRECTOR

AMANDA SHERIFF
ASSOCIATE EDITOR

CARRIE WOOD
ASSISTANT EDITOR

BRAELYNN BOWERSOX
STAFF WRITER

WWW.GEMSTONEPUB.COM

GEPPI'S ENTERTAINMENT MUSEUM

STEPHEN A. GEPPI
FOUNDER AND
CHIEF EXECUTIVE OFFICER

MELISSA BOWERSOX
PRESIDENT

WWW.GEPPISMUSEUM.COM

THE OVERSTREET GUIDE TO COLLECTING MOVIE POSTERS. OCTOBER 2015.
ISBN: 978-1-60360-183-2
PUBLISHED BY GEMSTONE PUBLISHING, INC., 1940 GREENSPRING DRIVE, SUITE I, TIMONIUM, MD 21093.

Coming Attractions

What Makes a Movie Poster Attractive?

Many key factors go into promoting movies. Trailer makers pore over footage to select the right clips that will embody the tone of the movie and offer just enough to tease the plot and entice audiences. Actors, directors, producers, and writers attend junkets and interviews to share on-set anecdotes, snippets of the story, and explain their motivations. And movie posters are framed in theaters, standees are displayed in lobbies, billboards are glued to signposts, and lobby cards are nestled in windows to advertise coming attractions.

By nature, movie posters are advertising material, designed to make consumers want that product. To entice audiences, they should be engaging and unique, while representing the storyline and the tone of the movie. Many factors that go into making a good movie poster are aesthetic, intrinsic, and sometimes incidental.

Artwork

Posters with beautiful artwork are always favored among collectors. Utilizing clever illusions to express the subject matter makes posters stand out. Vibrant colors, particularly those that aren't standard fare like the ones on the *Cimarron* one-sheet, draw attention. Unique fonts for the text of the title and the credits, such as *The Rocky Horror Picture Show*, can leave a lasting impression. Capturing the tone of the plot through how the actors are portrayed offers its own teaser for the movie. The mood of the film can be set through how much activity is represented on the poster. For a movie like *The Breakfast Club*, all that's needed is a collection of teenage stereotypes starring unwaveringly forward, whereas others are packed with film details, becoming their own storytellers.

Artistry is always a factor when it comes to movie posters. Some collectors will procure pieces based exclusively on who painted them. Popular artists establish fan followings for their brand of style, whether it's the minimalism of Robert McGinnis, the flamboyance of Bob Peak, or airbrushed realism of Drew Struzan. Even if collectors haven't seen the movie, they'll buy posters created by their favorite artists.

Art style has changed significantly over the last 30 years. Posters went from illustrated to predominately photo-based artwork in the mid-1980s because movie studios save money by using photos rather than hiring artists for the posters. This has left an artistic hole in many modern posters, as seen by the uniformity shared by posters of similar film genres.

However, creativity can still be found on photo-based posters. Studio designers can manipulate photographs of their stars to introduce artistic style and differentiate from bland contemporaries.

Rarity

It doesn't matter what type of collectible it is, if it's rare, it's favored. With movie posters, that predominately means vintage posters. Because movie posters were originally conceived singularly for advertising, they were often thrown in the trash after being displayed. During World War II many posters were recycled in paper drives to aid the war effort. Now, vintage posters that were initially collected by savvy pioneers of the hobby, or are being found in attics, old movie theater projection rooms, even stuffed in walls, are extremely valuable.

From the time of WWII through the 1980s, National Screen Service printed and distributed most movie posters. When they closed many of their warehouses in the '80s, millions of posters flooded the market, gaining new collectors. Since collecting became a mainstream hobby, newer posters are bet-

ter cared for after being displayed, and are therefore less valuable than the vintage ones. This means that rarer posters will bring the highest prices.

Film Popularity
No matter what the poster looks like, some will be favored with collectors because the movie is popular. There have been posters, both painted and photographic, that have bland art or graphics that simply missed the mark on accurately representing the film, but will still sell because of the movie itself. It can simply be a portrait of an action star, a painting that completely missed the point of the movie, or a couple holding each other close, and they will sell.

Actor, Actress, and Director
Similar to collectors who favor posters based on the artist, some procure posters for the director or stars. Popular directors that are collected include Alfred Hitchcock, Howard Hawks, Billy Wilder, and contemporaries like Steven Spielberg and Quentin Tarantino, among many others. For the star power, it's hard to beat Marilyn Monroe, Elvis Presley,

Cary Grant, Rita Hayworth, John Wayne, and Greta Garbo. As with the films themselves, the attractiveness of the stars on the poster can enhance popularity, so artwork featuring this batch – and several others – have won the hearts of many collectors.

Controversy
There are posters that are collectible for their controversial points. In some cases, posters are recalled or withdrawn. The *Pulp Fiction* Lucky Strike poster is a prime example. In the original one-sheet, a pack of Lucky Strike cigarettes is on the bed next to Mia. But because Miramax had not received permission to use the Lucky Strike logo, the cigarettes' producer, R.J. Reynolds, threatened to sue. The posters were ordered withdrawn, but several remain intact and have become favored among collectors. Another somewhat controversial example is the *Spider-Man* poster in which the Twin Towers reflect in the eyes of his mask. The posters were distributed before the 9/11 tragedy, and the studio requested that these posters be taken down after the events of that day.

Some posters draw controversy due to the death of someone involved in the film. The poster for *Enter the Dragon* is popular because it premiered just days after Bruce Lee's death. Sadly, *The Crow* poster is popular because its star, Brandon Lee – Bruce Lee's son – died on set after a gun misfired. *The Imaginarium of Doctor Parnassus* poster is often collected because Heath Ledger was in the middle of filming it when he died. A disturbing recent example is the *Deadline* poster which was released

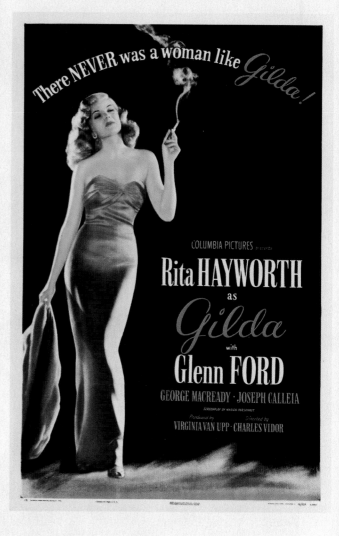

after Brittany Murphy had died, featuring the actress in a bathtub, eyes glazed over, appearing to be dead.

Controversy can also occur due to the nature of the art displayed. *The Outlaw* poster depicting ample amounts of Jane Russell's cleavage caused quite a scandal in 1943. The United Kingdom's first poster for 2011's *The Girl with the Dragon Tattoo* shocked some viewers by picturing the top-less form of Rooney Mara. Dozens of other posters that have shown nudity fall into this category, as well as horror and action film posters displaying graphic violence.

Country of Origin
Posters that originate from other coun-

tries where the movie was filmed are also popular. For instance, collectors of James Bond posters prefer the British versions vs the ones from the U.S. The same is true for Godzilla collectors, who prefer the Japanese posters over examples from the U.S.

Many factors determine what makes a movie poster attractive. In many cases those factors appeal to a wide swath of collectors because they find the art appealing or for the opportunity to own a rare piece. But sometimes they appeal to a small group of people who connect to the poster based on their personalities. Regardless of the reason, collectors can always find posters that will give them a happy ending.

MOVIE POSTER MARKET OVERVIEW

A *NEW* Walt Disney MICKEY MOUSE

UNITED ARTISTS PICTURE

The market for collecting movie posters and related art is currently thriving. Despite the dramatic downturn, improvement and subsequent ebbs and flows of the economy as a whole, movie poster collecting remained stable and has become increasingly stronger.

One of the greatest aspects of movie poster collecting remains its accessibility; anyone can do it. It doesn't matter which tax bracket you fall into or how much is in your take home pay. Original movie posters can be bought for $1 all the way up to hundreds of thousands. Great deals and record breaking sales can be made at every collecting level.

That doesn't mean that there aren't some seriously pricey posters out there. There are. Incredible prices for movie posters have been realized over the past decade. In 2013 eMoviePoster set a new auction record for a Harry Houdini poster when *The Grim Game* one-sheet sold for $67,166. Heritage Auctions made headlines in 2014 when they sold the only known copy of the U.S. release one-sheet for *London After Midnight* for $478,000.

The rare international version of the *Metropolis* poster from 1927 surprised the hobby twice in the

last decade. First, in 2005 when it sold for $690,000, gaining the world record for the sale of a single poster. Then in 2012, it was bundled with posters from *King Kong*, *The Invisible Man*, and *Arsenic and Old Lace*, along with the original painting of Elvis Presley for the *Jailhouse Rock* poster and sold for $1.2 million.

Posters from the days of silent film, very early Disney, and early Universal

Monsters can all garner six-figure sales, as well as many one-, three-, and six-sheets from before World War II. Inserts, lobby cards, window cards, and half-sheets from that period easily reach tens of thousands. Disney and Universal posters from the 1930s to 1950s also reach beyond the ten thousand mark.

From the 1940s to 1960s, such iconic titles like *Citizen Kane*, *La Dolce Vita*,

Breakfast At Tiffany's, *Vertigo*, and *Rebel Without a Cause* can sell for $10,000 or more. Similarly, subgenres like film noir, westerns, and musicals, comedy groups Three Stooges and Laurel and Hardy, as well as directors Howard Hawks and Billy Wilder can reach that level.

The $1,000 mark is regularly hit by posters for movies starring Cary Grant, Marilyn Monroe, and other popular stars from the 1950s and '60s. Posters by artists like Robert McGinnis and Saul Bass can sell for hundreds to thousands, particularly for their work on James Bond and Alfred Hitchcock movies.

Collectors can spend hundreds of dollars on a very wide variety of posters. They can range in age from the 1950s to modern, depending on condition and popularity of the movies. *Star Wars* posters are safe bets in this group, as are buzz-worthy releases like *Raiders of the Lost Ark* or *Titanic*. Great teasers, such as *Avatar* and *Ghostbusters* can sell beyond the regular one-sheets. Hot ticket items like recalled or banned posters insight bidding wars for the often rare pieces.

The market is flooded when it comes to purchasing posters for under one hundred dollars. Just about anything from the past 20 years sells for that amount, along with plenty from the '70s and '80s.

Anyone can build a collection of movie posters on whatever budget is available. Whether they are popular titles, sought after examples, or simply personal favorites the field is wide open. Some collect because they love movies, some because they just like the art, and others see it as a safe investment for the future. Whatever the reason, whatever the budget, fans can build a blockbuster collection.

Movie Magic: Collecting Disney

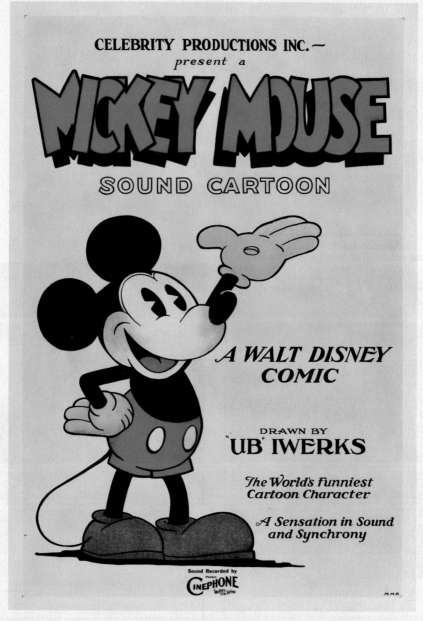

The Mickey Mouse stock poster, released in 1928, shows a very simple image of Mickey waving happily from the poster, boasting that it is a Walt Disney Comic, drawn by Ub Iwerks. It recently sold for $101,575

For almost 90 years Disney has been entertaining audiences with magical, enchanting stories. Animated, live-action, or a combination of the two, it doesn't matter. Disney's incredible stories, filled with funny follies, romance, adventure, and morality, have left fans enraptured. Once that familiar castle appears, that calligraphy text unfurls, and those melodious tones chime, audiences trust a spark of imagination will emerge.

The empire known as Disney began with an artist in Illinois. Not long after Walter "Walt" Disney was born on December 5, 1901 in the Hermosa section of Chicago, he began drawing and painting, and was soon selling pictures to neighbors and family friends. An ambitious artist from the start, he took drawing and photography classes and drew cartoons for the school paper at McKinley High School in Chicago while also taking night classes at the Chicago Art Institute. Disney dropped out of school when he was 16 years old to join the army during World War I, but was rejected for being underage. Insistent on doing something for the war effort, he joined the Red Cross and was sent to France to drive ambulances for a year.

After returning to the U.S. in 1919, he moved to Kansas City to become a newspaper artist. His brother Roy set him up with a job at the Pesmen-Rubin Art Studio, where he met cartoonist Ubbe Eert Iwerks, better known as Ub Iwerks. Disney then worked at the Kansas City Film Ad Company making advertisements based on cutout animation. He started experimenting with camera tricks making hand-drawn cel animation and decided to start his own animation business. He hired Fred Harman as his first employee and the first cartoons they screened at a Kansas City theater, *Laugh-O-Grams*, were huge hits.

This new found success afforded Disney the opportunity to open his own studio. Named after the cartoons, Laugh-O-Gram hired several employees and created a series of seven-minute fairy tales. However, studio profits couldn't cover the salaries and financial responsibilities, so by 1923 Laugh-O-Gram was dealing with significant debt and Disney had to declare bankruptcy.

Unwilling to give up on their dream, Disney, his brother Roy, and Iwerks moved to Hollywood, began Disney Brothers' Studio, and invented Oswald the Lucky Rabbit. Unfortunately, deal making left the Oswald trademark with producer Charles Mintz and Universal Pictures. Disagreements led to Disney Brothers' Studio losing the character, as well as all of their animators except Iwerks. A few years later Walt, Roy, Ub, and their wives produced three cartoons featuring Disney's new character, who would become the most famous cartoon in history. Mickey Mouse debuted in the silent films *Plane Crazy* and *The Gallopin' Gaucho*, which were not widely distributed. In 1928, *Steamboat Willie*, the first animated short with sound and music with Disney voicing Mickey, was released and became an immense success.

The milestones started coming fast and furious over the next few years. In 1929, Disney created *Silly Symphonies*, featuring other soon to be iconic characters Minnie Mouse, Donald Duck, Goofy, and Pluto. In 1932 Disney produced *Flowers and Trees*, the first cartoon in 3-strip Technicolor, which won an Oscar for Best Short Subject, Cartoons. These were followed by dazzling turns in *The Wayward Canary*, *The Mad Doctor*, and *Ye Olden Days*,

The Wayward Canary depicts an energetic image of Mickey playing a flute and Minnie singing and playing the piano while the canary soars above them. The one-sheet can sell for $26,290-$43,700.

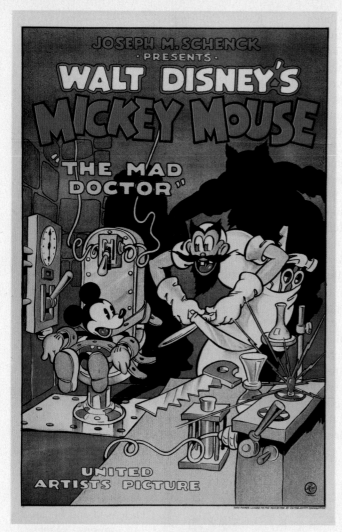

The Mickey Mouse **"The Mad Doctor"** one-sheet bears a more complex image of Mickey strapped to a chair while the Mad Doctor stands menacingly by his table filled with glossy, sharp images. In recent years the poster sold for $107,550-$138,000.

among others. Then, the hot tempered Donald Duck made his first appearance in *The Wise Little Hen* in 1934. Three years later in December 1937 Disney released *Snow White and the Seven Dwarfs*, the first full-length film. Even though the country was in the depths of the Depression, audiences fell in love with tale of magic and romance. *Snow White* made a staggering $8 million in theaters and won eight Oscars.

Walt Disney Studios opened a new location in Burbank, California in December 1939, following *Snow White* with two Disney classics in 1940. *Pinocchio*, about a sweet puppet who wants to become a real boy, was released early in the year, and *Fantasia*, an evolutionary tale filled with classical music and captivating animation was released a few months later. The following year *Dumbo*, the elephant with the flapping ears, flew into our hearts.

In 1942 audiences fell in love with *Bambi* a heartbreak-

The one-sheet for **Ye Olden Days** is delightfully colorful, in shades of green, yellow, and blue, with Mickey serenading Minnie in a tower with a grand castle in the background. The one-sheet can sell for $57,500-$59,750.

Dumbo had several successful posters. The style A one-sheet shows several of the characters in a parade around the poster with Dumbo's name written in circus type over a solid yellow background. The style B one-sheet features a circus of activity with Dumbo and Timothy, the crows, and the train with Dumbo's name in large, red text. The first post-war Italian 2-foglio shows Dumbo soaring enthusiastically between the parted curtains of the show, over the ring master. The three-sheet can sell for $3,585-$19,800, first post-war Italian 2-foglio for $14,340, style B for $3,680-$8,365, and style A for $3,910-$8,050.

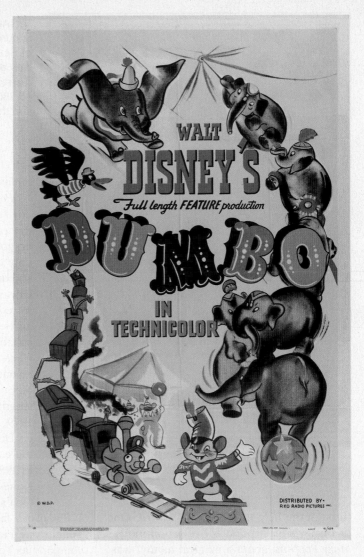

ing story about a fawn who must make his way in the world after his mother is shot by a hunter. During the mid-1940s Disney started creating packaged features with groups of short films that ran together as feature length.

By 1950 Disney started focusing back on full-length movies. They began with *Treasure Island*, their first fully live-action movie, based on the adventure novel by Robert Louis Stevenson. *Cinderella*, a quintessential Disney princess story about a girl treated poorly by her step-family who is granted a Fairy Godmother, meets a prince, and falls in love, was also released that year.

The next two big hits were both animated films adapted from contemporary literature. First, the wacky, fantastical *Alice in Wonderland* about a normal girl plunged into a peculiar world, based on the book by Lewis Carroll, came out in 1951; *Peter Pan*, about a mischievous boy who refuses to grow up, based on the play by J.M. Barrie, came out in 1953. A year later the early live-action hit *20,000 Leagues Under the Sea* was released, presenting an underwater adventure with a frightening sea monster.

Lady and the Tramp arrived in 1955, telling a romantic tale about two dogs that depicted the now iconic spaghetti sharing scene. In 1957 they released another dog-centered story with *Old Yeller*, a live-action film that presented the emotional timeline involved in loving a pet.

Disney ended the 1950s with *Sleepy Beauty*, a Brother's Grimm adaptation about a girl who falls into an enchanted slumber and must be saved by the kiss of a young prince.

Film production reached a fevered pitch in the 1960s. One of the earliest hits of the decade was *Swiss Family Robinson*, a live-action shipwreck story about a resourceful family adjusting to life on a deserted island. In 1961's *101 Dalmatians*, it's a dog's world, but the barbaric Cruella De Vil wants to turn the sweet dogs into coats.

Two years later *The Sword in the Stone* told the story of a young Arthur destined to become the fabled King of Camelot

The **Alice in Wonderland** one-sheet features Alice, the Mad Hatter, Queen of Hearts, and others sitting chaotically around a table for tea. Recently the six-sheet has sold for $1,550-$5,380, one-sheet for $540-$2,870, and three-sheet for $770-$1,075.

outlaws find gold.

Pete's Dragon, about an abused boy who tries to escape his adoptive parents with the help of a dragon, was released in 1977. Not only did it combine live-action and animation, it was also the first Disney movie to use the Dolby stereo process. One of the final movies of the decade featured a collaboration of the talents of Jim Henson with the imagination and resources of Disney. Henson's Muppets starred in their first full-length movie, *The Muppet Movie*, in 1979.

Disney took some gambles in the early '80s. First with *TRON* in 1982, the science fiction video game-inspired movie was high-tech special effects heavy. In early 1983 Disney launched the studio label Touchstone Pictures. It was a gamble for the company as Touchstone would release movies of out of Disney's typically G-rated fare.

In 1985, Disney released *Return to Oz*, sending Dorothy back to Oz in a movie inspired by L. Frank Baum's books. Also that year, *The Black Cauldron*, about a boy and his band of misfits who must fight the evil Horned King who seeks to rule the galaxy, was the first of Disney's animated movies to get the PG rating. In 1988, *Oliver and Company* told Charles Dickens' *Oliver Twist* with a twist of its own, starring adorable and scruffy cats and dogs. This was followed by Rick Moranis leading the wacky family comedy *Honey, I Shrunk the Kids*.

Following the release of *Robin Hood* through the next decade and a half, while they enjoyed some successes, there were many who pronounced the glory days of Disney animation as dead. In 1989, *The Little Mermaid* changed that when it took us under the sea with innovative animation

through the help of Merlin the wizard. One of Disney's most popular live-action movies, *Mary Poppins*, about a magical nanny, was released in 1964.

The innovative visionary Walt Disney was diagnosed with lung cancer in 1966. He died on December 15, 1966, but his empire continued to flourish, starting with *The Jungle Book*, about a little boy living with the animals in the jungle, released in 1967. A year later audiences were introduced to a Volkswagen Beetle with a mind of its own in *The Love Bug*.

The AristoCats, about three kittens who are bequeathed the estate of a famous opera singer, was released in 1970. It was the last Disney movie greenlit by Walt Disney prior to his death. Two more stories of poverty and wealth followed in 1973 and 1975. First was the timeless tale of robbing from the rich to give to the poor, this time by a clever fox in *Robin Hood*; then, *The Apple Dumpling Gang*, a family fun-filled movie about a group of kids trying to help inept

The one-sheet for **Robin Hood** depicts Robin Hood, Little John, and Friar Tuck hiding in a tree over greedy Prince John and the dastardly Sheriff of Nottingham. Disney also released door panels of Robin, Little John, the Sheriff, and Prince John. The door panels can sell for $40-$510, one-sheet for $10-$175, and Robin Hood wanted poster for $10-$100.

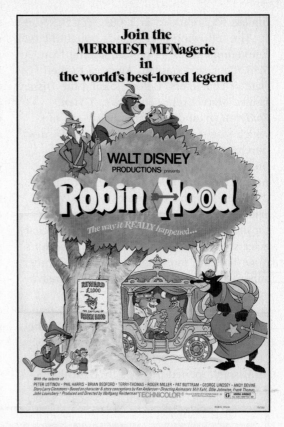

below the ocean's surface. The film rejuvenated the animated Disney magic and led to a string of very successful animated features, and it can at least be suggested that it played a major role in changing the studios' fortunes.

Beauty and the Beast was released in 1991, and became the first animated feature-length film to be nominated for the Academy Award for Best Picture. Disney took a bite out of Halloween in 1993 by working with Tim Burton to combine his style of fright with their fanciful adventures to make *The Nightmare Before Christmas*. *The Lion King* was released a year later featuring a grand scale opening sequence that captivated audiences of all ages and a story reminiscent of Shakespeare's *Hamlet*.

Toy Story was released in 1995 and has the distinction of being the first full-length computer animated movie and first full-length collaboration between Disney and Pixar (many Pixar animators were influenced by the storytelling in Disney classics). Boasting the voice acting of Tom Hanks and Tim Allen, the movie was very successful, producing two sequels, and an endless well of prospects for toys, clothing, and collectibles.

The same era saw many popular live-action hits as well. First was the slapstick comedy *The Mighty Ducks* featuring Emilio Estevez coaching a ragtag kids hockey team. In 1993 Disney released the future cult hit *Hocus Pocus*, about a trio of witches brought back to life. The next year they turned to Christmas with the first of three movies starring Tim Allen in *The Santa Clause*.

The late '90s were filled with sequels to *The Mighty Ducks*, *Angles in the Outfield*, *Air Bud*, and *The Lion King*, as well as remakes and adaptations of *Flubber*, *Rocket Man*, *George of the Jungle*, and *101 Dalmatians*. The company also added their first non-white Disney princesses in the '90s with Jasmine, the daughter of a Sultan in

Aladdin; *Pocahontas*, a Native American who interacted with European settlers, and *Mulan* a legendary Chinese warrior.

Disney started the 2000s by striking an historic chord with *Remember the Titans*. Based on the real story of an amazing 1971 season, the movie followed a high school football team while they dealt with racial tensions after schools were integrated.

The creatures under the bed became the protagonists in the 2001 movie *Monsters, Inc.* Then attitude and destruction infiltrated the PG-rated animated *Lilo & Stitch* in 2002 with an alien and his little girl best friend wreaking havoc on Hawaii.

In 2003 a Disney theme park ride became a highly successful movie starring Johnny Depp in *Pirates of the Caribbean: The Curse of the Black Pearl*. Two years later Disney hoped to tap into the success of the burgeoning young adult adventure subgenre with *Chronicles of Narnia: The Lion, the Witch, and the Wardrobe*, a big budget live-action movie based on the C.S. Lewis book.

In 2006 Disney acquired Pixar Animation Studios for $7.4 billion and celebrated by making the fast moving *Cars*. *Wall-E*, a cute love story between two robots that also told a cautionary tale of consumption and wastefulness was released in 2008.

The following year Disney bought Marvel Entertainment for $4 billion, adding Iron Man, Thor, and Captain America to their slate of characters. Before joining the Disney family, Marvel released *Blade*, *X-Men*, *Spider-Man*, and *Fantastic Four* – all of which saw successful sequels. After Disney purchased Marvel Entertainment, they produced movies based on Thor, Captain America, and Iron Man plus team films for the Avengers and Guardians of the Galaxy. The Marvel Cinematic Universe has plans for more sequels, team-ups, and single character stories for the next five years. *Editor's Note:* To learn more about Marvel and other superhero movies read our comprehensive coverage in this book.

In 2009 Disney made *The Princess and the Frog*, updating a classic tale and setting it in the vibrant, blues-infused world of New Orleans.

Disney opened the '00s by returning to *TRON* in 2010 for *TRON: Legacy* featuring cutting edge special effects and an electronic soundtrack composed by Daft Punk.

In 2012 Disney bought Lucasfilm, adding the *Star Wars* franchise to their immense collection of characters and properties. (*Editor's Note:* To read more about *Star Wars*, check out our comprehensive coverage article on the film franchise in this book.) Also that year *Wreck-It-Ralph* did for video game characters what *Toy Story* did for toys by telling the story of what happens after the arcade closes for the night and the game characters roam around.

Another hit from 2012 was *Brave*, which turned a Disney princess into the hero of the movie rather than a damsel. Then in 2013, *Frozen*, loosely adapted from a Hans Christian Andersen story, enchanted audiences with a story of sisters, one with icy powers, a rescue mission in the snow, the value of loyalty, and the fun to be had with a talking snowman. Despite its title, *Frozen* was a hot ticket at the box office, becoming the highest grossing animated film of all time and won Oscars for Best Animated film and Best Achievement in Music for "Let It Go." The summer of 2015 saw the release of *Inside Out*, a story that turns emotions into real characters inside a little girl.

Star Wars: Episode VII – The Force Awakens is on the horizon for December 2015 and is expected to break box office records. Between original characters, fairy tale adaptations, Pixar, Marvel, and Star Wars, there is no end in sight for the wonderful world of Disney.

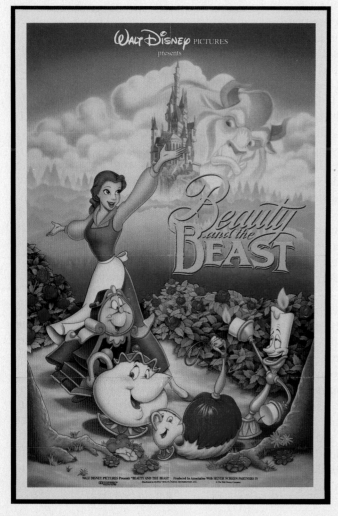

The whimsical **Beauty and the Beast** one-sheet shows Belle dancing with the bewitched staff of Beast while he peers grumpily from the clouds. The advance is a simple, romantic poster depicting the title characters dancing in the center, surrounded by glowing yellow light that radiates into shades of orange, red, and deep purple like a candle flame in a dark room. The one-sheet can sell for $25-$190 and the advance one-sheet for $15-$125.

The **Lilo & Stitch** advance poster came in lenticular 3-D, Stitch collared, or Stitch wearing his alien outfit. The top and sides of the poster are filled with Disney characters, both classic and new, looking frightened or appalled at Stitch who sits in the center. The lenticular 3-D advance can sell for $20-$335 and advance collar or alien clothes-style for $20-$70.

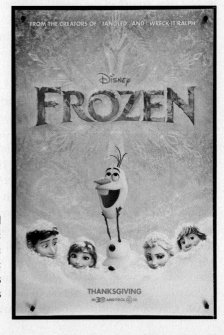

The **Frozen** advance one-sheet depicts the four lead human characters up to their chins in snow while Olaf, the snowman, stretches his head upward to the snowflake covered top portion of the poster. The snowflake advance poster is a gorgeously rendered snowflake in rich shades of blue and shimmering white. The snowman advance has sold for $30-$60 and snowflake advance for $15-$40.

JACK DAVIS

CARICATURIST TO THE STARS

Jack Davis is one of the most pro-lific, well recognized artists of our time. His work has been an integral part of the American pop culture landscape through a career that spans eight decades. The cartoonist and illustrator has a dynamic body of work in *MAD* magazine, advertising art, magazine covers, album covers, comics, and movie posters.

Born in Atlanta, Georgia in 1924, Davis took an early interest in cartoons. He read the Sunday comics voraciously and spent plenty of time trying to copy the art he found on newsprint. While his family listened to comedic radio shows like *The Jack Benny Program* and *Lum and Abner*, Davis would listen to the comedic routines and draw Mickey Mouse cartoons trying to produce something funny out of still drawings. His interest in comics was nurtured by the work of Hal Foster, who had been drawing *Tarzan* strips. Already successfully honing his sense of humor, Davis was published for the first time in

Tip Top Comics #9 in 1936, after he submitted a four-panel cartoon to the reader's page. Around that time he also had cartoons published in Georgia Tech's humor magazine *The Yellow Jacket*. He was just 12 years old at the time.

After serving in the Navy, he attended the University of Georgia where his career began to take off. He simultaneously drew for the campus newspaper, *The Red and Black*, and helped launch *The Bull Sheet*, an off-campus humor magazine filled with cartoons and risqué jokes. He served as a cartoonist intern at *The Atlanta Journal-Constitution* and during one summer he inked Ed Dodd's *Mark Trail* comic strip which he parodied later in *MAD* as Mark Trade. Through Dodd's encouragement, Davis continued studying at the Art Student's League in New York and worked on the *Herald Tribune* as an inker on *The Saint* comic strip.

Davis started freelancing for EC Comics in 1950 on their iconic titles *Tales from the Crypt, The Haunt of Fear, Two-Fisted Tales, The Vault of Horror, Crime SuspenStories, Shock SuspenStories,* and *Terror Illustrated.* He was well known for the way he depicted the Crypt Keeper, evolving the character from the simplistic version by Al Feldstein to a craggy, decrepit man with lank hair and warts. Davis also worked on Harvey Kurtzman's war comics, creating covers for *Two-Fisted Tales, Frontline Combat,* and *Incredible Science Fiction.* The style of scratchy lines and multi-layered layouts that Davis perfected, developed a following in the '50s with artists from rival companies attempting to copy his style.

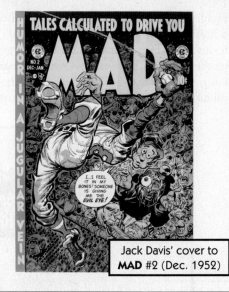

His comically exaggerated characters made him a perfect choice to be one of the founding cartoonists for *MAD* Magazine in 1952. It presented the opportunity to spoof some of the more grotesque imagery he had worked on at EC. Davis started spoofing sports figures and stars of Westerns as one of the early pop culture satirists. His work was featured in the first 30 issues of *MAD,* which led to his work on covers for albums, books, and *Time* and *TV Guide,* as well as movie posters. In 1961 he wrote, drew, and edited *Yak Yak* his own book for Dell Comics. He returned to *MAD* in the mid-1960s and his work appeared in almost every issue for decades.

In 1963 he was commissioned to create the movie poster art for the screwball comedy *It's a Mad, Mad, Mad, Mad World.* When he asked for a synopsis of the film he was urged to just go see it for himself. After watching the movie he was given the freedom to put everything

The style A one-sheet for **It's a Mad, Mad, Mad, Mad World** shows the globe over run by greedy, grabby people reaching for the elusive sack of money. In addition to the global chaos, the three-sheet also lists the impressive group of actors who vie for the money in this zany comedy. In recent years the one-sheet has sold for $30-$340 and the three-sheet for $80-$450.

imaginable into the art. The poster shows a litany of characters fighting like buffoons, climbing over one another to get to the case full of money. Over 50 years later, when the Criterion Collection made plans to release the movie on DVD and Blu-ray, he was sought to provide artwork for the accompanying booklet. The successful completion of the poster proved a turning point in his career.

His work on the Western comedy *Viva Max!* and war comedy *Kelly's Heroes* were

The Party style B poster embodies the momentum of a good party with a view of the event from the wide open doors as the focal point, while the top and bottom is blank space. Your eyes zoom in on the pink-hued fun with music, dancing, drinks, and other excitement-induced shenanigans. In recent years the three-sheet has sold for $70-$900, six-sheet for $115-$720, insert for $380, and one-sheet $25-$305.

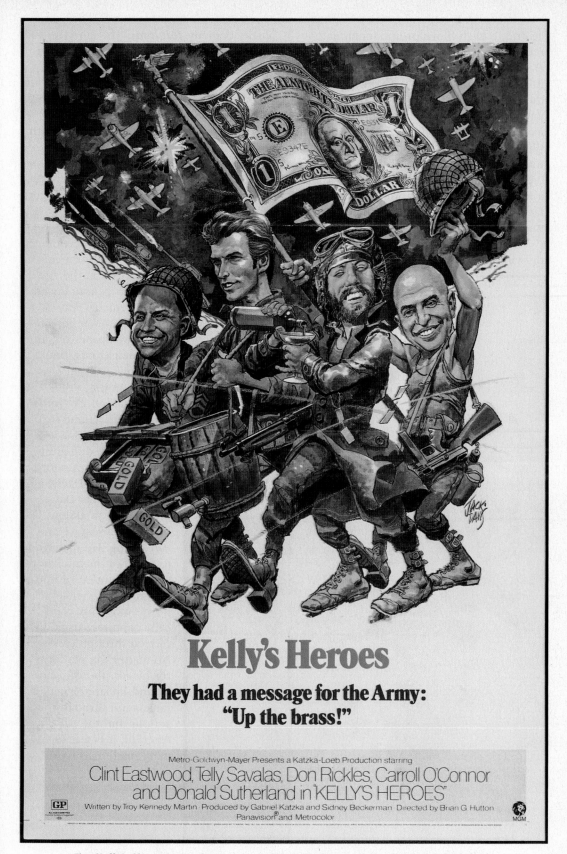

The **Kelly's Heroes** one-sheet style A shows Crapgame, Kelly, Oddball, and Big Joe front and center carrying gold and waving a dollar bill flag. Above them golden colored planes fly across the blue-black night sky while the foursome are all smiling, comically dancing with their loot. The one-sheet style A can sell for $35-$415.

central to each film's promotional material. The poster he produced for *Kelly's Heroes* was particularly impressive during this time period. Davis' artwork portrays the four lead characters in a cheesy grin parade carrying bundles of gold and a flag made from the one dollar bill. At this time Clint Eastwood had already developed an intimidating reputation for the hardened men he often played. For Davis to capture a look of silly-stupid happiness on the face of the man who usually glared from under a cowboy hat was comedic genius.

A year later he followed that up by drawing the poster for Woody Allen's plucky comedy *Bananas*. The story about a man who travels to a small Latin American country after his activist girlfriend breaks up with him and then becomes involved in a rebellion was, truly, bananas. Davis effectively captured the many facets of the film on the poster with protagonist Fielding Mellish, front and center.

Another of his beloved, and imitated, poster designs was for the Walter Matthau comedy *The Bad News Bears*. His work on this poster fit the tone of the movie perfectly, showing the team as a collection of preteen miscreants with a slob for a coach.

In 2014, at the age of 90, Davis announced his retirement. For almost 80 years he entertained everyone in comics to magazines, books, and movies. From fans of EC Comics to the *MAD* readers, *TV Guide* subscribers, comic strip collectors, and movie buffs, it'd be difficult to find a home in America without art by Davis.

The posters Davis drew were an assemblage of caricature and cartooning. He managed to focus on main characters surrounded by supporting characters and movie moments comically captured, usually filtered through chaos. No matter the platform for his art, the cartoonist and illustrator makes fans laugh through the serious and the silly. After all, it is a mad, mad, mad, mad world out there.

On the **Bananas** poster, Fielding Mellish is proudly holding up a gun and a banana with a slightly surprised, bemused look on his face with Nancy and Yolanda cheering him on. The background depicts a scene of chaos with fighting, chasing, yelling, and general insanity. The one-sheet sells for $10-$100.

The Long Goodbye style C presents a very different look at Philip Marlowe in a more amusing appearance as compared to other posters that feature him squinting menacingly with a gun in his hand. Davis' version has Marlowe eating a tin of Kat Phood, surrounded by the cast and crew. Word bubbles fill the top of the poster with amusing quips about who's who on the poster. The style C 30" x 40" can sell for $90-$220 and the one-sheet for $25-$140.

On **The Bad News Bears** poster, cartoonized versions of Walter Matthau and Tatum O'Neal are front and center, leaning on a broken team sign. The rest of the rag tag team surrounds them wearing their hats at odd angles, swinging bats, eating chicken, catching butterflies, and generally practicing ruffian behavior. In recent years the one-sheet has sold for $10-$150.

Mesmerized by the Movies: The Poster Collecting Journey

By Leonard Maltin

I trace my love of movie posters to my childhood, when I used to linger outside the theaters I attended every weekend in New Jersey. In those days, exhibitors displayed not only one-sheets but lobby cards and black and white stills in their showcases and inner lobbies. I should point out—though it makes me sound like a relic from the Stone Age—that this was back when most neighborhood theaters were located on main streets and not inside shopping malls. I would stand and stare at the images on the way in to see a double feature and on the way out, as well. Sometimes I'd even notice that a scene depicted in one of the stills or lobby cards didn't wind up in the movie!

When I was 12, I became aware that there were fanzines aimed at movie buffs, and from them I learned that it was possible to buy stills and posters. I was mainly attracted to stills and I started collecting them, partly because they were affordable: 25¢ to 50¢ each.

In time, I learned about a great mail-order outlet called Movie Poster Service in Canton, Oklahoma, that had a huge inventory. When I became a regular customer they would send me material on approval, which meant I only paid for the items I decided to purchase and returned the rest. Postage was cheap in those days.

I only bought a handful of posters, while amassing hundreds of stills. If I'd had foresight I could have built a world class collection of one-, three-, or six-sheets for a song. I wish I had!

When I was starting out, I collected purposefully: I loved cartoons and shorts, and set out to find one-sheets for each of the series I cared about. Thanks to that outlet in Oklahoma, I wound up with great posters for Looney Tunes, MGM cartoons, Robert Benchley one-reelers, Three Stooges comedies, and many others, for just $1.75 apiece. When I wrote a book about comedy teams, I decided it would be fun to have at least one poster for each of them.

When I got married, my wife Alice encouraged me to seek out one-sheets for films we both liked—and to pay considerably more than I'd been willing to shell out up to that time. (The market had expanded during the interim, so I didn't have much choice.) I remember the first time I laid out a hundred dollars for a

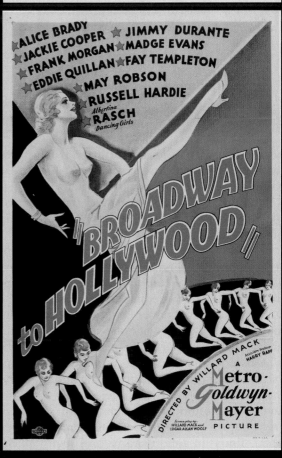

poster; that was a big deal to me. I paid twice that for a surprise birthday gift for Alice: a one-sheet of her favorite actor, Ronald Colman, in *The Man Who Broke the Bank at Monte Carlo*. It's still one of our favorites.

A good friend who built a connoisseur's collection on a schoolteacher's salary counseled me about trading, and trading up. His advice helped me acquire some pieces that I never could have gotten for cash, like a lovely one-sheet featuring silent-film star William S. Hart.

I also became very fond of window cards, which often replicate the image on the one-sheet but are much less costly— and easier to find room for on a wall.

In our travels we occasionally came upon "finds" in antique barns and such.

We also learned that some of the greatest films didn't have especially attractive posters, while some of the prettiest images happened to advertise odd or obscure movies.

I enjoy modern posters as well as vintage ones, but in recent years I've cut back on acquiring paper unless I have a specific place I think I can display it.

I only liquidated a handful of pieces in the Heritage auction, and sold off the items that seemed most likely to bring a good price. I still have hundreds of posters that I personally enjoy but don't have much monetary value.

When I was working for *Entertainment Tonight*, I had a lot of wall space in my office, which I delighted in filling with all sorts of pieces, old and new. I reserved a particular spot for one-sheets and considered that wall my temporary gallery. I deliberately displayed attractive posters for obscure movies from the 1940s and '50s—many of which even I hadn't seen. It gave me a perverse pleasure to have colleagues stop by and stare in wonderment at images of actors they'd never seen or heard of before. When I got tired of staring at the piece I'd switch it out for something new.

One of the reasons I've curtailed my collecting is that I don't have nearly enough display space. Most of the pieces I have were originally shipped folded in eight and I've kept them that way. I only linen-backed a handful of special posters that I earmarked for framing.

I wish I could say that I'd met great poster artists of the past, but I can't. I'm a huge fan of Al Hirschfeld and feel fortunate that I did get to chat with him on one occasion. I have a number of posters he illustrated over the years (usually without credit) for MGM and the Hal Roach studios. But I have no evidence that great poster art—be it by Alberto Vargas or Norman Rockwell—had any impact on a movie's box office success. That changed, along with many other things, in the 1970s when the "key art" played a major role in public awareness of movies like *Star Wars* and other mega-hits.

My wife and I still love our posters. They bring us great pleasure. And, having recently moved to a new house, I'm trying to find a dedicated space that I can turn into a new "temporary gallery" so I can enjoy even more of the pieces that otherwise spend their time folded up in a closet.

TARZAN SWINGS INTO THEATERS

The **Tarzan of the Apes** one-sheet features the barrel-chested Tarzan sitting among the trees with Jane at his side while lions growl in the background. The three-sheet has a more romantic image with Tarzan and Jane holding each other surrounded by the lush jungle foliage. The young Tarzan one-sheet shows an adolescent Tarzan with apes behind him. The one-sheet can sell for $19,120, three-sheet for $11,500, young Tarzan one-sheet for $10,350-$30,800, and lobby card for $260-$2,868.

The **Tarzan the Mighty** portrait style one-sheet depicts a central image of Tarzan carrying Bobby with Mary looking on, surrounded by action images from the movie. The general one-sheet features Tarzan holding onto Bobby on a cracking tree limb over sharpened spikes in the ground. In recent years the portrait style one-sheet has sold for $3,585-$5,290 and the general one-sheet for $2,990-$3,220.

The goal of any movie is escapism. Whether it's a bomb-blasting action film or thought provoking drama, we go to the theater to be entertained and to leave our lives for a few moments. We crave the excitement, the uncertainty, the conflict in film, which transports us to another world. One of the greatest escapism artists that has taken us there for nearly 100 years is Tarzan.

Edgar Rice Burroughs, Tarzan's creator, began his life in Chicago, Illinois in 1875. Burroughs was an ambitious man, serving as a private in the U.S. military, and hopping around to various careers. After his stint at Fort Grant in Arizona, he became a cowboy in Idaho, then a shoe-keeper, a railroad policeman, a gold miner, and an accountant. Frustrated by the different endeavors and failure of his own start-up businesses, he began drawing cartoons and writing fantastical stories to amuse his wife and himself.

After buying an agency that sold lead pencil sharpeners, and subsequently waiting for sales, he wrote his first story, "Under the Moons of Mars." Burroughs submitted it to *All-Story Magazine* and received positive feedback for the first half. He was encouraged that if the second half was as good, it would be published. Once the completed story was submitted, it was published, earning him $400.

Switching genres, he tried to follow "Under the Moons of Mars" with an historical novel, but it was rejected with the advice that he stick to fantasy writing. While mulling over possibilities, Burroughs came up with the idea for Tarzan, a story about a baby from a noble English family raised by an ape in African jungles. Taking the advice to heart he wrote *Tarzan of the Apes*, which was printed in *All-Story Magazine* in 1912, then became a bestseller when it was printed in book form two years later. Diving deeply into this new, exciting character, Burroughs wrote adventures that had Tarzan finding the lost cities of Opar and Atlantis, Pal-ul-don where dinosaurs and prehistoric humans still lived, the City of Gold, and habitable land in the center of the earth.

Movie producers showed interest in the character shortly after he was introduced in *All-Story Magazine*. But, studios faced several problems: how to film with the

The one-sheet for **Tarzan the Ape Man** is brightly painted, highly stylized, depicting Tarzan engaging in battle with a lion while Jane looks on frightened and an ape peers down menacingly. The three-sheet shows a risqué image of Tarzan and Jane entwined as he swings among the vines over a deep green background. The Austrian three-sheet features a mostly nude Tarzan carrying the lank form of Jane among a swirling thicket of vines. In recent years the one-sheet has sold for $20,700-$65,725, insert for $5,500-$9,775, Austrian three-sheet for $9,200, French double grande for $5,377, window card for $4,182, and lobby card for $1,092-$3,220.

Tarzan and His Mate style A one-sheet features Tarzan with a dagger in his hand pointed out a growling lion while Jane hangs onto him. The three-sheet is in shades of yellow and orange showing Tarzan dangling gracefully froma tree with Jane looking up longingly. The insert depicts a smoldering image of Tarzan and Jane holding each other with a menagerie of animals stampeding above. The style A one-sheet can sell for $2,777-$9,775, three-sheet for $5,750-$7,762, and insert for $2,629-$4,780.

menagerie of animals and jungle locales in Tarzan stories, and where to find an actor with the physical capability to swing from trees without being injured. Morgan City, Louisiana served as the jungle in the first movie and a large, muscular actor was found to play the hero.

In 1918 Tarzan was immortalized on film for the first time in *Tarzan of the Apes*. Starring Elmo Lincoln as Tarzan and Enid Markey as Jane, it was the first movie in history to gross $1 million. Other studios started making the movies as well with several muscular men sporting the loincloth, including Gene Pollar (fireman from New

York), P. Dempsey Tabler (opera singer), Jim Pierce (football player), and Frank Merrill (gymnast). Most of these movies were among the silent film era, distinguishing Merrill as the first to utter the famous Tarzan yell in a talkie. Unfortunately, it sounded more like he was in pain than invigorated.

Once the sound quality in movies improved, the yell would become a pivotal part of the character. In 1931, Irving Thalberg of Metro Goldwyn Mayer contacted Burroughs about making a series of movies with sound. Because Burroughs had sold the rights to *Tarzan of the Apes*,

MGM had the story rewritten. The new movie didn't explain how he ended up in Africa, the American Jane Porter became an English woman named Jane Parker, it took place in the jungle with no stateside trips, and Tarzan didn't really speak at all. The movie was filmed in Los Angeles and Crystal Springs, Florida with real footage from Africa spliced into the other scenes.

MGM found their perfect Tarzan in 27-year-old Olympic swimmer Johnny Weissmuller, whose athletic prowess and physical presence made him perfect for the role. He was matched with Maureen O'Sullivan, and the duo remain among the favorite couples in film history for their wonderful chemistry.

Tarzan the Ape Man premiered in 1932 to great success. It was an uplifting movie for Depression era people who needed to escape their own troubles into an imaginative world. Though Tarzan didn't speak much, Weissmuller created the yell that would cement him in the annals of movie history. That yell was echoed by children all over America, swinging from tree branches and yelling from apartment windows. The movie was a huge hit for MGM, revitalizing interest in the books and comics. In all, Weismuller starred in 12 movies as Tarzan, six of those movies with O'Sullivan.

Hollywood censors, however, were not enamored with the movie the way audiences were. They did not approve of Tarzan and Jane's revealing jungle outfits. As the series continued, their outfits covered more and more skin, to appease censors by desexualizing the leads. Another point of contention was their living arrangements, since it appeared that they were living together in the tree house without being married. Movie fans didn't seem to mind this anymore than they minded the revealing clothing, but later movies downplayed the romance between Tarzan and Jane to focus on the adventure story.

Burroughs died in 1950, after serving as a war correspondent during World War II. Following several health problems, he had a heart attack in March 1950. He had written almost 80 novels and was buried at Tarzana, Los Angeles, California. But, his imaginative legacy continued with new Tarzan movies, now shot in color in exotic locations around the world.

His company, Edgar Rice Burroughs, Inc. still retains rights to Tarzan, as well as rights to work still protected by copyright.

In the late 1950s Sy Weintraub bought the rights to Tarzan from producer Sol Lesser. He produced *Tarzan's Greatest Adventure* and eight more movies, as well as a TV series. Weintraub's version of Tarzan was closer to Burroughs' more articulate version than the "me Tarzan, you Jane" version usually seen on film.

Tarzan has left a lasting impression on the film industry. Since that first outing, he has appeared in almost 200 movies and TV episodes or specials. Starting in 1918, he has been through several actors in the '20s and '30s, a revitalization in the '50s, the Disney treatment in an animated film in 1999, and a new movie in the works, set for release in summer of 2016. Not too shabby for a man raised by apes.

The New Adventures of Tarzan was the only movie for which Burroughs acted as a producer. The style A one-sheet shows a stoic, bare-chested Tarzan with Nkima on his back. The three-sheet depicts a frightening Tarzan and a lion on the hunt for his friend d'Arnot bursting through the jungle. On the style B one-sheet Tarzan is in a fight with a jungle cat while Jane cowers in the weeds. The style A one-sheet sells for $60-$4,080, three-sheet for $3,565, style B one-sheet for $920-$2,325, lobby card set of 8 for $185-$402, and single lobby card for $10-$156.

PRESSBOOKS:
COLLECTING THE DETAILS

While promotional movie material is dominated by posters, throughout film history pressbooks have provided a meaty portion of the marketing equation. Also called showman's manuals, merchandising manuals, advertising manuals, and campaign books, pressbooks are distributed as part of press kits for film releases. Before the 1980s film studios did most of their own marketing, so pressbooks were given to exhibitors and theaters as an advertising aid.

Movie studios provide logistical details and general information about the film, the cast, and crew in pressbooks. They include release dates, synopses of the movies, biographies of the cast and crew, interviews with the actors, prewritten reviews and articles, and illustrated movie posters. Most provide background and behind-the-scenes exclusives, as well as history of the movie and some include articles about the actors' lives outside of the movies. The breadth of information varied from movie to movie and the pressbooks ranged in quantity from a one-page flyer, 2-page folded piece, pamphlet, booklet all the way up to 50-page bound book. Early versions were printed in different shapes and sizes, though usually from 8" x 14" to 15" x 24".

Pressbooks date back to the 1910s, well before movies received the type of media attention they do today. Since theater owners and film exhibitors don't have advertising backgrounds, studios issued the pressbooks to promote the films through the theaters and local media. They presented a breakdown of advertising material, merchandising and collectibles, even items available at the theaters such as souvenir giveaways. Some contained promotional suggestions for advertising on TV, radio, newspapers, and magazines. They included additional advertising inserts for newspapers to get audiences excited about upcoming movies. To offer more assistance, studios provided the dimensions of the ad inserts in inches or column size, to help theaters coordinate ad sizes with local newspapers. Some even shared ideas for contests and games surrounding the movie for the theater.

Though not as crucial to the marketing process as they previously were, they are still used for modern movies. They are more standard forms, often 8" x 11" and printed in black and white, usually stapled or in book form. Some include images from the movies and in the past few decades they have been released in electronic formats, such as videotapes and CDs. Now, they are mostly released in electronic form, featuring behind the scenes footage, videotaped interviews with the casts, as well as the material traditionally covered such as synopses, biographies, and still photographs.

Since they provide background details on the movies, they have become highly desirable collectibles. Some dealers even use them to help date other movie materials, especially those from earlier film days. They are not expensive, and many can be purchased for around $10, making them accessible to collectors at every level.

The futuristic cover of this German **Metropolis** pressbook showcases extravagant artwork

Photos are shared inside that can be used for press releases

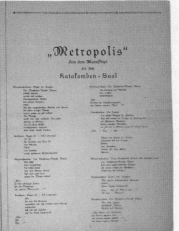

Advertising images are displayed as well as a portion of the manuscript

Cover for **Mickey Mouse and Silly Symphonies** single reel features

Images and descriptions of posters as well as artwork that can be cut out and used in newspapers

Another page features cartoon strips that can be used in newspapers

Descriptions of candy that will accompany the feature
and a picture from a campaign utilized in newspapers

The **King Kong** pressbook showcases the large posters available, including pricing

MGM tried to build up the scares with their pressbook for **Mark of the Vampire**

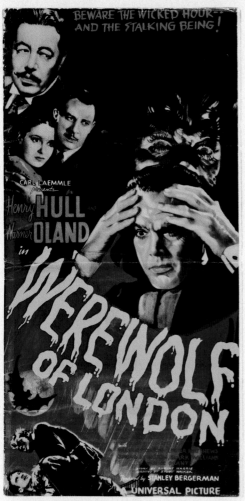

The **Werewolf of London** pressbook cover showcases the color art for the frightening flick

More posters are found inside

This page has a synopsis for the movie, a roto herald, display suggestions, options for display lines to draw in crowds, and information on midnight screenings

Potential newspaper articles are provided along with an image gallery of poster sizes

This basic **The Wizard of Oz** folder cover features drawings of the main characters and has been autographed

Cast and studio information is shared on the pressbook cover

Fun, animated image of the Dorothy and Co.

Table of contents page with MGM credits and radio script for on-air advertising

This complex page showcases what poster ads should be used where, lists where ads can be found in magazines, a sample herald with folding instructions, and information on the technicolor presentation and special exit music trailer

This page lists companies that are working with the movie on merchandising

A full page displaying the posters

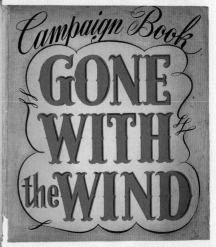

The foldout **Gone with the Wind** pressbook cover, examples of various posters for the lobby, and the advance herald.

Another page boasts the extravagant premiere of the movie

More **Gone with the Wind** artwork is featured on this page

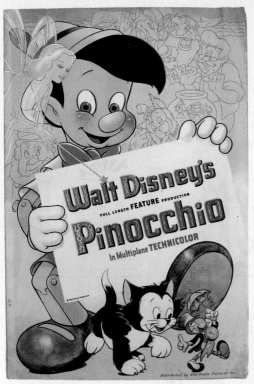

The **Pinocchio** pressbook displays a sweet image of the puppet with Jiminy Cricket and Figaro

This page showcases the various sizes of posters and their prices as well as listing the pressbook's contents

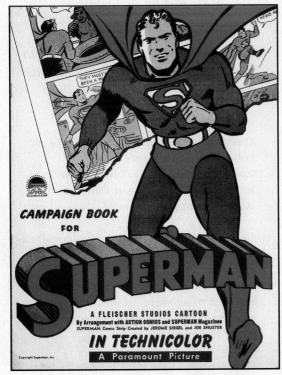

The **Superman** pressbook depicts the cartoon version of the Man of Steel

Inside the different ad mats are shown, along with the standee, one-sheet, and descriptions of other accessories

RALPH DELUCA:
AN EYE FOR DETAIL & BUSINESS

Ralph DeLuca is a world renowned movie poster collector and dealer who has been a part of the hobby since childhood. Over the years DeLuca has amassed an incredible collection of posters from the late 1800s to the 1980s. He has made headlines several times for his purchases of vintage movie posters, including in 2012, when he purchased the rare international **Metropolis** *poster along with four other pieces for $1.2 million.*

Overstreet: How long have you been collecting movie posters?
Ralph DeLuca (RD): I first started collecting movie posters in the early '90s while still in grade school.

Overstreet: What attracts you to collecting movie posters?
RD: I've been a lifelong collector of various things since age 5. Two great passions of mine were art and movies and movie posters, for me, combined both these interests.

Overstreet: Share with us a brief timeline of your personal and professional life buying and dealing in movie posters.
RD: I started collecting posters around 1990 when I was student and I would buy for my collection whenever I had

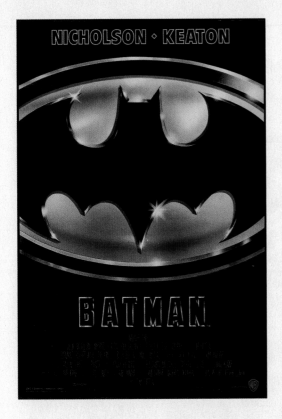

money to spend. After I graduated from school years later and was working in the business world I had considerably more discretionary income and started buying better quality posters. By the late '90s I realized it was much more advantageous to buy entire collections and groups of posters and to sell off the posters I didn't want to offset the cost of the ones I wanted to keep. Fast forward to the present and I am probably the biggest buyer of movie posters in the world.

Overstreet: What was your first movie poster?
RD: My first movie poster was for the 1989 *Batman* starring Michael Keaton and Jack Nicholson. I loved the movie, and when I saw it for sale in a comic book store I had to have it.

Overstreet: How did your collection grow from that point?
RD: I started buying new posters for films I loved until the point when I started reading *Movie Collector's World*, the largest hobby-related publication at the time, and then started saving up to buy older posters for films I cared about.

Overstreet: Which posters are on your want list right now?
RD: My holy grail would be a German poster for *Nosferatu*, the American one-sheet for *Cocoanuts* with the Marx Brothers and I'm sure I could come up with many others given the time.

Overstreet: Do you collect various sizes and/or other paper-related movie items?
RD: I collect all sizes and I also collect lobby cards, film stills, and original scripts.

Overstreet: Do you collect within certain genres/subgenres or by artist/actor/director?
RD: My favorite areas are horror, comedy, animation, and gangster films but my collection spans all genres and actors from 1896 through the 1980s.

Overstreet: Do you collect from a certain time period?
RD: The bulk of my collection is from the 1920s-1950s. I think posters from the '20s and '30s, otherwise known as the Golden Age of Hollywood, have arguably the best artwork and graphics.

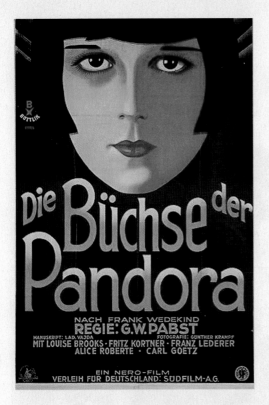

Overstreet: Do you collect international posters?

RD: Yes, I collect posters from all countries. I especially seek out country of origin posters for foreign films and international posters for American films with superior graphics.

Overstreet: Do you purchase rereleased posters?

RD: I purchase rereleases very infrequently and only if the poster doesn't exist as an original or if the graphics are vastly superior in the rerelease. For example *The Hustler* is a great rerelease poster that comes to mind.

Overstreet: What is the rarest piece in your collection?

RD: My collection has hundreds of very rare pieces, among the rarest would be the original poster for *Pandora's Box* starring Louise Brooks which, as far as research indicates, is the only known copy for this extremely important German expressionist film.

Overstreet: How do you feel about linen-backing?

RD: I linen-back a poster only if it's needed to preserve and conserve it. I have many posters that are in brand new-like condition and are folded and I will leave them as is.

Overstreet: How about restoration?

RD: Again, restoration will be performed if it will preserve the integrity of the poster long term. However I think there's a tendency for people to over-restore and make posters look brand new which they are not.

Overstreet: What are your thoughts on photographic posters vs. painted posters?

RD: I prefer painted posters because the artwork is generally superior but if I come across the use of a great photo montage which is often used in Russian constructivist movie posters, which I also collect, I can definitely appreciate them.

Overstreet: Do you think autographs add value or devalue posters?

RD: Ninety percent of the time I feel they devalue them, especially in the event that they're personalized. Exception would be a *Citizen Kane* poster signed by Orson Welles or a *Casablanca* poster signed by Humphrey Bogart but autographs require a whole other layer of authentication which can be problematic and can lead to fraudulent material.

Overstreet: What are the nuances in the artwork that attracts you to certain posters?

RD: I think if an artist can really capture the feel or the setting of the movie with graphics that piques my interest. Remember, the sole purpose of posters were to motivate people to buy tickets to the film so many posters have beautiful graphics even if the movie is not aesthetically pleasing in the end.

Overstreet: How do you store your posters?

RD: Whatever is not framed is in archival sleeves in fire-proof flat files. Posters too large for flat files are rolled in heavy PVC tubes.

Overstreet: How do you store lobby cards/glass slides/programs?

RD: Lobby cards are either in individual

Mylar sleeves or in binders organized by theme. Glass slides, the few I have, are in archival sleeves in a box. Programs are also in Mylar sleeves similar to the ones I use to store my comic books.

Overstreet: Are there any eras or genres of movie posters that you see improving in sales?
RD: I am seeing increased interest in animation, which has been slow for the last 10 years, and film noir is ever increasing in popularity. Also, silent movie posters with stunning graphics are still undervalued.

Overstreet: Right now, how is the market for buying and selling movie posters?
RD: Much like most art or collectible markets the high end is doing extremely well while the middle end seems to be having a much harder time than it has in the past. There will always be buyers for

low end items.

Overstreet: The economy has seen significant changes over the past 10 years. Has movie poster collecting fared well during that time?
RD: Again, the high end in good times and bad always does very well. As in our economy where we see a vanishing middle class, I see less and less of a market for mid-priced collectibles, posters included.

Overstreet: In an interview you did with BBC's *Talking Movies* you mentioned that movie posters have outperformed a lot of other investments in recent years, such as stocks. Can you expand on that?
RD: Shifting from investing in public and private companies to investing in movie posters I've seen astonishing returns in great, rare and expensive posters with very little risk not to mention the added

benefit of actually owning a tangible object which I enjoy. There are exceptions to every rule in both stocks and posters but with a combination of skill and a little luck one can do very well.

Overstreet: What type of posters (for instance time period, series, artist, etc.) are the highest sellers?
RD: The leader of this market has always been 1920s and 1930s horror films, especially Universal horror and German expressionist films like *Metropolis* and *The Cabinet of Dr. Caligari*, et cetera.

Overstreet: Does the availability of reprinted posters hurt the market for originals?
RD: Not at all, and in fact, in some cases an image becomes so popular it helps drive up the value of the original.

Overstreet: How do you spot reprinted posters when you are searching for originals?
RD: There are many telltale signs including size, markings, and paper stock.

Overstreet: What advice would you give to someone who wants to start collecting movie posters?
RD: Buy the best posters you can afford in the best condition. Be very disciplined and learn where to find the most trustworthy sources for business.

Overstreet: How about advice for people who want to transition from being a collector to a dealer?
RD: That's a very hard transition, that to do successfully takes an immense amount of knowledge, capital, and inventory. One must be an expert collector before they can be a beginner dealer.

TOP 10 SALES
AT eMoviePoster

eMoviePoster and its founder Bruce Hershenson have been selling movie posters since the early 1990s. The company began as a seller on eBay in 1998, and over the next decade they sold 330,000 posters and related pieces. In 2008 they left eBay to start auctioning on eMoviePoster.com.

The company had their most successful first half of the year in 2015 and they also sold their one millionth poster during that period. Below is a list of their top 10 sales in descending order by price.

1. *King Kong* (1933) one-sheet in fine condition sold in December 1994 for $97,100.

2. *Cleopatra* (1917) paper-backed one-sheet in very good to fine condition sold in September 2012 for $86,055.

3. *Flying Down to Rio* (1933) linen-backed one-sheet in fine condition sold in December 1996 for $81,700.

4. *King Kong* (1933) three-sheet in fine condition sold in December 1996 for $79,500.

5. *Dracula* (1931) one-sheet in very good to fine condition sold in December 1998 for $74,750.

6. *The Gold Rush* (1925) linen-backed one-sheet in fine condition sold in December 1993 for $70,700.

7. *The Birth of a Nation* (1915) two linen-backed one-sheets in very good to fine condition sold in December 2002 for $67,300.

8. *The Grim Game* (1919) straight jacket style linen-backed one-sheet in very good to fine condition sold in December 2013 for $67,166.

9. *Son of Kong* (1933) linen-backed one-sheet in very good condition sold in December 2005 for $60,100.

10. *The Phantom of the Opera* (1925) linen-backed six-sheet in good condition sold in December 1995 for $57,500.

ELVIS PRESLEY

THE KING OF ROCK GOES HOLLYWOOD

Some of the greatest contemporary music was produced in the 1950s and '60s, though few performers reached the plateaus of Elvis Presley. The King of Rock and Roll mixed musical genres, garnering the support of a fandom that bridged the racial gap. He was a sex symbol when the term was predominately reserved for actors. He had an angelic, smooth voice that could turn husky and haggard, driving fans into a tizzy. He had dance moves, style, and panache that teenagers loved and made parents wary.

Presley may have been one of the biggest cultural icons of the 20th Century, but he came from humble roots. He was born in Tupelo, Mississippi in 1935 to working class parents Gladys and Vernon Presley. The family moved around quite a bit while he was growing up, fostering a strong connection between Presley and his parents. They raised him with a devoted faith in God, attending the Assembly of God Church where he developed a love of gospel music.

Presley's mother gave him his first guitar when he was just 11 years old and he immediately exhibited prowess with the instrument. He was naturally talented, able to play the guitar by ear, rather than relying on typical musical training. Music became an even bigger part of his life and he spent a lot of time at record stores with jukeboxes and listening booths. A few years after he received that first guitar he won a talent show at Humes High School in Memphis, Tennessee.

Once he graduated high school

Presley took several odd jobs while pursuing his dream of breaking into the music business. In August 1953 he went to Sun Records, which later became known as Sun Studio, to record a two-sided disc that he intended to give to his mother as a gift. After hearing Presley record the songs, Sam Phillips, the person in charge of Sun Records, told the receptionist to get Presley's contact information. Phillips acquired a demo recording of a ballad called "Without You" that he thought would suit Presley. This led to the beginning of his music career in 1954 when he was 19 years old.

Presley was one of the earliest singers to perform in the rockabilly style, combining rock and roll with country, and adding the rhythm and blues. He began touring and recording, then signed with RCA Records in 1955. A year later he had his first No. 1 single and album with "Heartbreak Hotel." Through this rapid ascension, Presley was quickly established as the face of rock and roll. His live performances bolstered his popularity through high energy, unique dancing, and the controversial, sexually provocative stage presence that drove young girls absolutely wild.

He may have been known as the King of Rock and Roll but he also made his mark on film. In April 1956 he signed a seven year contract with Paramount Pictures and producer Hal Wallis, which allowed him to work with other studios. His film debut

The **Love Me Tender** poster marked the only time Presley was not given top billing on a poster, boasting the distinction "introducing Elvis Presley." The one-sheet has a large painted image of Elvis singing and holding his guitar then below the title is a close-up image of Presley kissing Debra Paget on the cheek with a stream of cowboys riding in the background. In recent years the one-sheet has sold for $250-$870, insert for $650, three-sheet for $900, 40" x 60" for $850, half-sheet for $190-$600, and British quad for $400.

came that year with the musical western *Love Me Tender*, in which he played Clint Reno, a young man who marries his brother's old girlfriend while his brother is fighting in the Civil War. While Presley liked the title track, which became the first single to pass the one million mark, he considered some of the other songs to be silly. Though it received mixed reviews from critics, his fans made it a box office hit.

Two of his most successful movies were released in 1957. In *Loving You* he played a delivery man turned musician who is discovered by another musician and a publicist. Then in *Jailhouse Rock* he starred as a young man serving time for manslaughter who becomes a rock star. *Jailhouse Rock* called for a more dramatic performance and the erotic dance sequence during the title song is considered his best on screen moment. Despite being a fan-favorite movie, Presley never saw it because costar Judy Tyler died before it was released and he found it too painful to watch the film.

After finishing *Jailhouse Rock*, he served a stint in the US military, which didn't stunt his blossoming career. He was drafted into the Army in 1957 where he served in Germany. Fellow soldiers have stated that despite his celebrity status, Presley wanted to prove his worth and be treated like an ordinary soldier. He was also generous to his comrades, donating his Army

salary to charity, buying televisions for the base, and buying extra fatigues for the men in his outfit. While there he also met Priscilla Beaulieu, whom he would later marry.

When he finished his tour in the Army, Presley headed back to America and spent most of the '60s making movies and their accompanying soundtracks. He kicked off the decade with *G.I. Blues* which set the tone for most of his movies of the '60s with both slow and up tempo songs, romance and humor. The film boasted more songs than his previous movies and the soundtrack was a chart topper. In 1961 he made his first beach movie, *Blue Hawaii* in which he played an army veteran who becomes a tour guide to avoid working in the family business.

Wanting to pursue more dramatic roles he starred in *Flaming Star* and *Wild in the Country*. Unfortunately, they were

The poster for **Jailhouse Rock** has a large image of Presley in 3/4 profile shot looking off into the distance. The bottom half is in vibrant red with an image of the guitar and jail bars with Elvis doing one of his signature dance moves from the film. The one-sheet can sell for $150-$3,300, three-sheet for $150-$3,000, six sheet for $3,400-$4,000, half-sheet for $500-$700, lobby cards for $350-650, French one-panel for $1,900, 40" x 60" style Y for $1,900, and insert for $500-$1,900.

not commercially successful, prompting the studio to want him to revert back to the "Elvis movies" formula. In 1962 to 1964 he filmed eight movies, including *Kid Galahad*, *Girls! Girls! Girls!*, *Fun in Acapulco*, and *Kissin' Cousins*.

Viva Las Vegas was the final film of '64 and proved to be one of his biggest hits. In addition to Presley, the movie featured Hollywood starlet Ann-Margret. Presley admitted that he was nervous while filming because Ann-Margaret was as big of a star as he was at the time. Adding to the star power, David Winters, who had famously choreographed *West Side Story*, choreographed *Viva Las Vegas*. His talent combined with Presley and Ann-Margret made it the most successful movie at the box office. It made more than dou-

ble what the average gross was for other Presley movies.

The films Presley made in the latter half of the '60s could not live up to his earlier work. He starred in three films each year from 1965 to 1969 for a total of 15 movies in just five years. Critical reviews were not often favorable, labeling Presley's performances as automatous, which is understandable considering the exhausting filming schedule he endured. Presley was also not shy about expressing his dislike for some of the songs in his movies. While there were plenty he enjoyed, there were others that he considered irrelevant to plotlines. Still, the movies were the only way for many of his fans to see him perform and they continued to support Elvis Presley, the movie star.

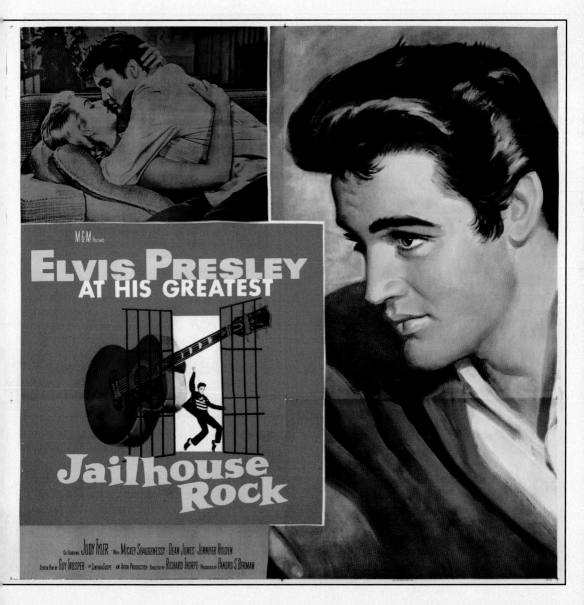

His life off-screen was also filled with difficulty. He and Priscilla got married in 1967 and had their daughter Lisa Marie the next year. Unfortunately their marriage was tumultuous, leading to divorce just a few years later in 1973. Presley was dealing with an addiction to prescription drugs and the usually thin rock star was also battling a weight problem. His destructive lifestyle led him to being hospitalized for his drug problem. He died in August 1977 as a result of heart failure after years of prescription drug abuse. He was only 42 years old. Presley was buried at Graceland near his mother, father, and grandmother.

Presley starred in 33 films from 1956 to 1969. Though his movies received mixed reviews from critics, audiences flocked to see the King on screen and rushed to buy his soundtracks. Fifteen of his movies came with soundtracks and another five by soundtrack EPs. In the first half of the '60s, three of his soundtracks hit number one, including songs like "Can't Help Falling in Love," "Return to Sender," and "Viva Las Vegas." In addition, he won three Grammys for gospel records, had 18 No. 1 singles, and many gold and platinum albums. He was one of the first performers inducted into the Rock and Roll Hall of Fame in 1986 and was also inducted into the Country Music Hall of Fame and the Gospel Music Association's Gospel Music Hall of Fame. All hail the King of Rock and Roll.

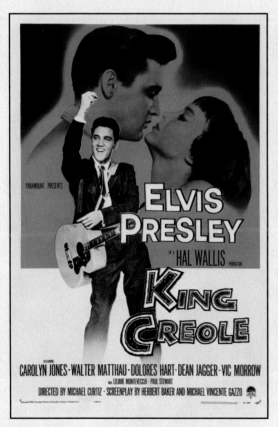

The **King Creole** one-sheet features a black and white image of Elvis smiling with his guitar slung over his shoulder in the foreground and the top portion is dominated by smoldering burnt orange profile shot of Elvis and Carolyn Jones about to kiss. In recent years the one-sheet has sold for $100-$1,380, three-sheet for $380-$900, six-sheet for $675, half-sheet for $140-$700, insert for $100-$650, British quad for $470, and French one-panel for $60-$260.

The **Blue Hawaii** one-sheet is extremely colorful harkening to the beautiful setting of this classic Elvis film. The poster shows the blue Pacific Ocean, palm trees flowing in the breeze, golden sand, even purple mountains. Cleverly splitting the image is a bright white surf board bearing the credits for the movie in blue and pink with a full length picture of Elvis is at the bottom of the image, much smaller than most posters for his films. The one-sheet has sold for $200-$1,500, three-sheet for $600, insert for $200-$700, and window card for $100.

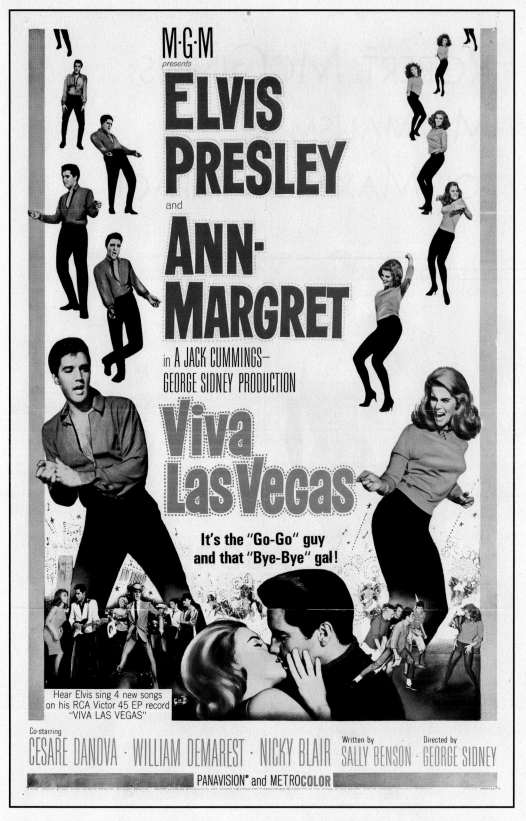

The central image of the **Viva Las Vegas** one-sheet is a full length image of Presley and Ann-Margaret dancing, centered over four smaller images featuring scenes from the film, including comical images, larger than life performances, and a romantic kiss. The one-sheet has sold for $85-$1,200, three-sheet for $500-$1,000, six-sheet for $1,500-$2,000, half-sheet for $300, set of eight lobby cards for $950, British quad for $575, 30" x 40" for $500, insert for $240-$380, French one-panel for $120-$380, and Japanese B2 for $120-$180.

ROBERT McGINNIS:
MINIMALISM
FOR MAXIMUM IMPACT

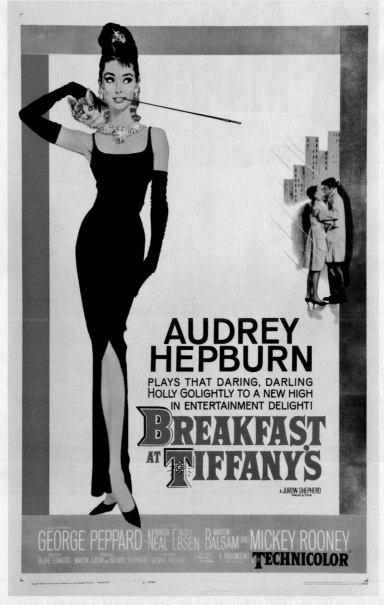

The **Breakfast at Tiffany's** poster has a sexy, full length image of Holly Golightly, with her cat perched on her shoulder and long cigarette holder in her mouth with a small romantic scene playing out off to the side. In recent years the one-sheet has sold for $955-$13,145, 40" x 60" for $10,160, and 30" x 40" for $3,565-$6,500.

The bold full length poster of **Barbarella** pictures her as simultaneously sexy and strong while embracing space age campy charm. The 24-sheet can sell for $1,910, six-sheet for $775-$1,430, subway poster for $490-$990, three-sheet for $140-$660, one-sheet for $20-$400, half-sheet for $60-$240, and insert for $50-$180.

Painter and illustrator Robert McGinnis is a man of style. He has drawn magazine covers, designed title sequences, illustrated over 1,200 paperback book covers, and painted more than 40 movie posters with a sense of coolness permeating all of his art. His work on movie posters has been featured in goofy comedies to spy thrillers, mod hits of the 1960s to Blaxploitation of the 1970s, family friendly musicals to sexually charged European films. The common thread that has always linked McGinnis' work is his ability to use minimalism to punch up the effect of his art.

McGinnis' love for art began at an early age. After he left school in 1943, he studied at the Academy of Commercial Art in Cincinnati, where he was born. During the early days of his career, he worked as an apprentice at Walt Disney, studied fine art at Ohio State University, and served in the Merchant Marine.

In 1958, while he was working in advertising, McGinnis had an unplanned meeting with artist and illustrator Mitchell Hooks, which earned him a job at Dell Publishing. He started by drawing paperback covers for authors such as Donald Westlake, Edward S. Aarons, Richard S. Prather, Carter Brown, Erle Stanley Gardner, and Michael Shayne. He also provided artwork on *Ladies' Home Journal, Good Housekeeping, Time, Guideposts, Women's Home Companion, TIME, Argosy*, and *The Saturday Evening Post* as well as working as the main title designer for *The Hallelujah Trail*.

PARAMOUNT PICTURES
presents

Jack
Lemmon
and
Walter
Matthau
are
The
Odd
Couple

...say
no
more.

Produced by HOWARD W. KOCH • Directed by GENE SAKS • Screenplay by NEIL SIMON Based on his play
Music NEAL HEFTI • A HOWARD W. KOCH Production • PANAVISION® TECHNICOLOR® • A PARAMOUNT PICTURE

McGinnis used the mini-malistic style to perfection on **The Odd Couple** one-sheet with contrasting images of Felix clean and pristine, holding a feather duster and spoon while Oscar slouches in dirty, ragged clothing holding a beer. In recent years the one-sheet has sold for $20-$315.

In 1985, McGinnis was recognized for his work on romance novel paperback covers by being awarded with the title of "Romantic Artist of the Year" by *Romantic Times* magazine. Since 2004 he has created cover illustrations for the *Hard Case Crime* paperback series. He is a member of the Society of Illustrators Hall of Fame and was the subject of the documentary *Robert McGinnis: Painting the Last Rose of Summer* by Paul Jilbert.

McGinnis' heyday for poster art began in the '60s, with momentum due in large part to how he painted the female form. His first poster assignment came in 1961 for *Breakfast at Tiffany's*, where he broke away from the ostentatious trends of the time period by using a minimalist style. The artwork of Audrey Hepburn as the central image, with a small romantic scene off to the side, draws the viewer into Hepburn's attractive, curvaceous form, yet focuses on her refined, elegance.

McGinnis was able to do this again while working on the poster for the 1966 thriller *Arabesque*. He requested that Sophia Loren's tiger stripe dress be sent to him so that a model could wear it to provide an accurate appearance of how the dress looked on a woman. The result was a sizzling, mod image so good that it was repeated on the poster three times.

Two years later he followed up by painting another favorite from the '60s.

The central image for the **Cotton Comes to Harlem** poster is a collage with Gravedigger Jones and Coffin Ed, guns drawn, among scantily clad women posing confidently and a sparking gold car ready to drive off the poster. The three-sheet can sell for $45-$215, insert for $30-$130, one-sheet for $15-$120, and half-sheet for $25-$60.

His poster for *Barbarella* portrayed Jane Fonda as both a sexy bombshell and strong woman with defined, muscular tone and a gun. His paintings of the feminine form have a signature look that fills much of his work, including in James Bond and Matt Helm films with male protagonists.

McGinnis provided the main imagery for James Bond posters throughout the '60s and '70s. His first Bond poster came in 1965 with *Thunderball*, which showcased the cornerstones of what people love about a Bond movie: a confident spy, impressive action sequences, and beautiful women. His Bond posters featuring Sean Connery and Roger Moore are among the most highly sought-after posters in the col-

lecting hobby, which are vibrant without distracting backgrounds. McGinnis would often add significant shots from the movie into his posters, allowing them to serve as stationary trailers, yet he'd do so without overloading the poster with superfluous additions. On one poster, he was able to draw beautiful women, provocative weapons and gadgets, and always portrayed that 007 swagger.

His talent, however, was not limited to painting sexy women and secret agents. In 1968, McGinnis painted the poster for *The Odd Couple*, epitomizing the stark contrast between Oscar and Felix with two, hilarious images. His poster for *Avanti!* took on an even more comedic tone portraying a

On the **Diamonds Are Forever** poster James Bond and two ladies are astride the arm of a crane, surrounded by helicopters while the oil rig explodes below. The background of the poster is mostly blue adding eye appeal to the images in the foreground. The three-sheet can sell for $80-$1,195, 40" x 60" for $135-$1,015, quad for $285-$750, one-sheet for $75-$740, insert for $40-$580, and six-sheet for $260-$480.

chaotic scene with cartoonish characters. He was able to capture the zany, desperation and frustration of Willy Clark on his poster for *The Sunshine Boys* with contrasting imagery of four characters and little else.

During the '70s McGinnis infused his style into the subgenre of Blaxploitation. His work on the poster for *Cotton Comes to Harlem* harkened back to his portrayals of Jane Fonda and Raquel Welch, drawing several ladies in self-assured poises, daring the viewer to give them attitude. In 1972 his poster for *Come Back Charleston Blue* presented a collage, focused on the

refined central imagery, surrounded by playful scenes and action shots of the film. He embraced the comedic presence for *The Bingo Long Traveling All-Stars & Motor Kings* painting the characters as a triumphant pyramid of entertaining baseball players.

No matter the genre, McGinnis was able to bring out the essence of the movie without bogging it down with extraneous details. He could embody the tone succinctly and with such flair that it drew audiences simply because of the poster. McGinnis used minimalism to achieve the maximum effect.

The flashy art for the **Live and Let Die** poster shows suave James Bond standing confidently with his gun in front of an explosion with other characters displayed on fortune telling cards. Beneath them a crocodile sets upon a boat which is crashing into a car while boats explode above them. Recently the six-sheet has sold for $155-$1,550, quad for $90-$895, one-sheet for $50-$570, three-sheet for $105-$540, and insert for $50-$260.

United States Movie Poster Sizes

*Movie promotion takes on many guises and styles.
When it comes to movie posters, an all-encompassing term
this book uses to reference the art form at large, there are dozens.
Below is a simple guide of terminology to define movie poster
sizes in the United States.*

One-Sheet

One-sheets are the most popular movie poster size. They are 27" x 40" or 27" x 41", printed on thin paper stock, and are displayed on both exterior and interior theater walls. They include teaser or advance posters before film releases and regular editions that include film credits. Many studios produce several styles for one film. Before the 1980s one-sheets were often folded into eighths, but are now rolled.

Half-Sheet

Half-sheets are 22" x 28", half the size of a one-sheet, made from card stock. Studios usually print two styles for this size: one is the same as the title lobby card and the other is often a combination of art and photography. They are displayed in theater lobbies and pictured in pressbooks, usually called displays.

Three-Sheet

Three-sheets are 41" x 81", printed on a thin paper stock. They are created to display outside of theaters. Usually only one style is printed, but movies with bigger releases have two different styles. Early versions were printed in two or three segments, then in the early 1970s studios started printing three-sheets as one piece. They have been printed less often since the 1980s.

THREE-SHEET (41" x 81")

ONE-SHEET (27" x 41")

LOBBY CARD (11" x 14")

HALF-SHEET (22" x 28")

SIX-SHEET (81" x 81")

Six-Sheet

Six-sheets are made of thin paper stock, measuring 81" by 81". They are displayed outside of theaters, often issued in four pieces and folded. Six-sheets usually have different artwork than the regular posters. Older versions were displayed with wallpaper glue, which meant that they were not reusable, therefore few survive. They are printed in much smaller numbers than one-sheets and three-sheets.

Twenty-Four Sheet

Twenty-four sheets are 246" x 108", billboard art, printed in 12 sections on standard paper. They are often destroyed after use. Very few are still in existence, especially for films made before 1950.

Insert

Inserts are 14" x 36", printed on card stock. They are usually used with one-sheet posters, often a mix of photographic and artwork, whereas one-sheets primarily display one or the other. They are usually folded into thirds and are among the favorite types of posters.

Lobby Card

Lobby cards are 11" x 14", on card stock, usually printed in sets of eight. The title card displays credits and one-sheet artwork and the others feature scenes from the movie. Lobby cards are used in theater lobbies.

Jumbo Lobby Card

Jumbo lobby cards measure 14" x 17". They are usually created for blockbusters and higher profile releases, printed on linen or glossy stock. They do not include a title card and are much rarer than regular lobby cards.

Window Card

Window cards made on heavy cardboard stock. They are considered to be small posters, measuring 14" by 22". The top of the cards have a 4" blank white area for the theater's name and date of the showing. They are usually displayed in store and shop windows.

Mini or Midget Window Card

Mini or midget window cards are 8" x 14" and were printed prior to 1940. They are smaller versions of window cards, depicting the same artwork. Mini or midget window cards also had the blank white area used to display the theater's name and showtimes. They were printed in smaller quantities and are thus rarer than window cards.

Jumbo Window Card

Jumbo window cards are oversized versions of the regular window cards, measuring 22" x 28". They are printed on cardboard stock, produced in smaller numbers and are rarer than regular window cards.

Door Panels

Door panels are displayed vertically, measuring 20" x 60", printed on thin stock paper. They are sold in sets of four for regular releases and six for larger releases to be displayed on theater doors. Door panels usually have different artwork from the regular one-sheets. The first panel depicts the title of the movie and other panels feature stars and/or scenes from the movie.

Paper Banners

Paper banners are 24" x 80", silk-screened pieces. They usually have photographic images and are made after posters are printed. They are hard to find in good condition.

Subway Posters

Subway posters earned their name because they were posted in New York subways. Measuring 45" x 60", they are similar to two one-sheets, set in landscape format. They are printed as advance posters before movies are released.

Glass Slides

Glass slides are very small, 3.5" x 4", from the early silent film period through the 1940s. They were used in film projectors to advertised upcoming movies and local businesses. They usually had a blank space to mark the date the movie was playing.

8" x 10" stills

8" x 10" stills are photographs from movies, made on thin glossy paper. Printing of these stills began in the 1910s. Because 8" x 10" photographs are easy to reproduce, they can be hard to distinguish original theater-used stills from reproductions.

11" x 14" stills

11" x 14" stills were made during the earliest days of cinema and few were produced after the 1920s. They are made of a higher quality paper stock than 8" x 10" stills. The photographs were usually shot by famous photographers.

30" x 40" and 40" x 60" Posters

30" x 40" and 40" x 60" posters are made on heavy paper stock similar to post-1940 lobby cards. They crease easily when being rolled or unrolled, but were often issued without being folded.

One-Stop

One-stops are about the size of three-sheets. They consist of two different styles of one-sheets with eight lobby cards in the middle. These rare pieces were used for international promotion.

Two-Sheets

Two-sheets are rare pieces that resemble 40" x 60" posters. They are 41" x 54" and were printed for low budget movies from the 1940s to the 1950s.

Pressbooks

Pressbooks were primarily made from the 1910s to the 1970s, though some are still produced now. They are filled with details about movies, specifically synopsis, credits, profiles on cast and crew, prewritten reviews, posters, contest suggestions, and advertisements for local media. They vary in sizes from 8" x 11" to 15" x 24".

Programs

Programs are paperback leaflets that feature scenes from the movie and offer production notes, similar to pressbooks. They were usually created for big releases and sold in lobbies.

Herald

Heralds are paper flyers, printed on both sides, varying in size from 5" x 7" to 6" x 9". They were printed as both single-page and multi-page pieces. Theaters gave them away to promote upcoming movies. They were printed primarily between the 1910s and 1980s.

HERALD

International Movie Poster Sizes

The world of movie posters expands far beyond U.S. shores to creative outlets all over the globe. Most international movie posters are produced in a plethora of sizes not found in the U.S. and often feature different or original artwork.
The following is a breakdown of popular international sizes that can often be found in auctions and movie poster collections.

Australian

Daybill
Daybills have varied in size from 15" x 40", commonly called the long daybill, to 10" x 30", 13" x 30", and 13" x 26". They can be compared to U.S. inserts and were originally printed using hand litho or stone litho process. From WWII through the 1960s color daybills were often accompanied by duotone versions.

Belgian

14" x 22"
The 14" x 22" posters are similar to a U.S. window card and usually include space for the theater to list showtime information. Prior to WWII they were usually 11" x 17".

22" x 34" to 23" x 32"
Posters measuring 22" x 34" to 23" x 32" are rare and were primarily printed before WWII.

AUSTRALIAN DAYBILL

British

Quad

Quads are the most popular British poster size, measuring 30" x 40". Early British posters were not commonly issued in specific sizes, until the quad. Quads in vertical format were originally called quad crowns and those issued in horizontal format were called broadside quads. The broadside quad dominates the style.

British Half-Sheet

British half-sheets are 22" x 28", similar to the American half-sheet. They are issued both rolled and folded.

Double Crown

Double crowns measure 20" x 30" and are printed on paper stock.

Front of House

Front of house or FOHs are movie stills, measuring 8" x 10". They are often sold in sets of eight to be displayed in theater lobbies.

Underground Poster

Underground posters are also called giant flies. They usually measure 65" x 40" and are used on the walls of transit stations such as subways and bus shelters.

Billboard

Billboards are large British sizes, measuring 80" x 90". The top ten inches are left blank so that theaters can add their showtime details, like U.S. window cards.

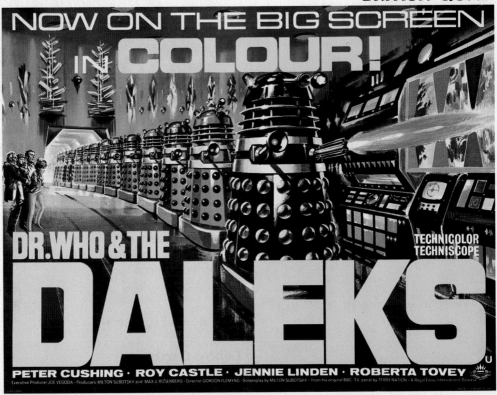

BRITISH QUAD

French

One-Panel
One-panels are also called French grandes. They are 47" x 63", though size does vary slightly.

Two-Panel
Two-panels are also called double grandes. They are 63" x 94" and almost always folded.

Half-Grande
Half-grandes are 31.5" x 47.2", roughly half the size of a one-panel. They are usually set horizontally, similar to U.S. half-sheets.

Pantalon
Pantalons are also referred to as door panels, door posters, or French inserts. Measuring 23" x 60" to 23" x 63", they are half the size of a one-panel set vertically.

Moyenne
Moyennes are 23" x 31", usually considered a medium sized poster. They can also be referred to as petites or petite affichettes.

Petite
Petites are also called minis, measuring 15" x 21" to 16" x 24, and are usually issued folded.

Eight-Panel
Eight-panels are also called eight panneaux. They are billboards, measuring 160" x 120", usually issued in eight pieces and often folded.

FRENCH ONE-PANEL/GRANDE

German

A1
A1s are 23" x 33" and are the most common size in German posters.

A2
A2s range in size from 16" x 23" to 17" x 24".

A3
A3s range in size from 11" x 16" to 11" x 17".

A0
A0s are rare sizes at 33" x 46". They appear regularly in both vertical and horizontal formats.

A00
A00s are rare sizes at 46" x 65".

Lobby Cards
Lobby cards are printed on paper, varying in size from 8" x 12" to 12" x 18".

Two-Foglio

Two-foglios, also known as a two-sheets are 39" x 55". This is the most common
Italian size and they are almost always folded.

One-Foglio

One-foglios, also known as one-sheets, are 28" x 39" and are usually folded.

Four-Foglio

Four-foglios, also called four-sheets, measure 55" x 78". They are usually printed in
two pieces and almost always folded.

Locandino

Locandinos range in size from 13" x 27" to 13" x 28". They are similar to a U.S.
insert but are made on paper stock.

Photobusta

Photobustas are
also known as
fotobustas. They
range in size from
19" x 27" or 20" x
28" and are glossy
lithographs, simi-
lar to U.S. lobby
cards. They appear
as both vertical
and horizontal for-
mats. Before the
1960s they were
14" x 20".

Double Photobusta

Double photo-
bustas are 28" x
40" for pre-1960s
examples and 40"
x 48" for post-
1960s copies.

ITALIAN TWO-SHEET/2-FOGLI

B2

B2s are 20" x 29" and are the most widely used size for Japanese posters. They are printed single sided and not automatically folded after printing. There is often several kinds of artwork for each film.

B1

B1s are 29" x 40", approximately double sized versions of the B2s. They usually display vertically but sometimes horizontally. The vertical ones typically have the same artwork as B2s and horizontal B1s have unique designs. Most are printed single-sided but in recent years they have been double-sided.

B0

B0s are also called B-bai or two-sheets, measuring 40" x 58". They consist of two B1 sheets and are designed in both vertical and horizontal format. Vertical ones share design with B2s and the horizontal ones feature different artwork.

B3

B3s are also called Nakazuri. They measure 14" x 20", about half the size of B2s. They are used in bus and train stations and are similar to a mini-sheet. They are typically one-sided and often displayed information about the theater showing the film.

B4

B4s are 10" x 29", though smaller versions do exist. They are sometimes called a Japanese insert or "speed" poster, used to announce movies before they opened. Some versions in the '60s had two purposes: one side was the speed poster the other was a press sheet. Theaters would display the speed poster before the movie ran then use the backside to advertise the movie in local newspapers.

B5

B5s are also called chirashis with varying measurements, though usually they are 7" x 10". They are small promotional posters like fliers, often printed with information on the back of them.

STB

STBs, sometimes called Tatekan posters, measure 20" x 58". Only a small number are printed for each title, making them very rare and more valuable than B2s.

JAPANESE B2

Collecting, Film Making, Poster Selling: The Expertise of Grey Smith

Grey Smith is the director of the movie poster category for Heritage Auctions. He began working with the company in 2001 as their first movie poster expert. Prior to that he worked in the film industry for 20 years. He is a lifelong movie lover and has been collecting movie posters since childhood.

Overstreet: How long have you been collecting movie posters?

Grey Smith (GS): I have been collecting for 47 years.

Overstreet: What was your first poster?

GS: I bought a group of posters at a nostalgia convention, so there were probably six or eight posters. Most of them were B-westerns, so they were modestly valued material. But at the time I had no knowledge of what anything cost or significance among collectors. But I was an avid student of watching TV and of course in those days the airwaves were full of old movies because TV stations were trying to fill their programming time and they didn't have a lot of material so they'd run older movies constantly.

At that time movie poster collecting was in its infancy. I was 11 years old when I bought my first poster. Older, savvier people had a better idea of what was classic material. Some of those early pioneers in the hobby knew what was

good and what wasn't. I was just a kid with very little money and these were just things to put on my wall.

Overstreet: So you are a film lover?

GS: That's how I started collecting posters by really loving films. I went into college and studied film. When I left college I worked in film for 20 years. That was really my love. But, poster collecting was always a passionate hobby for me. I loved old films and I wanted to collect posters since I loved the art form and all that. But, film itself was really where my heart was and I wanted to make a career of it with the movies I worked on in the '80s and '90s.

Overstreet: Can you elaborate on your career in movies?

GS: I started out editing after college because that's what I learned as a craft. Once I got into the professional arena I realized that wasn't what I wanted to focus on. I found my way into the art department and started working as a prop master, then a set decorator, then an

art director. So I climbed up in the ranks and when I retired from that business 15 years ago I was working as an art director.

Overstreet: Has your experience working in films impacted how you feel about movie posters?
GS: No, I don't think there's been any change in that respect. They really were two separate things. With movie posters it's more of a nostalgic love for the movies. I've been fortunate enough to sell so many posters over the years from so many other countries. In many instances I have to go by previous sales and knowledge of demand. I saw many classic films as a child or through my study in college. In college I was exposed to a whole lot of foreign cinema which gave me a greater knowledge of the hobby overall.

Overstreet: What do you think about autographed posters? Does it make a difference whether they are originals or reprints?
GS: I don't really specialize in autographed posters. Our entertainment and memorabilia division handles them more as autographs are their area. But, I have nothing against them and rather like them if the autograph is from an actor of note, for instance Cary Grant or Sean Connery. Those are hard autographs to get.

I know that there's a certain faction in movie poster collecting that don't really like it, because they feel like it's defacing the poster. But, I'd say that's a pretty small faction of the hobby. I think for most people having something they love, for instance a *Rear Window* one-sheet signed by James Stewart can only be a plus factor. I think it does help the value.

In a number of instances I sold posters signed by stars that have long since passed away that have sold really well. We don't really specialize in them, so consequently if

someone is offering me an autographed reissue or reprint, especially a reprint, in many instances I wouldn't take it or steer away from it. Just because our real focus is on the posters themselves and we don't want to offer reprints. From time to time we'll put something in a sale because it was in a larger collection, but we clearly state that it is a reproduction from the 1990s or 2000s.

Reissues are a different story. If a film has been rereleased 10 years after the original release we're happy to offer that because they're actually theatrically released posters. That's what we aim for.

Overstreet: What are the nuances that make a good poster?
GS: There are really three things that drive demand for a movie poster. One being the film itself. The title. Collectors that love a film would like to have an original release poster.

Second, it's probably the star or stars. For a collector who wants to complete a run of all of the films done by Clark Gable, they will buy a poster just for that.

Finally, but certainly not least of all, is the graphics. I've sold a number of posters that were not big films, not terribly high demand titles, but just have really outstanding graphics. As an example, I'll point to the exploitation films like *Marijuana* or *Assassin of Youth* that were done in the '30s and '40s. The graphics are so much fun. They're so over the top. That sort of thing will really draw in collectors. I think a lot of collectors will look at the catalog and think, "Wow, what would that look like framed in my house?" That also goes for some of the 1950s titles like *Attack of the 50 Ft. Woman*. The film itself is not noteworthy but the graphics are.

Overstreet: How do you safely store your posters?

GS: I'm also realistic as to a person's space limitations for storing posters. If I were to speak to a museum group, I'd tell them to keep the one-sheets lying flat and buffer both sides of them with a non-acidic paper to protect them from the migration of acidic material. But realistically most people don't have that in their homes, so I would suggest that if you're framing something spend the extra money to have someone museum frame it. If the poster is not mounted, first of all, it runs the risk of being too close to the glass and having moisture migrate onto the poster and causing mildew or being exposed to sunlight and fading. There are things in a museum framing that you can do to minimize that.

But generally in storing, I'd suggest that people invest in an architectural file, if they have the space. Lay them flat on top of each other. I don't necessarily believe they need to be separated by other paper. If you are looking through these posters on a regular basis – meaning maybe twice a year – they aren't going to brown and diminish over that time period. It's a way to keep them from being exposed to the elements. Keep them in a tempered climate – nothing really hot and nothing with moisture. Everyone has their different circumstances for where they live. So if it comes down to just folding the posters and putting them in a Mylar sleeve, that's fine too. Keep them as well preserved as you can.

Overstreet: Do you consider restoration an acceptable way to preserve posters or do they lose some value, monetary or intrinsic?

GS: In general restoration is a good thing. Frankly many of these posters would be more damaged unless they are stabilized and restored. You have to remember that most of these posters were printed with a cheaper paper stock that was just two or three grades above wood pulp paper. Consequently, the paper does have a tendency to brown and degrade. When you wash and de-acidify a poster and put it on Japanese acid-free paper and then linen or cotton duck fabric that stabilizes it.

The French were really the first poster collectors 150 years ago. They realized that by taking posters and putting them on linen fabric it would preserve them. Many of those posters remain to this day in decent condition.

The science of restoration has really come a long way in recent years to increase the overall appearance of posters once they've been conserved. Many posters don't need to be restored, they need to be conserved because they have splitting at the folds, browning, etc. Washing them and put them on linen is really conservation. Restoration involves paper replacement, painting, etc. In my opinion they are made more presentable, they are easier to handle to transport and sell them.

If a poster arrives to me that is in nice shape, folded, with maybe just blemishes such as pinholes and fold-wear, I won't begin to restore it. I think that it's not broken, so why do I need to fix it? My job really is difficult in that respect, because I need to walk that fine line judgement of what is best restored and what is not. As far as value is concerned, if a vintage poster is in good condition and hasn't been restored, theoretically, it'll do better than one that has been restored. But, if it's rare enough, people are going to want the poster regardless.

Overstreet: What are your thoughts on

linen-backing?

GS: People ask me if they restore their posters and put them on linen will it decrease the value. If the poster really needs it, then you're probably stabilizing it for someone to buy in a more solid manner so that the poster is not crumbling.

Overstreet: How long have you been working with Heritage?

GS: I started with Heritage in the fall of 2001, so 14 years.

Overstreet: You were Heritage's first movie poster expert and now you are the director of the auction category. What are some important things you've learned about movie poster collecting during that time?

GS: Oh gosh, that's difficult. I've certainly learned a tremendous amount about posters and about the broader collecting community. I was fortunate enough to have bought and sold posters during my career in film and even in my younger years. So, I was pretty well versed in it.

I didn't know much about the auction business other than having participated in auctions throughout the years. All of those things were new knowledge to me. As far as the hobby itself, it's been an incremental thing. I've learned a good bit about the demand for various titles and foreign issue posters. It's been a great experience.

Overstreet: What are some of the poster sales highlights that Heritage has made?

GS: I think of some fun things that have come through the door, which have been highlights. Some years ago a woman and her husband contacted me about some silent film posters that they had that were left in a home they bought. She sent me a list of titles and I was blown away. She had found me through the internet when Heritage was younger, as far as movie posters. She had reached out to a few other auction houses and there wasn't a quick response. There were two styles of one-sheets for *Wings*,

which is the first Academy Award winner for Best Picture. A number of Douglas Fairbanks posters, things like that. They were a great find to see, some of which had never appeared on the market before. So that was a highlight.

A few years ago a man contacted me and he had a list of posters he had collected in the '60s. He sent me a list and it was a little bit more mundane material from the late '40s and the '50s. So I called him and before we hung up the phone he said, "Oh, I have one other poster that's really my favorite, but I'm wondering if you can tell me something about it. I have a full size poster to the *Bride of Frankenstein*."

So I said, "That's interesting. Can you describe it for me?"

I asked if it had Universal's name written on it. He said yes that it had the logo for Universal. I was sitting there wondering if it was the undiscovered style one-sheet and knowing it's never been on the market before except in a foreign version. I asked him to measure it for me and he said that he knew it was the size of a one-sheet and it had been framed. I asked him to send a picture but he needed to wait for his wife to get home. I waited this grueling 36 hours to get it wondering if he was asking other people about it and shopping it around. He sent me a picture and of course, I was delighted. The sale was good. Those things are always exciting.

More recently we sold a *Frankenstein* three-sheet which a man had gotten out of an attic of an old theater when he was a teenager. He took it home and didn't really know what he had.

The Berwick discovery of all of those one-sheets from *Little Caesar, The Public Enemy, Cimarron, Dracula*. Those were all one find. That was an exciting find.

I love for people to see new images. Even if

they are not new images, they are fresh to the market. Last fall a gentleman contacted me about his grandfather who had collected Lon Chaney, Sr. to see if they were worth anything. I asked what titles he had and he listed a few that were not his biggest titles. He sent me images and one included the one-sheet for *London After Midnight*, which we sold for $470,000.

Overstreet: How does Heritage authenticate movie posters?

GS: Purely and simply we look at the material, examine it closely, look for anything that throws us that it might not be what it's meant to be. We certainly use black lights and light tables. Between myself and Bruce Carteron [Auction Coordinator at Heritage], my assistant, we have probably 90 years of experience between us. That really works in our favor regarding what these posters look like, feel like, and what their characteristics are to determine that they are authentic. Even if they've been linen-backed.

Overstreet: How do you approach grading posters?

GS: Grading is really a subjective art. There's no way it could be objective. In all instances a poster is graded by two people that are good about knowing what to downgrade for and trying to come to a consensus using techniques I've discussed.

The beautiful thing about Heritage is that if we sell something to somebody there's a trust factor involved. They expect us to be accurate in what we are doing and if they disagree with our grade, then I'm more than anxious to hear from them to try to resolve it.

We use what was essentially the comic book grading scale. The reason I began using that is that when I was brought into Heritage they were just branching out from numismatics and moving into comics. So they had set up a program using the comics grading

scale and I thought that was best to adapt to use for posters as well. We have a legend on our site and in each of our catalogs that tells you what that grade entails. We give lots of details in our catalog about the condition. The best thing for us is to give the most information we can because that makes for a happier buyer.

Overstreet: The economy has seen significant ups and downs in recent years. How has movie poster collecting fared during that time?

GS: Well, posters have really continually risen in value through the years. Now, there was a drop or set back in 2008-2009, which we saw in late-2009 to 2010. It was sort of a correction because the market had been climbing pretty dramatically and it took about a 15 to 30 percent drop in value. But since then it has come back quite well. All sorts of fluctuations in the market which translates into the general economy will have some effect on collectibles. It's a nonessential spending, so it's going to be one of the first things people cut back on in a bad economy. Some consignors won't want to sell their posters during that period of time, but for collectors, there can be some really good buying opportunities.

Good material will find higher value at any time because collectors realize that if they don't buy a poster now they may never have another chance.

It's different than investing in stocks, bonds, and commodities. Those are things you can't look at and enjoy. With any sort of collectible you have the pleasure of owning it and what those of us in the collecting industry call bragging rights.

Overstreet: Many of the posters that reach the highest prices are Universal Monsters or Disney. Are there other eras or genres that are more valuable than others or that are increasing in value?

GS: I see shifting trends with various genres. Of course, I always think horror and science fiction always tend to have a fairly strong following because people tend to remember those films. They really make an impression, especially when you are young. In years to come, I'd say that for the horror films of today, the posters will be more valuable.

Other genres that are collectible and really desirable always includes great classic cinema like Academy Award winners, like Frank Capra to *Gone with the Wind*. All across the various genres. Those posters tend to hold a greater demand. Those are posters that you really want to pay attention to because they have great cultural significance. As far as genres in general, film noir be it the classics from the '40s, such as *The Postman Always Rings Twice*, the [Alan] Ladd and [Veronica] Lake films tend to have a pretty good demand.

Animation tends to bring out good, strong bidding.

James Bond is another. Bond always seems to do well, specifically the earlier films with Sean Connery. There's a good demand there because it kind of crosses over cultural barriers from British to Japanese to American buyers.

Within the last 10 to 15 years posters for foreign films have really taken off. Especially the Italian posters for American titles, for instance the Italian poster for *Casablanca*. The appreciation for that post-Second World War artwork has really grown. It's a lot of fun to see that demand go up.

Overstreet: Which posters from, say the last 20 years, are the most valuable?
GS: Quite frankly, I think that if you look

on our website and pull up our auction archives and look at the years between 2000 and today you will see that there are bigger sellers through those years. Some that come to mind are *Pulp Fiction, Reservoir Dogs* – the Quentin Tarantino movies. They are just big favorites with buyers. Some of the superhero stuff. They are more widely collected for the films. It's hard to say that there is one specific genre that does better than others.

There are some instances where films have come out and posters that were released with them have been withdrawn for whatever reason. Those tend to bring a greater demand, because collectors see those as being more scarce. For instance, *Revenge of the Jedi* instead of *Return of the Jedi*. The *Pulp Fiction* Lucky Strike poster is one because of the cease and desist by R.J. Reynolds because the movie was using their tobacco company image on the artwork. Those are things collectors gravitate toward.

The *Aliens* one-sheet that depicts Sigourney Weaver with child was withdrawn because it showed endangerment to a child.

Newer posters have a demand if they are known to be in limited quantities.

Overstreet: What advice would you give to someone who is starting to collect now?
GS: Really, really do the research. Go out there and look at websites selling posters, try to educate yourself. There are so many sources now online. In that respect try to figure out your direction in collecting that is near and dear to your heart. I always think it's good to have an area you want to focus on initially. With the education and with the focus you'll make better buying decisions. You'll probably do better in years to come when it comes time to sell.

UNIVERSAL MONSTERS
THE GOLDEN AGE OF HORROR

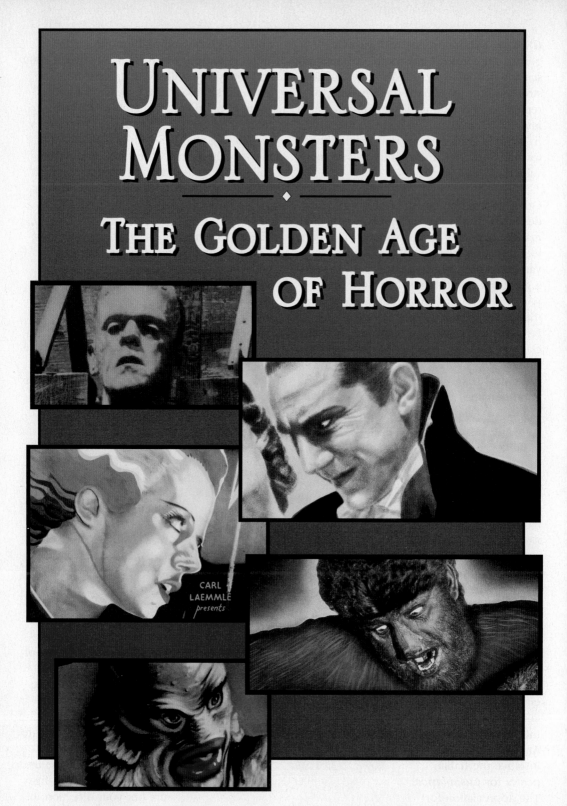

Universal Studios has produced some of the greatest and most iconic monster movies of all time. Beginning in the 1920s, "Universal Monsters" became a household name distinguishing the series of horror, suspense, and science fiction films produced through 1960.

These films, led by Dracula, Frankenstein's Monster, the Wolf Man, the Invisible Man, and plenty more were some of the studio's greatest early successes. They put actors Bela Lugosi and Boris Karloff on the top of the horror heap, along with genre actors like Dwight Frye,

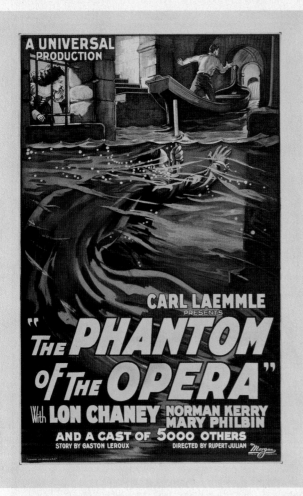

John Carradine, Lionel Atwill, and Edward Van Sloan. Composers Frank Skinner and Hans J. Salter, and make-up artists Jack Pierce and Bud Westmore earned lasting reputations for their work on several of these films. Universal Monster movies also developed horror tropes like cobwebs, fog and mist, creaking staircases and doors, and frenzied mobs of torch wielding people that are still used copiously today.

The Universal Monsters subgenre started with silent films *The Hunchback of Notre Dame* and *Phantom of the Opera*, both starring Lon Chaney. *Hunchback* was released first, in 1923 with Chaney in the title role of Quasimodo. Production was impressively designed as 15th century Paris, with a recreation of the Cathédral Notre-Dame de Paris. *Hunchback* was a great success in theaters, prompting Universal studio head, Carl Laemmle, to greenlight *Phantom of the Opera*. Though *Hunchback* was the first Universal Monster movie, *Phantom* had more in common

with the movies produced in the '30s and '40s. The 1925 film based on the novel by Gaston Leroux told the story of the mysterious music loving Phantom turned violent toward those who kept him from enjoying the music of the woman he adored. This movie is visually celebrated for Chaney's complicated make-up as the Phantom, which was so grotesque that it can still repulse modern day, desensitized audiences. Once again production was key and Universal recreated the inside of the Opéra de Paris Garnier as setting for the Phantom and his muse.

The next crop of films, prominently starring Lugosi and Karloff, were some of the studio's most successful. The 1930s laid the groundwork for the way monsters should look, sound, behave, and move to terrifying effect. Even though the country was gripped by the Great Depression, it didn't stop movie fans from buying tickets to see *Dracula* and *Frankenstein*, making both huge successes in 1931.

Tod Browning's version of Bram Stoker's *Dracula* wasn't the first adaptation for the king of vampires, but it is the archetypal version. He utilized the best parts of Stoker's book, which itself used bits of historical folklore and legends, and the Broadway production, adapted from the novel by Hamilton Deane and John L. Balderston, to tell the story. Browning then cast Lugosi, the original Broadway stage actor to play the count, as the mysterious vampire onscreen. Using Broadway theatricality and his intimidating, hypnotic stare, Lugosi terrified audiences. Cameraman Karl Freund accentuated the vampire's powers with expressionistic effects through the lighting, camera angles, and focus on how things moved in the shot. The film combines stage and silent film style performances with the ominous tension created by Dracula and the wide-eyed, desperate lunacy portrayed by Frye as Renfield. Many Dracula films that have followed mimic elements and styles of the film collaboration between producer Carl Laemmle, Jr., Browning, Lugosi, and Freund, though few have caught lightning in a bottle the way they did.

Universal's next project was to bring life to Mary Shelley's *Frankenstein*, though it was different than originally intended. Lugosi was set to star as the Monster with the plan to portray Frankenstein's Monster as a vicious killer with no regard for life. When director James Whale joined the project he changed the tone drastically, then cast the towering Karloff to play the Monster. Karloff's size made the Monster intimidating, but his demeanor gave him a childlike, naive quality. Whale's interpretation of Shelley's narrative about the dangers of irresponsible scientific exploration, evolved into a story about a misunderstood misfit who will forever be an outsider. This style was further accentuated by depicting the humans, particularly the crazed

The **Dracula** style A one-sheet shows a large image of Dracula's head with an expression of predatory rage. The background is a mix of blue and gray and the title comes three-dimensionally off of the page in orange and red. The style F one-sheet design presents a larger than life picture of Dracula, cape flowing, eyes bulging as he gets ready to pounce on the cowering figure of Renfield with the moon shining behind him on a rocky boat with the title boldly shown in bright red text. On the 1947 rerelease three-sheet the top half is dominated by a close-up of Dracula getting ready to put someone under his thrall. The bottom half shows John trying to comfort Mina as Renfield hunches beside the crate holding his master. The 1960s rerelease one-sheet is dominated by bright red background, Mina's dress is red, and looks like it is smeared by blood. By stark contrast Dracula and Mena are in black and white and Dracula is about to bite her as she lies helpless in his arms. The style F one-sheet can sell for $75,000-$310,700, 1947 rerelease three-sheet for $71,700, title card for $65,725, lobby cards up to $45,000, the 1938 rerelease one-sheet for $20,000-$33,400, insert for $33,000, 1947 rerelease one-sheet for $26,000, and 1960s rerelease one-sheet for $450-$1,600.

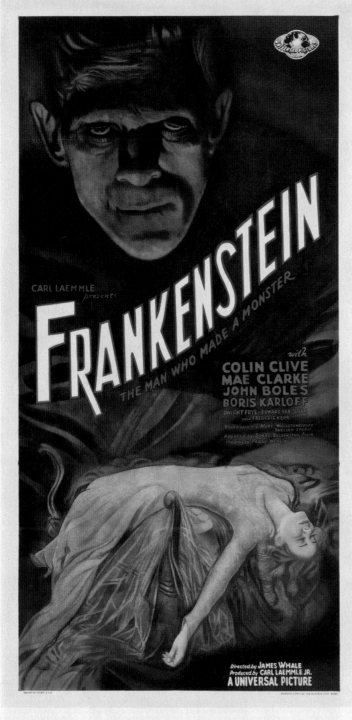

ally defining the look of the Monster.

The success of these movies logically prompted Universal and executive Laemmle, Jr. to continue in the genre. *The Mummy* came out in 1932, following quickly after *Dracula* and *Frankenstein*. Karloff traded his flat-top for bandages and a fez to portray Imhotep, the Mummy. Once again, Karloff played an isolated monster, this time with a soft-spoken demeanor and obsession with a modern woman who reminds him of someone he loved during his life. Freund, who traded his camera for the director's chair, gave the film a dream-like quality and Karloff embodied a sympathetic Imhotep who was lonely like Frankenstein's Monster. Despite long lasting imagery of the bandaged Mummy, Karloff only wore that costume for the opening minutes of the film. Once in contemporary clothing, this allowed Imhotep to hide in plain sight, though the chill inducing moment when the Mummy's glistening eyes first open is hard to replicate later in the movie.

Next, the studio turned their attention to Edgar Allan Poe for a trilogy of movies based on his stories and poems. *Murders in the Rue Morgue* came out in 1932 starring Lugosi, then *The Black Cat* was released in 1934 and *The Raven* in 1935, both with Lugosi and Karloff. *Murders in the Rue Morgue* was filled with acts of more realistic horror by Dr. Mirakle, including murdering a prosti-

scientist Dr. Frankenstein, played by Colin Clive, as desperate monsters. As the make-up artist Pierce completed the Monster's chilling image by creating his flattop head, bolts in the neck, and grotesque scarring. Pierce's technique is so beloved by the horror community that it has been duplicated innumerous times on film, television, in books, and Halloween costumes, liter-

The **Frankenstein** one-sheet art is captured along the sides of this poster. The monster is pictured in the bottom corner, dull-eyed and flat-headed looking grotesque with bolts protruding from his neck. Henry Frankenstein, Elizabeth, Victor, and Fritz are pictured around the monster with Elizabeth shown in full figure, looking swept by the wind blowing across the center of the poster to the top. The top half of the insert shows a close-up of the monster lit from below by orange light with deep shadows across his face. The bottom half shows Elizabeth lying supine across the bed. The 1938 rerelease three-sheet is a painted image of the monster running through the village with red and white background, and slender, long lightning bolt scorches from the top corner to the ground below the monster. The title crackles in white at the bottom of the poster with trees blowing and windmill turning above. In recent years the style C three-sheet has sold for $358,500, insert for $262,900, one-sheet sells for $189,750, and the 1938 rerelease three-sheet for $29,000-$38,000.

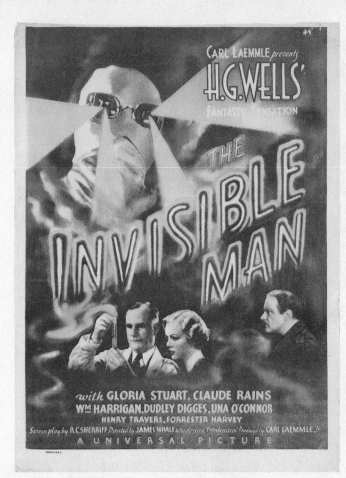

On **The Invisible Man** one-sheet, the titular character is hovering at the top of the frame projecting what looks like beams of light from his glasses. Flora, Dr. Cranley, and Dr. Kemp desperately test chemicals at the bottom with the title stretching eerily across the center, separating the Invisible Man from those he is tormenting. The advance one-sheet is very mysterious, depicting a close-up, barely visible image of a man's face, painted in shades of orange and black with vibrant gold eyes in the center. The window card is similar to the primary one-sheet, yet colored in purple and gold showing the beams of light coming from his eye as much more vivid and electric. Smoke seems to swirl around the poster adding to the mystery. Recently the one-sheet sold for $55,200, advance one-sheet for $48,300, window card for $1,250-$9,560, lobby card for $6,380-$7,765, 1951 rerelease insert for $1,955-$3,735, and 1951 rerelease one-sheet for $1,315-$1,555.

tute, and overt allusions to bestiality and sexual assault. Robert Florey directed this film and worked with Freund as cinematographer, infusing the movie with horrifying tones played out through expressionistic style. That, combine with Lugosi's unnerving portrayal as the mad scientist, made this a disturbing movie. *The Black Cat* was one of the last movies before the Motion Picture Production Code was strictly enforced, shocking audiences with scenes of torture, satanic rituals, and other dark elements. With Karloff and Lugosi together in their first costarring role as a pair of antagonists, the weight of Dracula and Frankenstein was felt throughout the movie. Their collaboration in *The Raven* was not as well received, disturbing viewers through the heavy revenge theme portrayed through torture and disfigurement.

After the first Poe adaptation, Universal produced *The Invisible Man* in 1933 based on the book by H.G. Wells. Whale helmed the film presenting another recognizable look with the bandaged Claude Rains as the Invisible Man. Even though his face is not visible, Rains' performance was so grandiose that a solid presence was felt throughout the movie. Unlike some of the sympathetic monsters in Universal movies, Rains played the Invisible Man as nasty, witty, and cunning with an unmistakable air of intellectual superiority. The menacing erudite uses his new state of being to wreak havoc on the people around him. *The Invisible Man* featured groundbreaking, state of the art special effects for the time period and led to four sequels.

Frankenstein produced the rare sequel that surpassed the original when *The Bride of Frankenstein* was released in 1935. In addition to being a great sequel, it also featured the first female Monster in the world of Universal horror, played by Elsa Lanchester. As the director, Whale pushed the visual effects more in this film and infused dark humor, which wasn't in its predecessor. What makes this movie so memorable is the emphasis on the Monster's emotions and humanity. The Monster wanders through the countryside seeking companionship and feeling lonely.

The Black Cat one-sheet style B is done in red and black with white popping vibrantly throughout the poster. The faces of Hjalmar and Dr. Werdegast float at the top of the poster, brows furrowed, sinister expressions in place with an arch-backed cat poised between them. Peter and Joan look frightened and paranoid at the bottom of the poster and the title is painted brightly across the center of the poster in white. The style D one-sheet has a central image of Thamal carrying a limp Joan while Werdegast lurks from above and Hjalmar looks up from below. A giant black cat dominates the background with beams of glowing yellow light emanating from its eyes. The half-sheet features the faces of Hjalmar and Werdegast with the cat slinking behind them over a black background. The style B one-sheet can sell for up to $334,600, style D one-sheet for $286,800, the half-sheet for $89,625, the Swedish one-sheet for $805-$12,650, title card for $15,810, lobby card for $50-$12,360, and pressbook for $3,585.

He finds his creator's old mentor and they concoct a plan to create a mate for the Monster. The scene when the Bride meets the Monster has become one of the most iconic scenes in monster movies.

Werewolf of London also came out in 1935, six years before its more popular counterpart *The Wolf Man*. Though it's the first significant werewolf movie, it was not the biggest. What sets it apart is Pierce's make-up which presented a feral beast inducing plenty of nightmares. *Dracula's Daughter* followed in 1936, which was an impressive sequel among the many they released. This one focused on the Count's daughter but followed the theme of vulnerable monsters and humans as monsters seen in *Frankenstein*. It is also noted for having lesbian overtones, which Universal hinted at in early advertising.

The first round of these Universal films ended in the late 1930s when the Laemmles left the studio after box office flops and other financial issues. Part of the problem came because Britain put a temporary ban on American horror films

after MGM's *Mad Love* and Universal's *The Raven*. Universal stopped making monster movies for a few years, though *Dracula* and *Frankenstein* were rereleased garnering impressive box office results.

New executives at Universal moved forward with *Son of Frankenstein* in 1939 with Karloff, Lugosi, and Basil Rathbone. Directed by Rowland V. Lee the movie was visually impressive and focused on how the sins of the past can haunt the next generation. Rathbone played Dr. Frankenstein's son, Lugosi played the twisted Ygor, and Karloff starred as the Monster for the last time on film. Throughout the 1930s, Lugosi, Karloff, or both starred in 13 out of 17 Universal Monster movies.

In 1941, *The Wolf Man* introduced another of Universal's most well recognized characters. Chaney had been one of the biggest stars of their horror in the '20s and this movie established his son Lon Chaney, Jr. as the new face of Universal. Unlike favored monster predecessors, *Frankenstein* and *Dracula*, this film was

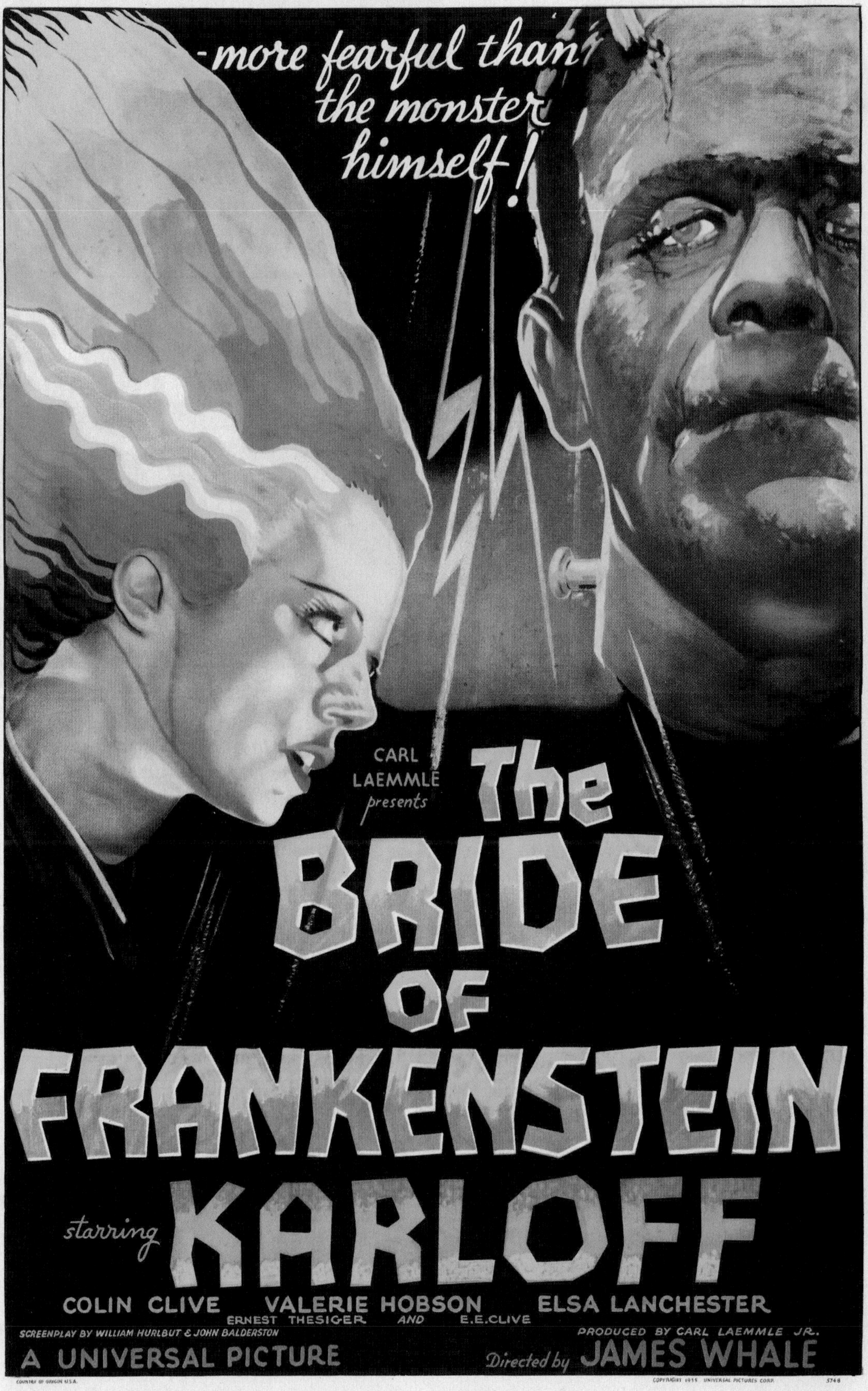

-more fearful than the monster himself!

CARL
LAEMMLE
presents **The
BRIDE
OF
FRANKENSTEIN
KARLOFF**

starring

COLIN CLIVE **VALERIE HOBSON** **ELSA LANCHESTER**
ERNEST THESIGER AND E.E. CLIVE
SCREENPLAY BY WILLIAM HURLBUT & JOHN BALDERSTON PRODUCED BY CARL LAEMMLE JR.
A UNIVERSAL PICTURE *Directed by* **JAMES WHALE**
COUNTRY OF ORIGIN U.S.A. COPYRIGHT 1935 UNIVERSAL PICTURES CORP. 5748

based on myths from enduring legends and those created by writer Curt Siodmak, rather than literary texts. Director-producer George Waggner and Siodmak sped up the pace for their werewolf movie, having Chaney, Jr.'s character Larry Talbot find out about the werewolf's curse within minutes of the movie beginning. As Talbot, Chaney, Jr. didn't have the same charisma as other Universal Monster actors, but when he transformed into the Wolf Man he took on a feral, beastly quality both threatening and frightening.

The '40s saw the largest volume of Universal Monster movies, though they were primarily sequels. It started out with franchise sequels *The Invisible Man Returns* and *The Invisible Woman*, both in 1940, as well as *The Mummy's Hand*

which followed with another sequel *The Mummy's Tomb* in 1942. Chaney, Jr. played Frankenstein's Monster in *The Ghost of Frankenstein* in 1942. Then Lugosi played the Monster with Chaney, Jr. as the Wolf Man in *Frankenstein Meets the Wolf Man* in 1943, followed by Chaney, Jr. as Dracula in *Son of Dracula* in 1943. With the exception of the Mummy, Invisible Man, and the Bride of Frankenstein, all of the Universal Monsters appeared in *House of Frankenstein* and *House of Dracula*.

After churning out a list of sequels, the studio released the horror comedy *Abbott and Costello Meet Frankenstein*, which was a big hit near the end of the decade in 1948. Despite the title, the movie featured more Universal Monsters than it promised. In addition to Frankenstein's

The Bride of Frankenstein one-sheet style D bears the tagline "More fearful than the monster himself!" The bold image shows close-ups of the figures of the monster and the bride. The color is brilliantly contrasted with the bride in shades of orange while the monster is painted in shades of green. Syncing them together are subtle streaks of green in her hair and blazing orange in his eyes and between the pair is a lightning bolt leading down to the title in a rickety font. The style D one-sheet has sold for up to $334,600, half-sheet for $65,725, jumbo window card for $1,775-$55,200, title card for $46,000, insert for $31,900, pre-war Belgian poster for $20,315, lobby card for $110-$13,740, and Argentinean poster for $11,950.

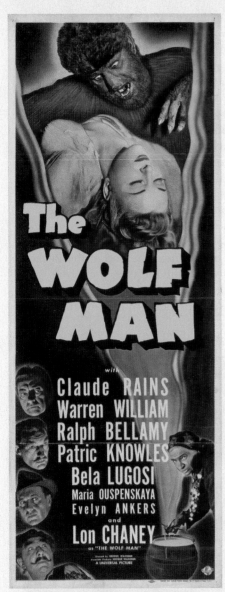

The **Abbott and Costello Meet Frankenstein** three-sheet is green-hued larger image of the Monster comically holding the terrified Abbott and Costello by the backs of their shirts. Dracula and the Wolf Man lurk at the top of the poster ready to spook the comedy duo. The inside of the image filled with Dracula mid-bat transformation is at the top of the poster with large close-ups of the Monster and the Wolf Man lit from below by spooky green light while Abbott and Costello are at the bottom of the poster looking ready to run. The poster looks like a cartoonish chase scene marrying the concept of horror-comedy. The poster seems to move with Abbott and Costello at the bottom of the poster followed by a smiling Monster, snarling Wolf Man, and glaring Dracula running from the rickety old house. The three-sheet can sell for $15,535, 24-sheet for $11,500, insert for $4,600-$7,700, lobby card set for $6,900, one-sheet for $3,940-$6,675, half-sheet for $1,670-$3,880, and a lobby card for $160-$4,255.

The **Wolf Man** one-sheet is fairly basic with the Wolf Man's fur covered face dominating the top of the poster in front of a hillside displaying creepy, foreboding trees. Beneath the title Gwen lies unconscious. Her vulnerability is accentuated by significant exposure of her throat and cleavage. On the insert the Wolf Man is about to pounce on the defenseless Gwen. They are encased in the mysterious smoke produced by Maleva's cauldron. Other principle cast members are stacked along the side expressing different levels of fear and concern. The insert can sell for $38,835-$47,800, one-sheet for $13,800-$24,150, half-sheet for $10,155-$23,900, lobby card for $715-$9,775, and window card for $3,585-$8,625.

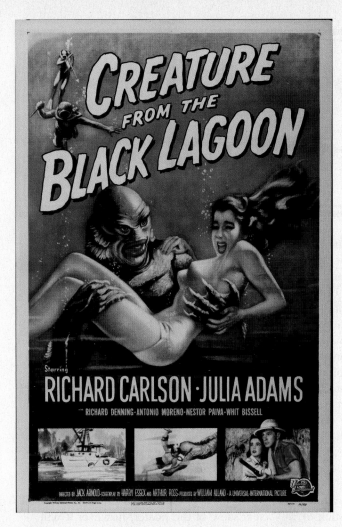

Creature from the Black Lagoon has a large central image of a terrified Kay being carried underwater by the Creature with smaller images of David and Mark above with weapons aimed at the Creature with three stills at the bottom of the poster. The coloring on the poster gives it an underwater effect, darker at the bottom and lighter at the top. The three-sheet shows a large image of the Creature looking down at a terrified Kay while small divers swim near his head with a very green and blue background as if it's in a lagoon. The one-sheet has sold for $4,025-$25,100, the three-sheet for $2,225-$19,000, six-sheet for $7,190-$17,925, and half-sheet for $1,980-$7,760.

Invasion of the Body Snatchers, Forbidden Planet, and *The War of the Worlds*. Universal embraced the trend in 1953, releasing *It Came from Outer Space*. While the movie features a different kind of monster than usually produced by Universal, the theme of misunderstood monsters and depiction of humans behaving monstrously followed into this science fiction horror film. The movie also served as a scary story about 1950s paranoia that aliens will come to our planet.

Monster, played by Glenn Strange, Lugosi returned as Dracula, Chaney, Jr. as the Wolf Man, and a cameo from the Invisible Man voiced by Vincent Price. The movie was able to reinvigorate Universal Monster movies by playing on the nostalgia for their most beloved monsters. Chaney, Jr. picked up the mantle as the go-to monster actor, starring in 17 of the 35 Universal Monster films in the '40s.

By the '50s, Universal's horror movies no longer included most of the original monsters, with Dracula, Frankenstein's Monster, and the Wolf Man retired in the 1948 Abbott and Costello movie. The comedy duo were back in 1951 for *Abbott and Costello Meet the Invisible Man* and in 1955 for *Abbott and Costello Meet the Mummy*, helping to keep the Invisible Man and the Mummy popular with audiences.

The 1950s saw other studios release a crop of very popular science fiction films like *The Day the Earth Stood Still*,

Creature from the Black Lagoon revived the genre for Universal in 1954 and was the last great Monster introduced by the production house. *Creature* told a story of evolution with archaeologists finding a fossilized appendage from a being that was part fish, part human before encountering the Gill-man himself. What drew people to the movie was the beauty and the beast plotline with the Gill-man falling for Kay, the girlfriend of a scientist who is searching for him. Director Jack Arnold was able to capture the interesting story with fright but also sympathy and beauty, particularly in a chilling underwater swimming sequence. The rest of the '50s comprised many one-shot horror films.

The Dos and Don'ts of Framing

Buying movie posters, particularly vintage posters, is quite an investment. Many posters sell for tens of thousands and a select group can sell for hundreds of thousands. With that kind of investment, it is crucial that you have the poster framed properly, using the best possible materials.

The most important thing to consider with the frame is what is in front of and what is behind the poster. The first thing to know is that glass is not the best material for framing. Glass can break easily during moving and transportation and will likely scratch, gouge, tear, or outright destroy the poster. Glass acts as a heat conductor which can cause the poster to fade and decay. It can trap moisture, creating mildew, and can cause the poster to stick to the glass. Spacers can help to separate the poster from the glass, but because of the size of one-sheets and larger posters, they can buckle in the center and will touch the glass anyways. Some framers use conservation glass because it has archival properties, but it can still break and damage the poster. Another negative aspect is the weight of a frame with glass, which makes the poster more cumbersome and difficult to transport.

Plexiglas is the best material to use for framing, with many benefits over glass and other plastics. It does not stick to the poster like glass, protecting it from damage. High grade Plexiglas has higher UV protection levels which block the sun's harsh rays. Note that it should be about 1/8" thick and the most important thing is to always use acid-free Plexiglas. When properly installed, it should be polished with antistatic cream or similar material to repel dirt and dust.

It is available in clear and non-glare types. Clear is just that: it presents a crystal clear view of the poster, however it will pick up the glare of lights. Non-glare glass is etched on one side which can cause the poster appearance to be somewhat out of focus, particularly if the poster is matted. However, it repels light glare, giving it a vivid appearance.

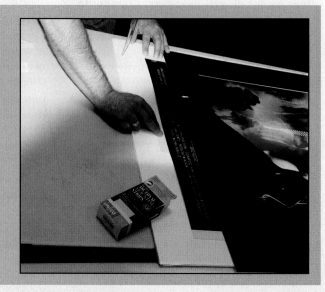

Be sure that it is indeed Plexiglas, not plastics like styrene or Lucite, which do not have UV filtering or other archival qualities. Use high grade Plexiglas, that won't yellow or become opaque. Lower grade plastics that are too thin can also warp and become distorted if they don't lay flat in the frame.

For the backing use artboard or foamcore, but be sure that the material is acid-free. Whether the poster is linen-backed or not, it's important to use acid-free backing. If the poster is just backed with cardboard, it will absorb the acid from the cardboard and become yellow and brittle.

After the poster is properly framed and hung proudly at home or in the office, do not use ammonia-based cleaners to clean the surface. Ammonia can cause clouding on the surface ruining the beautiful appearance you've worked to achieve. Use water or special cleaners without ammonia.

A Note on Framing
By Eric Bradley

Do-it-yourself framing can be done on the cheap. A quick web search uncovers affordable, aluminum frames with a basic acrylic covering to protect the poster from surface dust and grime that can be had for roughly $60. The flexible PVC lens is thin – extremely thin – and does not promise UV protection, although makers do say the film protects the poster from yellowing.

Having a poster framed by a professional can run $100-$500, but the frame is usually much sturdier and it accommodates the full size of the modern one-sheet of 27" by 41". The service includes Plexiglas and dust paper, which seals up the back of the poster neatly. It's a nice, professional service that is absolutely worth the cash and time.

When I had a 27" by 41" poster framed recently, I opted for a solid wood frame and UV filtering Plexiglas acrylic. The cost tipped in at $300 simply for the protective, high-end acrylic. But it was worth it. I can move the poster as many times as I need to without worry of shattering anything or exposing the 80-year-old poster to harmful sunlight.

Having posters linen-backed can cost up to $150 per poster. Experts usually do not advise the service for posters created from 1970 to the present simply because they can be easily replaced. Pre-WWII posters are generally candidates for linen-backing, but even the most advanced collectors would rather own a poster in its most original condition.

Sing a Song, Dance All Night, and Make 'Em Laugh

For over 85 years Hollywood has entertained audiences with movie musicals. Showcasing the talented triple threats who can act, sing, and dance, these movies transport viewers to the utmost fantasy lands where characters break into song when emotions overflow, sometimes accompanied by elaborate, synchronized dancing. They can be modern or period pieces, prodigious epics or simple stories, fitting into drama, comedy, even horror. With theatrical flair, emotional performances, and beautiful songs, musicals account for some of the most entertaining movies of all time.

The Jazz Singer, released in 1927, was the first movie musical. Starring Al Jolson as a Jewish Cantor who wants to set aside his family's religious traditions to become a jazz singer, it was also the first movie with sound.

Seeing the impact of *The Jazz Singer*, studios started cranking out musicals to duplicate the success. One of the early hits was *The Broadway Melody* in 1929, about a vaudeville duo who head for Broadway where their plans for stardom become complicated by love. The romantic comedy became the second winner of an Academy Award for Best Picture.

During the 1930s, many successful musicals were directed and/or choreographed by Broadway dance director Busby Berkeley. Utilizing his stage knowledge and work ethic, he created intricate dance routines that wowed audiences. One of his most noted films is *42nd Street*, often considered among

The Broadway Melody one-sheet is primarily white with the three leads in the center surrounded by high-stepping dancers. In recent years the one-sheet sold for $1,725-$31,070, lobby card for $480-$2,630, and program for $50-$390.

The Wizard of Oz style A three-sheet features basic sketch images of Dorothy and friends making their way along the winding Yellow Brick Road. The style D one-sheet includes three images: one photographic of Dorothy and Co., one of the two witches, and a wacky drawing of the leads as they would appear in a children's picture book. The style D one-sheet can sell for $25,300-$65,725, half-sheet for $9,775-$19,800, Australian one-sheet for $7,475, and Swedish one-sheet for $4,065.

Gaiety! Glory! Glamour!

THE WIZARD OF OZ

with
JUDY GARLAND
FRANK MORGAN
RAY BOLGER
BERT LAHR
JACK HALEY

BILLIE BURKE
MARGARET HAMILTON
CHARLEY GRAPEWIN
and **THE MUNCHKINS**

A VICTOR FLEMING Production
SCREEN PLAY BY NOEL LANGLEY, FLORENCE RYERSON AND
EDGAR ALLAN WOOLF FROM THE BOOK BY L. FRANK BAUM
Directed by
VICTOR FLEMING· MERVYN LEROY
Produced by

It's
**METRO-GOLDWYN-MAYER'S
TECHNICOLOR TRIUMPH!**

the best musicals, about a producer planning what could be his final Broadway show who must replace the star with a chorus girl.

Singing and dancing duo Fred Astaire and Ginger Rogers began their dynamic partnership in 1933. Their first outing was supporting roles in *Flying Down to Rio*, about a band leader and pilot who gets his group fired for flirting with the wrong woman. In 1934 the duo took the lead in *The Gay Divorcee* with Rogers as Mimi, a woman seeking divorce by hiring someone to make it appear like she's cheating and Astaire as Guy, the man Mimi mistakenly thinks has been sent to her for the faux affair. It featured the Cole Porter hit "Night and Day" and "The Continental," which was the first song to win the Academy Award for Best Original Song. In 1935, they starred in *Top Hat*, about an American dancer falling for a model who has mistaken him for his producer. They also had a hit in 1936's *Swing Time* with Astaire playing a performer and gambler engaged to a woman when he meets

Rogers as Penny, a dance teacher, with whom he reluctantly becomes smitten. It featured the gorgeous Jerome Kern and Dorothy Fields song "The Way You Look Tonight." A year later the duo's *Shall We Dance* featured the first score by George and Ira Gershwin and included the song "They Can't Take that Away from Me."

L. Frank Baum's beloved children's novel *The Wonderful Wizard of Oz* was brought to the screen in 1939. *The Wizard of Oz* is a visually dazzling tale about young Dorothy Gale on a quest to get back to Kansas, with her dog Toto, the Scarecrow, Tin Man, and Cowardly Lion. It is considered by the American Film Institute (AFI) to be the third greatest musical of all time and the ballad "Over the Rainbow," with music by Harold Arlen

The colorful **Singin' in the Rain** one-sheet depicts the three leads in yellow raincoats on a jaunty walk in the rain, under blue skies. In recent years the six-sheet has sold for $3,110-$12,650, three-sheet for $510-$4,180, and one-sheet for $520-$3,700.

and lyrics by E.Y. Harburg, won an Oscar for Best Original Song.

In the 1940s the music became more integrated into the larger story, rather than primarily as stage numbers. Rita Hayworth and Gene Kelly shared the spotlight in 1944's *Cover Girl* about a woman who wins a contest to become a cover girl which threatens her romance with her dance mentor. That same year, Bing Crosby starred in *Going My Way* as Father O'Malley, a clergyman who led a life of sports and music before joining the church, then uses his street smarts to

connect with the rebellious youth of the neighborhood.

The first half of the 1950s featured some of the most enduring musicals. In *Singin' in the Rain*, Kelly stars as a silent film star during the film industry's complicated transition into the era of sound. The 1952 movie is considered by AFI to be the best musical of all time. Two years later, Crosby, Danny Kaye, Rosemary Clooney, and Vera-Ellen told a Christmas story of romance, loyalty, and honor in *White Christmas*, featuring Irving Berlin's Oscar winning song of the same name. In

Using minimalism, the **West Side Story** poster is mostly red, featuring the title in large block letters beside dancing figures on the fire escape. The six-sheet recently sold for $2,600, three-sheet for $260-$1,550, and one-sheet for $95-$1,025.

1955 Marlon Brando, Jean Simmons, Frank Sinatra, and Vivian Blaine starred in *Guys and Dolls*. In Brando's first and only musical, he and Sinatra play criminal and gambling rascals, one trying to woo a straight-laced woman and the other hiding from the pressure of his girlfriend and the cops.

A trend of the late '50s to '60s showcased musicians transitioning into movies. Elvis Presley began with *Love Me Tender* in 1956, making other hits like *Jailhouse Rock*, *Blue Hawaii*, and *Viva Las Vegas*. Presley's musicals capitalized on his fame rather than substance of the songs he was singing, though they did produce several hits. (*Editor's note:* For more on Elvis Presley movies see our comprehensive coverage in this book.)

The Beatles began their movie career in 1964 with *A Hard Day's Night*. It was followed by *Help!*, *Magical Mystery Tour*, the animated *Yellow Submarine*, and *Let It Be*, a documentary about the making of an album which inevitably filmed tension within the band, capturing the beginning of their break-up.

The '60s started strong with *West Side Story*. In this *Romeo and Juliet* style story, Natalie Wood and Richard Beymer starred as two young adults from rival New York gangs who fall in love, causing additional tension between their respective groups. The 1961 film is considered AFI's second best musical of all time and won ten Academy Awards, including Best Picture. Three years later, *My Fair Lady*, based on George Bernard Shaw's *Pygmalion*, was released. Audrey Hepburn played Eliza Doolittle, a flower girl who takes speech lessons from a snobby professor to become a woman of high society.

That was also the year of *Mary Poppins*, one of Disney's most popular musicals, starring Julie Andrews and Dick Van Dyke in the story about a magical nanny who helps the family of an unhappy banker. Andrews captivated audiences again in 1965's *The Sound of Music*. As a woman who leaves an Austrian convent,

On the exciting **The Sound of Music** poster, Maria is running across the hill while the Von Trapps look on, painted in shades of pink, yellow, and tan it evokes warm tones and high energy. The three-sheet can sell for $260-$1,610, six-sheet for $885-$1,315, and one-sheet for $80-$860.

and becomes the governess for children of a widower in the Navy. The beautifully shot film won five Oscars, including Best Picture.

Broadway star Barbra Streisand made her film debut in the 1968 movie adaptation of *Funny Girl*. Loosely based on the life of Fanny Brice, the movie tells the story of a plain woman who becomes a star in New York while dealing with the complications of her marriage to a gambler. It includes two of Babs' biggest hits: the high energy "Don't Rain on My Parade," and the softer emotion-filled "Funny Girl."

A different kind of style prevailed in musicals of the 1970s. In 1972 Bob Fosse had people talking about the steamy *Cabaret* with the ever theatrical Liza Minnelli and Michael York. The story of a club entertainer in Berlin romancing two men at the same time with interludes by Joel Grey as the master of ceremonies, was equal parts sexy, burlesque, and intrigue. Minnelli's powerful rendition of "Maybe This Time" resonates as a defining moment of her career.

Midnight screenings became a staple after *The Rocky Horror Picture Show* debuted in 1975. Another musical for an adult audience, the plot starts when, after

their car breaks down, a couple seeks sanctuary in the weird residence of scantily clad Dr. Frank-N-Furter. Portraying sexuality in open, fluid terms, this envelope-pusher featured brilliant performances by the ensemble cast that included Tim Curry, Susan Sarandon, Barry Bostwick, Patricia Quinn, Nell Campbell, Richard O'Brien, and Meat Loaf. It has pumped up the theatricality with songs like "The Time Warp" and "Sweet Transvestite."

Musicals went to high school in 1978's *Grease*. Set in the late '50s Sandy, a square beauty from Australia falls for greaser Danny, but their summer love hits a snag when school starts and he becomes too cool to be the guy she fell for. As Sandy and Danny, Olivia Newton-John and John Travolta had terrific chemistry that was sweet, funny, and infectious. Another great ensemble cast, they performed excellent songs like "Summer Nights," "You're the One that I Want," and "We Go Together."

Audiences fell for a little girl with curly red hair in 1982's *Annie*. Set during the Great Depression, little orphan Annie is chosen to stay with a billionaire to help his image and ends up changing him instead. As Annie, Aileen Quinn's infectious smile and demeanor won fans with performances of classics "Tomorrow" and "It's a Hard Knock Life."

In 1983, Streisand starred in, directed, co-wrote, and co-produced the film adaptation of *Yentl*. The dramatic story about a Jewish girl who disguises herself as a boy to enter a religious school features Streisand hits "Papa, Can You Hear Me?" and "The Way He Makes Me Feel."

Three years later *Little Shop of Horrors* combined musical, comedy, and horror for a bizarrely entertaining movie. Using

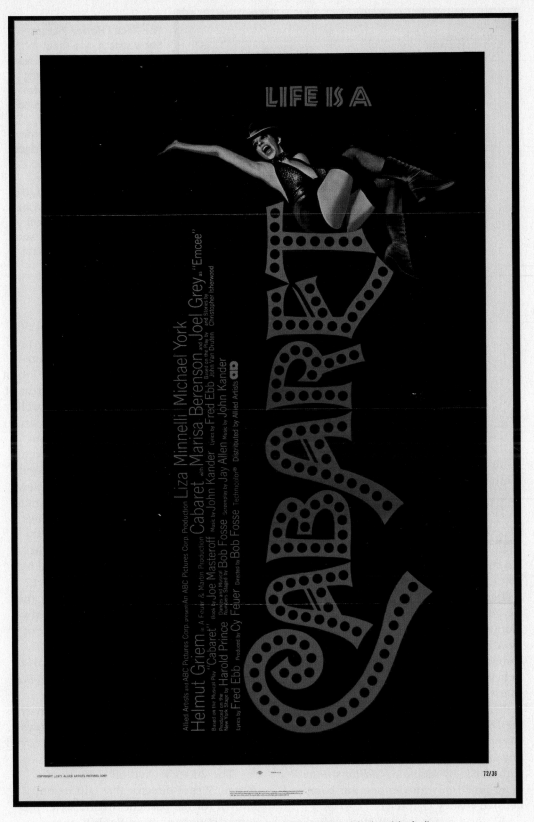

The marquee style **Cabaret** poster is solid black with the title fading
from purple to orange with Sally lounging on it in her burlesque outfit.
The Polish A1 features the master of ceremonies singing from Sally's
spinning legs in the form of a Swastika. The Polish A1 can sell for $895-
$1,800, Czech poster for $100-$825, and one-sheet for $25-$250.

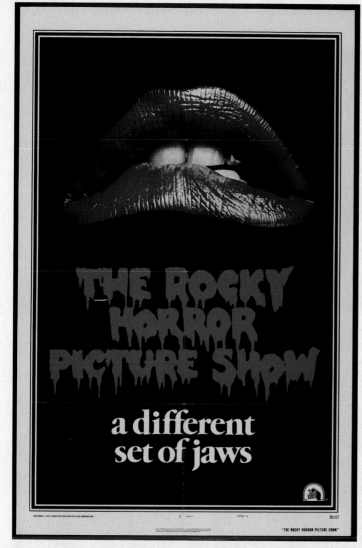

of both their social circles. Johnny Depp, already tired of his heartthrob reputation, did an excellent job of mocking it, with the rest of the cast acting delightfully over the top.

Two of the standout musicals of the '90s were stories of historical significance. Based on the New York City newsboy strike of 1899, *Newsies* follows a group of young newspaper sellers who fight the establishment and are challenged by domineering big business. Including 12 songs by brilliant composer Menken, the 1992 Disney movie also featured a baby faced Christian Bale as Jack, a leader of the newsies.

Madonna showed off her powerful voice and acting prowess in 1996's *Evita*. Based on the life of Evita Duarte, an Argentinian actress who eventually marries President Juan Perón, the movie follows her journey becoming both the most loved and hated woman in Argentina.

The 2000s kicked off with *Moulin Rouge*. Writer-director Baz Luhrmann, known for his pastiche artistic style, presented the story of an English poet who falls for a terminally ill cabaret star of the Moulin Rouge. The 2001 jukebox musical reimagined and mashed-up pop songs from "Lady Marmalade" to "Your Song,"

his charming nerd persona, Rick Moranis plays Seymour the unintentional owner of a plant with the ability to talk and a taste for human flesh. Directed by Yoda and Muppets voice actor Frank Oz and music by Alan Menken, the musical has great comedic cameos by Bill Murray, James Belushi, John Candy, and Christopher Guest.

The late '80s into the early '90s saw the Disney renaissance with *The Little Mermaid*, *Beauty and the Beast*, *Aladdin*, *The Lion King*, and *Pocahontas* – most with music by Menken. (*Editor's note*: For more on Disney movies see our comprehensive Disney chapter.)

Writer-director John Waters poked fun at society in the 1990 musical *Cry-Baby*. Set in the '50s, Baltimore bad boy Cry-Baby wins the heart of good girl Allison, much to the dismay of several members

On the **Chicago** one-sheet Roxie and Velma smirk over their shoulders while holding pistols behind their backs with Billy in between them in front of a large neon "C". The "13 Nominations" poster has a white background with the three leads facing forward in front of the "C". The one-sheet sells for $10-$70, "13 Nominations" style for $10-$110, and teasers for $10-$80.

"Diamonds Are a Girl's Best Friend" to "Smells Like Teen Spirit."

Chicago, director and choreographer Rob Marshall's masterpiece, was released in 2002. Set during the 1920s Jazz Age, two women – one a successful nightclub singer, the other a would-be singer dreaming of fame – kill their husbands. Once locked up in the same jail, the merry murderesses seek the legal help of a flashy lawyer. Renée Zellweger, Catherine Zeta-Jones, Richard Gere, Queen Latifah, and John C. Reilly lead the talented cast in song and dance numbers that were high energy, sexy, and rich with jazz.

Three years later, Chris Columbus adapted *Rent* from the stage musical by Jonathan Larson. The rock opera explores the complications of love, sexuality, drugs, life with AIDS, and the struggle to pay rent while living a bohemian lifestyle in the East Village of New York City. The music itself transitions dramatically from song to song covering everything from rock to performance art to tango and hymnal.

Dreamgirls, the journey of a trio of female soul singers topping the charts and navigating personal struggles within the group, was released in 2006. Featuring the powerhouse voices of contemporary pop/R&B singers Beyoncé Knowles and Jennifer Hudson, the movie churned out beautiful songs with emotional resonance.

The most recent successful musical was *Hairspray* in 2007. Based on Waters' original 1988 comedy that became a Broadway musical in 2002, it challenges traditions in Baltimore when Tracy, a pleasantly plump girl earns a spot on the local TV show and fights for racial integration during the early '60s. The high energy musical is filled with an all-star cast that includes Travolta, Queen Latifah, Michelle Pfeiffer, Christopher Walken, and Zac Efron.

Musicals may currently be in a period of stagnation, but with such a rich history of wonderful musicals, audiences have plenty that will have them singing along, tapping their feet, and falling in love. After all, the hills are alive with the sound of music. And all that jazz.

The Subjectivity of Movie Poster Grading

By Eric Bradley

Movie poster grading is still subjective for the most part and big league collectors don't see that changing any time soon. "Unlike comic books and coins, restoration and conservation in movie posters is a generally accepted practice," said Ralph DeLuca, a high profile movie poster collector. "All of these posters came folded and were printed on pulp paper and were never at all intended to be collected or saved or sold to the general public. They are very fragile so the chief qualifying factor for conservation and restoration is rarity."

The movie poster hobby has seen incredible growth in prices since 1990 as fresh finds came on the market and an affluent collecting public saw them as a more approachable form of pop culture art. The generally accepted grading guideline follows a 10-point scale ranging from "Mint" to describe the very best quality posters to a grade of "Poor" to describe a poster that's badly torn and in need of restoration just to be presentable.

Grading of collectible movie posters is subject to interpretation and opinions may vary. Any value estimate or past auction price may have little relevance to future transactions. Such factors as changing demand, popularity, new discoveries, strength of the overall market, and economics conditions are influences, according to poster collector Jim Halperin in his book *Collectible Movie Posters* (Whitman Publishing, 2010).

Rare discoveries such as one-sheet

variety from the 1931 Universal Studios classic *Dracula*, which DeLuca bought for $310,700 in a 2009 Heritage Auctions sale, qualify for conservation work because only three copies are known to exist.

The rare poster, from actor Nicolas Cage's collection, was presented with a grade of Very Fine on linen. The grade represents the poster's condition before it was sent to a restoration expert, who repaired several tiny holes, minor tears, and minor cross-fold separation and slight

paper loss before preserving the integrity of the poster with a linen-back. DeLuca was happy to spend hundreds of thousands to own the rare survivor because, he said, he sees condition and rarity as a pyramid: "If something's really rare – maybe one to three copies – I and other collectors are much more lenient when buying posters that need restoration. The more common a poster then the more critical I am that it be as close to perfect as possible."

Unlike the encapsulation, a/k/a "slabbing," of vintage comic books and coins, movie posters present a series of

challenges for that form of preservation. Chief among them is the size. Standard one-sheet sizes measure in a 27" wide by 41" high, but the size is a relatively recent phenomenon. Sizes can vary from an inch or more on the height to 40" by 60" for 1960s releases and a host of differences for posters produced in Denmark, Italy, and Poland. Lobby cards are encapsulated, the collectibles grading company Certified Guaranty Company leads the industry, but only because they are a manageable size of 11" by 14".

"In the silent era of the 1920s and '30s there's not even a real size unity," DeLuca said. "Other than lobby cards and most post-1960s or 1970s paper it would really be impossible to have any kind of slabbing system for that reason."

DeLuca said he and many other dedicated collectors prefer to buy posters in unrestored condition. He sees the same mentality among comic book, coin, and stamp collectors who seek out vintage movie posters from time to time. Fold lines on posters – caused by the distributor as the poster was sent to theater owners – are not considered detrimental to the poster's overall condition for pricing purposes, however some collectors work to have them removed during the framing or restoration process.

"Some people can't stand to see the fold lines in a poster so they have it sprayed or flattened when they really don't need to be," he said. "Posters from the 1950s or earlier are a sweet spot and I don't think a poster should ever be perfect. It should be conserved and presented in the best way to preserve the presentation, but I don't mind a tiny stain or fold marks because that's endemic to the poster. It shows originality."

Collectors who seek out restoration

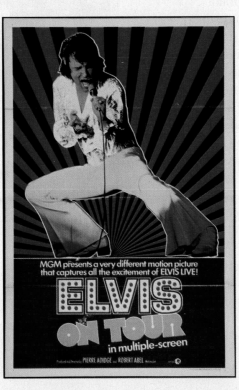

have a duty to take several pre-restoration photos of the movie poster, DeLuca advises. The images can come in handy when it's time to sell. Reputable auction houses and dealers should always state grades on all restored items as pre-restoration grades.

"[Collectors] that are coming at them from the poster art angle tend to want posters over perfect and a fine with linen-backing," DeLuca said. "Generally, you only linen-back a poster if it needs it."

HERITAGE AUCTIONS MOVIE POSTER GRADING GUIDE

Mint: A never-used poster. May show minor signs of age and wear at folds due to storage. No holes, no tears.

Near Mint: A generally unused poster with fresh, saturated colors. May have minimal tears at folds. Has no significant holes, no paper loss. May have minor tears along edges, and fine pinholes.

Fine: A poster with bright colors, clean, with general signs of use. May have minor tears at folds with minor paper loss. May have fine pinholes. May have restoration.

Good: An average poster with overall fresh color. May have tears, minor paper loss, minor hazing. Paper may be brittle due to age. May have minor stains or a small amount of writing in an unobtrusive place. May have medium or major restoration.

Fair: A poster with faded colors and brittle paper, showing significant signs of use. May have tears and paper loss, and tape, writing, and stains in image area. In need of restoration or has undergone major restoration.

Poor: A poster that is worn, torn, and damaged. May have staining, cracking, dry rot, and large tears. May be heavily soiled, with pieces missing. In need of major restoration.

MINT
THE TAIRA CLAN
JAPANESE B2

FINE+
THE CATMAN OF PARIS
ONE-SHEET

POOR
DON'T BET ON BLONDES
ONE-SHEET

CGC Grading Scale on Movie-Related Collectibles

Certified Guaranty Company (CGC) employs a 10-point grading scale for movie lobby cards and mini window cards that is based on the industry standard used for comics and magazines, and was pioneered by CGC in 1999.

CGC Grading Scale

10.0 Gem Mint

9.9 Mint

9.8 Near Mint/Mint

9.6 Near Mint +

9.4 Near Mint

9.2 Near Mint -

9.0 Very Fine/Near Mint

8.5 Very Fine +

8.0 Very Fine

7.5 Very Fine -

7.0 Fine/Very Fine

6.5 Fine +

6.0 Fine

5.5 Fine -

5.0 Very Good/Fine

4.5 Very Good +

4.0 Very Good

3.5 Very Good -

3.0 Good/Very Good

2.5 Good +

2.0 Good

1.8 Good -

1.5 Fair/Good

1.0 Fair

.5 Poor

*Presented courtesy Certified Guaranty Company, certifiedguaranty.com

eMoviePoster.com
Basics of grading

Movie posters, generally being made out of a paper product, are not "minted" like coins. With few exceptions, they are either displayed in movie theaters or sent to movie poster exchanges, where they sit for decades, unprotected, on dusty shelves. Because of this, almost all show some signs of age and wear. Even most of the ones that never made it to a theater show wear, and almost all of the ones that were used for display have a good amount of use.

Therefore, we at eMoviePoster.com use a grading system all our own, not derived from ones used in other hobbies. Our top grade is "fine," which means the poster is virtually defect-free. Our next grade is "very good to fine," to indicate a poster with just a few defects. After that is "very good," a poster with clear defects, but ones that are not very distracting, making it a poster that collectors would display "as is."

Next comes "good to very good," with defects that are more significant but are not the sort that are difficult to repair, or are not terribly distracting. Then comes "good," where the defects are significant enough that you would only display the poster if it were restored. Below that are "fair" and "poor" where the defects are really significant, and it might be quite costly to repair them. And of course, there are all the in-between grades, for all of those posters on the edge between two different grades.

Fine
The poster is virtually defect-free.

Very Good to Fine
A poster with just a few defects.

Very Good
A poster with clear defects, but ones that are not very distracting, making it a poster that collectors would display "as is."

Good
The defects are significant enough that you would only display the poster if it were restored.

Fair/Poor
The defects are really significant, and it might be quite costly to repair them.

The Apex
of Elegance
and Class

DREW STRUZAN: AIRBRUSH WITH SUCCESS

The Thing one-sheet is electrifying and mysterious with bright crystals of light exploding from the face of the figure who appears to be encased in ice. In recent years, the one-sheet has sold for $30-$450 and the insert for $75-$300.

Snake Plissken, Indiana Jones, Princess Leia, Rambo, Marty McFly, Harry Potter, and Tinkerbell. What do these infamous, famous, and beloved characters have in common? They were all immortalized on movie posters by Drew Struzan.

Throughout his extensive career, Struzan has illustrated more than 150 movie posters. He is known as a favored artist of icons George Lucas and Steven Spielberg.

The neon-tinged **Blade Runner** one-sheet has close-up images of the main characters Rick Deckard, Rachael, and Roy Batty with flares of light raining down on the image. The one-sheet can sell for $30-$100.

Struzan's **Indiana Jones and the Last Crusade** one-sheet features close-up images of Indy and his dad with a horse-riding action sequence in the center of the poster. The tan background mirrors the sandy structures of the architectures they visit. In recent years the one-sheet has sold for $20-$260.

He utilized his realism-focused style on memorable posters for many box office blockbusters and cult favorites including multiple *Star Wars* episodes, the *Back to the Future* trilogy, *Harry Potter and the Sorcerer's Stone*, *Hook*, *First Blood*, and *The Thing*, among many others.

In addition to his movie posters, Struzan is also well known for his painted album covers, collectibles, and book covers.

Born in Oregon City, Oregon in 1947, when it came time to enroll in higher education, he chose to attend the Art Center College of Design in West Los Angeles, California in 1965. During a session with his guidance counselor, he was told that he could major in fine art or illustration. The counselor explained that majoring in fine art meant that he could paint what he wanted and that majoring in illustration meant that he'd get paid to paint.

The hungry artist chose to become an illustrator. While working his way through school, Struzan sold artwork and accepted small commission work. After five years he graduated with a Bachelor of Arts degree with honors. He completed two years of graduate studies and eventually went back to the school for a short time years later to teach.

Following graduation he stayed in Los Angeles, working as a staff artist for the design studio Pacific Eye & Ear. He spent his time designing album covers, creating artwork for Black Sabbath, Tony Orlando and Dawn, the Bee Gees, the Beach Boys, Bach, Roy Orbison, Glenn Miller, Liberace, and Earth, Wind and Fire. Among his most celebrated covers was the illustration for Alice Cooper's *Welcome to My Nightmare*.

The **Back to the Future** poster features Marty McFly standing next to his DeLorean time machine with flames marking the tire tracks. In recent years the one-sheet has sold for $40-$500, subway for $490, and French eight-panel for $265.

On **The Goonies** one-sheet, the kids hang from a stalactite in cascading order, clutching onto one another over an image of the map that guides their course. The one-sheet can sell for $40-$300.

The next step in his journey was the beginning of his movie career. He started Pencil Pushers, a small company with a friend who had a background in the movie industry, which lasted eight years. During this time he honed his skills, providing artwork for one-sheets with an airbrush style, which would become his signature. His first posters were commissioned in 1975, mainly for B-movies like *Empire of the Ants* and *Food of the Gods*. Then things took a dramatic turn for the best in 1977 when George Lucas hired artist Charles White III to design a *Star Wars* poster for the 1978 rerelease.

White, who was well known for his airbrush style, asked Struzan to help with the portraits of the characters on the poster. White focused on the ships, Darth Vader, C-3PO and mechanical details, while Struzan worked on the human characters using oil paints. White and Struzan painted several action images with Luke clutching Leia in one hand and a rope in another, Leia shooting a blaster, a portrait of Han Solo, Darth Vader wielding his lightsaber, and C-3PO and R2-D2 cruising in a land speeder. When the artists learned that there wasn't enough room to list the film's credits, they manipulated the image to make it appear to be a torn bill posted on plywood. They added Obi-Wan on the lower left side to make it look wider and deeper. The *Star Wars* style D poster became popularly known as the circus poster.

He continued working with George Lucas by designing the original logo for his special effects company, Industrial Light & Magic. A few years later he created a post-release poster for the Steven Spielberg directed, Lucas co-written and produced, *Indiana Jones and the Temple of Doom*. Struzan's post-released poster became the primary image for the film, replacing the one-sheet in theaters. Continuing with the series, he provided all the promotional art for *The Last Crusade* and video box covers

Struzan's **Adventures in Babysitting** one-sheet is done in similar style to The Goonies poster. Chris and the kids in her charge are scaling the side of a building in various stages of exhilaration and fear with vibrant skyscrapers behind them. The one-sheet can sell for $10-$75.

for *Young Indiana Jones.*

In addition to creating poster designs for new movies, he was sought after to paint artwork for rereleases, reissues, video releases, book covers, theme park rides, and video games. His work became the defining imagery for *Star Wars* and *Indiana Jones.*

Throughout the 1980s he was creating about ten poster designs each year, including those for some of the biggest films of the decade. In 1982 he was commissioned to work on concepts for Ridley Scott's sci-fi movie *Blade Runner.* His poster design was shelved, but years later he was contacted to provide art for a director's version of the film. He updated the art and it was used for the DVD cover in 2007.

Then in 1985, he created his first *Back to the Future* poster featuring time traveling teen Marty McFly checking his watch as he gets ready for an adventure. He followed that up with the *Back to the Future Part II* poster in '89 depicting Marty in his futuristic clothing, joined by Doc Brown. A year later he provided art for the last chapter in the trilogy, giving it a Wild West theme with Marty and Doc in cowboy clothing, joined by Doc's love interest Clara. The second and third posters follow the format of the first movie, presenting a seamless transition from one to the next. Some of his other works throughout the '80s included *Cannonball Run, Police Academy, Coming to America, Risky Business, An American Tail, The Goonies,*

The **Coming to America** poster depicts Prince Akeem, larger than life in resplendent African style, as he towers in front of the gritty buildings of New York City. In recent years the one-sheet has sold for $20-$40.

and *Adventures in Babysitting*.

When computer imagery started dominating the poster industry, design work offers began to decline. Due to the rise in popularity for computer-designed images on posters, work hadn't been as steady for Struzan, stunting the Neoclassic style that dominated the '70s and '80s. Despite having fewer job offers, Struzan still created iconic poster art for films like *Hook, The Shawshank Redemption, Hellboy,* and the American version of *Harry Potter and the Sorcerer's Stone*.

With the decline of commissions for movie poster art, Struzan branched out into other types of media and venues for his art. He worked on comics, drew for games and collectibles, and providing limited edition art. He illustrated the art for U.S. postage stamps of Jimmy Stewart, composer Dimitri Tiomkin, and Yoda, drew the cover for Parker Brothers' new edition of Clue in 1996, and produced Franklin Mint collectible plates, including a 12-piece set commemorating Princess Diana.

After completing the extensive artwork for *Indiana Jones and the Kingdom of the Crystal Skull* in 2008, he announced his retirement. But that hasn't stopped him from completing more work, including producing the DVD *Conceiving and Creating the Hellboy Movie Poster Art* with a step-by-step process, creating an image of Mattel's Barbie for *Kurv* magazine in celebration of the doll's 50th birthday, and early in 2015 he designed a poster for the documentary *Batkid Begins*. Many of his fans have been hoping that he'd come out of retirement again to produce one-sheet designs for the new *Star Wars* movie, and he did not disappoint. As of the writing of this book, Struzan designed a one-sheet teaser for *The Force Awakens* for Disney's 2015 D23 Expo.

Struzan's distinct style has become a favorite among movie poster collectors. His detailed process started with sketching out drawings on illustration board, then tinting the draftsmanship with airbrushed acrylic paint, finishing with highlights and details with colored pencils, and finally more airbrushing. His work honors the film rather than just trying to promote it by simultaneously presenting an imaginative look at the movie while realistically connecting fans to the characters.

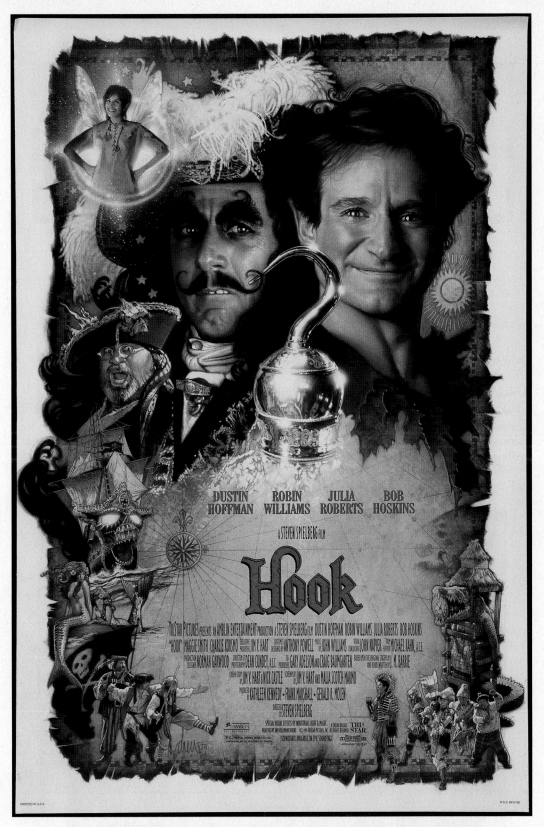

On the **Hook** one-sheet, Peter Pan smiles mischievously and Captain Hook glares menacingly with the title character, his hook, glistening brightly in the center of the poster. Tinkerbell, Smee, and the lost boys frame the edges of the poster in various states of action in this one-sheet that can sell for $10-$45.

BRUCE HERSHENSON
THE eMoviePoster WAY

Bruce Hershenson has been collecting movie posters for nearly 50 years and has been selling them since the early 1990s. He founded the movie poster auction company eMoviePoster in the late '90s, which sells tens of thousands of posters, and other paper-related movie memorabilia each year.

Overstreet: Let's start with the basics: Why do you love movie posters?
Bruce Hershenson (BH): I was a major comic book collector and dealer in the 1960s and 1970s. But those only appeal to a certain segment of the population. Movie posters appeal to absolutely everyone!

There is no one who does not have at least a few "favorite movies."

Overstreet: How long have you been collecting them?
BH: I started collecting in the late 1960s. I quit collecting in the mid-1970s and I sold

JAMES DEAN in "REBEL WITHOUT A CAUSE"
CINEMASCOPE AND WARNERCOLOR   A WARNER BROS. PICTURE

all my comic books, but I kept my movie poster collection. In the early 1980s, I investigated selling my movie posters, but instead, I became a collector again! In 1990, I started auctioning them in a major way, and that quickly became my sole source of income as well.

Overstreet: What was the first piece you purchased and what made you want to acquire it?
BH: It was a lobby card from *Rebel without a Cause*. I loved the movie, and I loved that I could buy an item from the movie and frame it on my wall. Soon all my walls were covered with framed lobby cards!

Overstreet: How long was it after that first acquisition that you began to consider yourself a collector?
BH: Pretty fast. But that was because I was already a major comic book collector.

Overstreet: Are you a movie buff or just a fan of the art?
BH: I am both. Some posters I solely appreciate for the movie (because the poster itself is bland), and in some cases, I love the art and have no idea what the movie is about!

Overstreet: Could you give us some examples of each?
BH: A good example of a great movie with much lesser art is the *Casablanca* one-sheet. A good example of a bad movie with a great poster is *The Clan of the Cave Bear* one-sheet. There are many more of each! One can go into our Auction History at http://www.emovieposter.com/agallery/archive.html and look at the posters by highest price first, and quickly see ones that fit each category (you can go to the posters from each decade at this page http://www.emovieposter.com/sales/decades.php).

Overstreet: What is the most valuable piece in your collection?

BH: I don't think in those terms. I am a collector, not an "investor"! That might seem funny since I auction them for a living, but I think people should collect for the "love" first, and put the investment element second.

Overstreet: Do you know how many pieces are in your personal collection?
BH: Only a few dozen posters, but tens of thousands of other items!

Overstreet: What are the perimeters of your collection? For instance, do you collect certain sizes or from certain artists?
BH: For 30 years I have been trying to get a pressbook from every movie ever made, and also all the studio yearbooks. It is an unending job! I also collect some oddball other stuff that is movie-related but not standard sizes.

Overstreet: A pressbook for every movie? That must be an arduous task. What other kind of movie-related memorabilia do you collect?

BH: The only other items I collect are the yearbooks that studios put out each year telling theater owners what movies they were planning for the coming year. Each studio made one of these for almost every year. I have hundreds of them, but I have been collecting them for over 35 years! There are many where the one I have is the only one I have ever seen, and there are many I have searched for and never seen even a single example.

Overstreet: You founded eMoviePoster in 1998. Did it start out as its own website straight out of the gate?

BH: Yes. As soon as I went online, I hired Eli Post to create a website. It looked like most 1998 websites, but it served its purpose well. At that time, we solely auctioned through eBay, so the website was just an informational place, with lots of images, designed to drive traffic to our auctions. In 2008, we left eBay completely (after 330,000 auctions there), and we started running the auctions on our own site, and we recently held our one millionth auction!

Overstreet: Can you give us a highlight reel about the company's growth over the past 17 years?

BH: Between 1998 and 2002, we auctioned one and a half to two million dollars per year. In 2003, we had our first two million dollar year. In 2008, we had our first three million dollar year. In 2012, we had our first four million dollar year, and the very next year we had our first five million dollar year. We are on track to pass that this year,

but we don't know by how much, because we never know exactly what we will be consigned over the coming months. Unlike most auctions, we don't own any of the items we auction, and our auctions are 100% consignments.

Overstreet: What effect does being 100% consignment based have on eMoviePoster's relationships with consignors and buyers?

BH: I think it is extremely helpful that we don't auction our own items in competition with our consignors' items, as so many other auctions do. Certainly, when an auction owns a lot of the items it sells, there must be a great temptation to favor those items over the consignors' items. Our consignors and buyers know that we are 100% consignment, and I am sure that is a significant reason for why we auction so many more items than any other auction.

Overstreet: What are your goals for the future of the company?

BH: I just want to keep doing what we do, and any ways there are to improve what we do, I want to embrace. It is hard to predict what the future holds, because the Internet, and the global economy, keeps changing in so many ways!

Overstreet: eMoviePoster starts auctions at very low prices. Why is that?

BH: All our auctions start at $1 with no reserve. We have all of the major dealers of the entire world following our auctions avidly, and many of them purchase their inventory through our auctions, picking up the bargains that fall through the

THE CLAN OF THE CAVE BEAR

COMING THIS FALL

cracks in every set of auctions. Because of this, it is rare for an item to auction for under half of a realistic retail price. But the possibility exists on all our items! We know that some people won't consign to us because they are unwilling to gamble on this, but the buyers love it so much that it results in higher prices overall, so the consignors who take the risk are usually well rewarded for their gamble.

Overstreet: The website sells a lot of international posters. Was this a plan of yours from the start?
BH: Initially we were primarily U.S. posters, just like every other U.S. auction. But over time, we learned a huge amount about how to identify international posters, and how to tell what release they were

from, so we have become the leading auctioneer in the U.S. of international posters, by a wide margin. Not only that, but a lot of our international posters are sent to us from other countries, because we often do a better job of auctioning them than the auctions in those countries do.

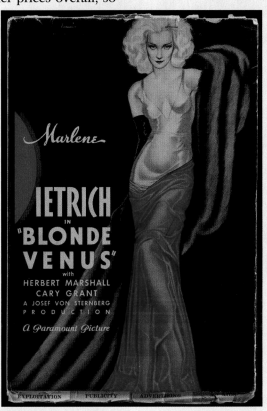

Overstreet: Is there a significant U.S. market for international posters?
BH: It is steadily growing. The primary market for any country's posters is the residents of that country, because people like to buy the posters they saw in the theaters when they went to the movies. But there are a lot of people who like to buy posters with great art no matter where they come from. This is especially true with Eastern European countries, especially Poland. Our auc-

costs. We put as many items into each package as can possibly be safely done, while we still pack more securely than any auction we know of. We use only custom-made tubes and boxes, and the people who pack our packages have worked for us for many years, and they are truly experts in packing movie-related memorabilia!

Overstreet: What are the criteria regarding condition for the posters you sell through eMoviePoster?
BH: This is what sets us apart from every other auction of movie posters! We grade on a far harsher scale than any other auction, and we go to great pains to describe every defect. We also provide supersized unenhanced images of every item, something that many auctions do not do.

tions have exposed lots of collectors to posters they were unaware of, and we create a lot of new collectors of international posters that way!

Overstreet: Do you have a lot of international customers?
BH: Approximately 40% of our auctions sell to international customers. This is far greater than any other U.S. auction. We allow our international customers six weeks in which to combine all their purchases. Over that time, we have auctioned around 15,000 items, so sometimes we are sending them a dozen or more posters in a single package. This saves them a huge amount over purchasing the same items from a dozen different auctions, and it results in many dedicated buyers for us!

Overstreet: I'm guessing it cuts down on shipping costs?
BH: It drastically cuts down shipping

Overstreet: How do you grade them?
BH: We have three people who spend all of their day grading movie posters, and that is all they do. They have done so for a long time, and have more expertise in doing this than virtually anyone else on the planet!

Overstreet: With reprinted posters so easily accessible, how do you verify that posters are the originals or authentic rereleases?
BH: We have a massive database, including images, of original posters, and also information and images about fakes. We also have people who have handled originals for many years, and have also seen many fakes, and have been trained in how to spot the differences. Some of them are very small differences. But one thing that is often true of fakes is that the paper stock is often different, and the printing quality is often not as high as that of originals.

Overstreet: If you had to categorize which type of posters (genre, time period, artist, etc.) are the highest sellers, how would you do so?

BH: The top classics of the 1930s are the highest selling items in terms of sheer dollars, but those posters are extremely rare and hardly ever come up for auction. Some auctions repeatedly offer the same posters over and over, and I don't know the explanation for why the buyers want to keep reoffering them. But in terms of popularity, some of the very most popular are the James Bond movies, the Star Wars movies, and other top franchises of the 1960s and 1970s. They don't sell for as much money as the much older classic posters, but there are far more collectors of those posters.

Overstreet: Is there a pricing difference between painted posters and photographic posters?

BH: Absolutely! Almost every collector prefers an artwork poster over a photographic one. That is why one-sheet posters from the 1930s to 1950s, which usually have artwork, usually sell for far more than the smaller posters and lobby cards, which usually are photographic. Unfortunately, in the last few decades, the majority of posters are floating heads, or other boring photographic designs. Thankfully, there are a few exceptions!

Overstreet: What advice would you give collectors to avoid overpaying for posters?

BH: One great piece of advice is to differentiate between "asking prices" and "selling prices." Just because you see a poster listed for $300 does not mean that anybody ever has paid close to that, and even if someone did, maybe that person was misinformed and vastly overpaid. The best resource for checking poster prices is our Auction History database on our website, eMoviePoster.com. It has almost every item we have ever auctioned – well over one million – and you get the image, the condition, and the actual selling price. Unlike every other similar online database, we drop out all results where the item was canceled or returned. That means you know that the price you see on the above database is one that was actually paid in cash. Also, many items have been auctioned by us dozens of times, so you can see a very wide range of actual selling prices, which gives you a better sense of what it really sells for.

Overstreet: How has movie poster collecting fared during the ups and downs of the economy over the last several years?

BH: Like with all other collectibles, some items have gone down and some have gone up. It doesn't seem all that related

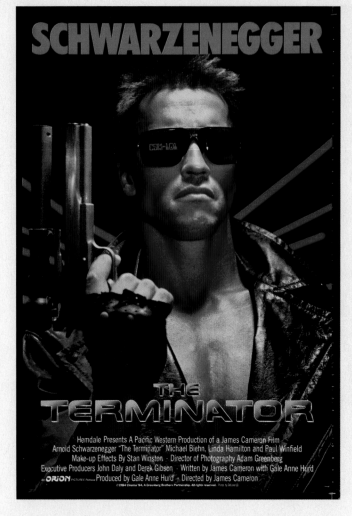

Hemdale Presents A Pacific Western Production of a James Cameron Film
Arnold Schwarzenegger "The Terminator" Michael Biehn, Linda Hamilton and Paul Winfield
Make-up Effects By Stan Winston · Director of Photography Adam Greenberg
Executive Producers John Daly and Derek Gibson · Written by James Cameron with Gale Anne Hurd
An ORION PICTURES Release Produced by Gale Anne Hurd · Directed by James Cameron
©1984 Cinema '84, A Greenberg Brothers Partnership. All rights reserved. Printed by DeLuxe ®

company's history. What do you attribute to that success and growth?

BH: A major factor was that two different long time collectors began consigning very large collections to us. That provided us with an excellent nucleus of material for our auctions over the first six months of 2015, which has given us sales of $2.8 million during that time. Of course, we would love for the second half of the year to match that, but that all depends on the consignments we receive! Also, our business continues to expand thanks to the virtual complete implosion of eBay. Where there were once hundreds of sellers auctioning quality vintage movie posters there on a weekly basis, there is now only a tiny number remaining. It is in no way the fault of those sellers. eBay has continued to change their site in negative ways. The movie poster section is overrun with repros and fakes, and eBay does nothing to change that. Many of those people who used to sell on eBay now consign to us, and many of the people who used to search eBay now find they are happy to solely search our site.

Overstreet: Unlike some popular collecting fields, movie posters have both a very pricey high end and a very accessible entry level. In your opinion, does that keep new collectors coming into the market?

BH: Obviously, few people will start out buying a $10,000 or $20,000 poster. You can purchase posters on any price level. One thing that differentiates the poster hobby from all other collectible hobbies is that the posters were never openly sold to the public, even to the present day. In every other collectible field, you could have purchased the items brand new when they were created. This means that every attic has potential to have a collection of

to the economy. It seems more related to the aging of collectors, and the changing tastes. A great example is B-westerns, from the 1940s, with stars like Roy Rogers and Hopalong Cassidy. Most of the people who grew up watching those movies are now no longer with us, or have reached an age where they are no longer collecting. So many of those posters have dropped considerably in price over the last 15 years. Conversely, 15 years ago, you could purchase a lot of posters from the 1980s and 1990s for next-to-nothing, and the ones from the best movies of those decades now sell for quite respectable prices. In 1994, you could easily purchase the one-sheet poster from *The Terminator* for $20 or less. Now, it auctions for around $100 to $150 in nice condition!

Overstreet: From January 2015 through June 2015, eMoviePoster.com had their most successful first half of the year in the

comic books or baseball cards or whatever, but only a tiny percentage of attics may have movie posters, because only people connected to movie theaters ever had access to them. Also, there are virtually no stores that sell movie posters (new or old). This helps create new collectors in all other hobbies, but the lack of them helps to keep the movie poster hobby much smaller than other collectible hobbies.

Overstreet: If you were starting out right now, what posters do you think you'd collect?

BH: Absolutely, it would be some of the better posters of the past 30 years. They tend to be in a price range of $20 to $300. When you see something sold over and over for $20, you think it can't rise in value, but look at my example of *The*

Terminator above. In spite of being sold many hundreds of times, the price has risen steadily from under $20 to around $100 to $150. It will likely continue to rise over the coming years, as it becomes more difficult to find. But, as I said above, one should only collect these posters (or any posters), because you love owning them, not just solely in the hopes that the price will rise!

Overstreet: Thanks so much for talking with me, Bruce. Do you have any final comments or advice you'd like to share?

BH: We are trying hard to have our best year ever in 2015, and we continue to look for any way possible to improve every aspect of our business and our website. We are not satisfied with staying where we are. We always want to get better!

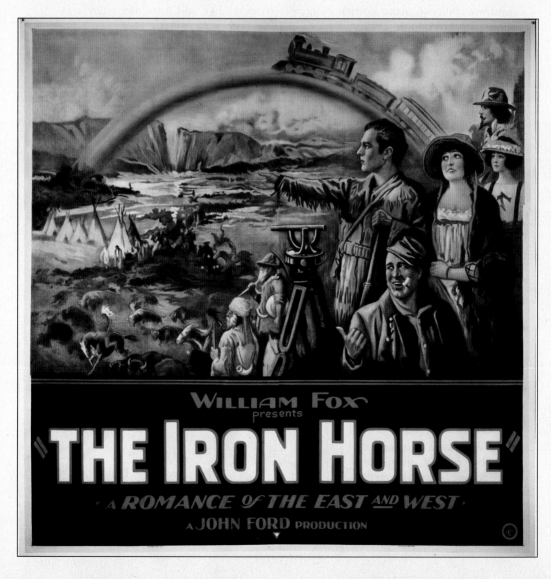

THE WONDERFULLY WEIRD WORLD OF TIM BURTON

Tim Burton has developed a reputation as the maker of strange movies filled with bizarre characters. He directs through the lens of peculiarity with gothic architecture, moody lighting, and pale actors in ostentatious wardrobes. He has the uncanny ability to make normal behaviors seem strange and bring normalcy and compassion to oddities.

The **Pee-wee's Big Adventure** one-sheet shows the high energy man-child Pee-wee Herman kicking his feet up in the air and shouting happily as he hangs onto his prize bike. The one-sheet can sell for $10-$180 and the presskit for $60-$180.

Like many great directors, Burton's love of film is traced back to his childhood. Born on August 25, 1958, he was raised in Burbank, California, where he grew up watching Roger Corman horror flicks starring Vincent Price. In addition to his love for movies, he had an affinity for art, which he pursued at the California Institute of the Arts, where he majored in animation. After graduating in 1980, he started working as an apprentice animator at Walt Disney Studios, though he only stayed for a year. In 1982 he released the stop-motion short *Vincent*, about a boy who pretends to be like horror actor Vincent Price. Not only did Burton immortalize his childhood idol, he got Price to narrate the film.

His next short film came two years later with the live-action version of *Frankenweenie*, a Frankenstein story about

a dog. Impressed with the film, actor Paul Reubens, the man-child who entertained children as Pee-wee Herman, asked Burton to direct his upcoming feature length film, *Pee-wee's Big Adventure*. Reubens and Burton made a great team, and the film was a success, which opened many doors for the aspiring director. In 1988 he directed the quintessential Burton movie, *Beetlejuice*, starring Michael Keaton, Geena Davis, and Alec Baldwin as housebound ghosts. It cemented Burton's reputation for combining horror and fantasy with bizarre humor and gothic visual style, fast-tracking him on Hollywood's radar.

Burton's next project was Warner Bros.' mainstream adaptation of *Batman* in 1989. His casting choice of Michael Keaton cre-

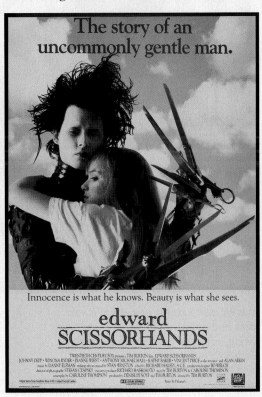

The **Beetlejuice** one-sheet shows the larger than life ghost with the most sitting on the house, flanked by Adam and Barbara Maitland in their wedding clothes. Betelgeuse holds Adam's head in his hand and ghosts seen throughout the film hang out on the front of the house with the Deetz family standing frightened at the bottom of the poster. In recent years the one-sheet has sold for $15-$100, Australian daybill for $20-$30, presskit for $50-$90, and set of 8 lobby cards for $30-$60.

The **Edward Scissorhands** one-sheet shows the up close profile of Edward's heavily scarred face, counterbalanced by his beautiful, delicate features, with a few of the very sharp blades from his scissorhands below, reflecting an image of his face. The international one-sheet shows Edward and his love Kim, her arms wrapped protectively around him while he holds his dangerous scissorhands away from her back. The one-sheet can sell for $20-$170, British quad for $15-$60, international one-sheet for $20-$60, advance style A one-sheet for $15-$70, and advance style B one-sheet for $15-$20.

The **Batman Returns** one-sheet is very dark and moody in tones of black, blue, white, and gray depicting a scowling Batman, Catwoman ready to scratch, and Penguin leering out of the poster at the viewer. The "Oswald Cobblepot for Mayor" printer's proof is a poster that is used throughout the film with Oswald shown proudly facing the light ready to usher Gotham into a new day. The one-sheet sells for $10-$115, "Oswald Cobblepot for Mayor" printer's proof for $340-$1,015, Japanese B2 for $360, advance one-sheet of Batman for $20-$80, advance one-sheet of Batman logo for $10-$60, advance one-sheet of Batman's head for $20-$205, and subway poster of Catwoman for $100-$520.

ated a clash with studio executives and drew ire of Batman fans who fervently believed that comedic actor Keaton was not right for the role. But Burton was convinced that the superhero didn't need to be physically intimidating since he had the cunning and intellect of Bruce Wayne with Batman's gadgetry. He swayed the studio to stick with Keaton, then cast the animated, intimidating Jack Nicholson to play the Joker and Kim Basinger as Bruce's lady love. His casting gamble paid off and *Batman* produced $100 million in box office results during the first 10 days.

The hits came fast for Burton in the 1990s. He opened the decade by directing the odd, yet sweetly affecting *Edward Scissorhands*, marking his second collaboration with wide-eyed Winona Ryder and the first of many with Hollywood heartthrob Johnny Depp. *Edward Scissorhands* is celebrated by critics and fans alike, for satirizing suburbia and vilifying intolerance, while telling a simple love story of longing for companionship. His next project was a sequel for the Caped Crusader with *Batman Returns*, reteaming with Keaton, and adding in the talents of Michelle Pfeiffer, Danny DeVito, and Christopher Walken. In 1994 he directed the black and white biopic *Ed Wood*, portraying the life of low budget science fiction director Ed Wood, with Depp playing the title role and Martin Landau in an Academy Award winning performance as Bela Lugosi. In 1996 he directed the alien invasion flick *Mars Attacks!*, based on the 1960s trading cards. The sci-fi campfest boasts an A-list ensemble cast led by Nicholson, DeVito, Glenn Close, Annette Bening, Pierce Brosnan, Martin Short, Sarah Jessica Parker, and Michael J. Fox. Three years later he directed an interpretation of Washington Irving's *Sleepy Hollow*, casting Depp as Ichabod Crane and Christina Ricci as Katrina Van Tassel.

In the early 2000s, Burton spent most of his time on adaptations and remakes. In 2001 he directed a remake of *Planet of the Apes* with Mark Wahlberg; in 2003 he directed *Big Fish*, based on the novel *Big Fish: A Novel of Mythic Proportions* by Daniel

The **Big Fish** one-sheet isn't a big seller but it is one of the best posters for a Tim Burton film. "Big Fish" is painted across the center of the poster with tree branches sprouting from the top of the letters with young Ed walking between them and the rest of the scenery is a beautiful winding road and hillside under a mild, blue sky. The Japanese B2 is an off-kilter image of Ed and Sandra laying in a field of bright yellow flowers that swirls up the sides of the posters to show other images from the film curling around the edges. The one-sheet can sell for $25, Japanese B2 for $20, and deluxe set of ten lobby cards for $45.

The international **Ed Wood** one-sheet is black and white with Dolores handing Ed a bright pink sweater with the quirky tagline "Movies were his passion. Women were his inspiration. Angora sweaters were his weakness." The U.S. one-sheet is also a black and white shot from behind the director sitting in his chair with "Ed Wood" written across the back and Ed smiling in profile. In recent years the international one-sheet has sold for $15-$240, U.S. one-sheet for $10-$65, ten lobby cards for $105, and British quad for $50-$90.

Wallace; then in 2005 he directed *Charlie and the Chocolate Factory* based on the novel of the same name by Roald Dahl. Also in 2005 he made his first full-length stop-motion film as a director with *Corpse Bride*, featuring favorite collaborators Depp and Helena Bonham Carter voicing the two main characters. It received an Academy Award nomination for Best Animated Feature Film. Burton's next project was the horror-musical adaptation of *Sweeney Todd: The Demon Barber of Fleet Street* with Depp, Bonham Carter, and Alan Rickman. His actors gave passionate performances of deviant characters willing to cut throats, literally and figuratively, and bake cannibalistic meat pies – all while singing. *Sweeney Todd* won an Oscar for Best Achievement in Art Direction and was nominated for two more.

Burton directed two more adaptations in 2010 and 2012 with a live-action version of Lewis Carroll's *Alice in Wonderland* and one

of *Dark Shadows*, based on the 1960s TV show. Also in 2012, he directed a full-length animated version of his early career project *Frankenweenie*. In 2014 he directed Amy Adams and Christoph Waltz in *Big Eyes*, telling the story of real life 1950s painter Margaret Keane and her husband Walter, who took credit for her work. He is currently working on *Miss Peregrine's Home for Peculiar Children* and a long-awaited sequel to *Beetlejuice*.

Whether he is directing a new project or making adaptations and remakes, Burton excels where many directors cannot. Every project is stamped with the Burton-esque kaleidoscope of bizarreness, affection for the oddities, mythic Halloween-like energy, and marriage of darkness with light. Animated or live-action, lighthearted or serious, ghost with the most or boy with a golden ticket, you'll know it's a Burton movie as soon as the title sequence begins.

Protecting and Storing Your Posters

*How to store movie posters so that little children (or **Star Wars** fans) won't pick them up and use them as swords (or lightsabers)*

Movie poster collectors don't stop collecting after available wall space has been covered by frames. Once those prized few have been chosen for display it is crucial that the rest of the collection is stored properly to protect the investment.

Posters can be stored rolled or laid flat. Collectors should understand both formats, and determine which fits their needs and practical storage spaces.

Storing Rolled Posters

Rolled posters should be stored differently for short-term or long-term time periods. If they will be handled often, they should be placed individually inside acid-free plastic sleeves and heavy cardboard tubes. These tubes can be easily organized by writing the title on a mailing label and sticking it on the tube, not the poster. That way one poster can conveniently be unrolled and viewed without potentially damaging several posters.

Posters in short term storage can be stored standing on end or laid flat. If rolled individually and laid flat, but not in cardboard tubes, do not store more than 10 posters on top of each other. The weight can cause waving in the posters on the bottom of the stack. If a larger number needs to be stacked, store them in heavy cardboard tubes to protect from waving. If stored standing on end, place them gently into a storage box or other location so that the ends don't get damaged.

Posters that are rolled for long term storage can be layered into larger tubes. First, decide if they will be stored standing upright or laid flat. If they will be standing upright, round, square-shaped, or triangular tubes are acceptable. However, if rolled posters will be placed in multiple tubes and stacked, then square-shaped tubes are much easier to use. If they are stacked, it is important that three or four layers of tubes is not exceeded – depending on how many posters are inside the tubes – because the weight will weaken the integrity of the bottom stacks. If the tubes bend posters inside will become warped and possibly creased.

Before storing posters, examine them to

These rolled posters are housed in round and triangular tubes as well as a rectangular box. Since they will be viewed often they are kept in individual tubes for easy access.

make sure they are clean and free of any debris that could damage them while stored. For cataloging purposes, make a list of the posters on a mailing or packing label to display on the cardboard tube. When rolling posters together make sure that all edges match up so that none are creased inside the tube. After the posters are rolled, put them in an acid-free, high quality plastic bag. Tuck the acid-free bag around the ends of the poster roll to ensure that the cardboard tube will not touch any part of the posters. Taping the ends is a beneficially way to ensure protection, as long as the tape does not touch the posters. Place the rolled posters inside of the tube to determine if there is any more space left in the tube. If there is still room, the roll can be padded with newspaper or similar materials to protect it from bouncing in the tube and causing damage. Store them in a cool, dry place away from excessive heat, moisture, animals, and every day in-house traffic.

Storing Flat Items

The best way to store flat items is to seal each poster in a Mylar sheet with acid-free backing board. After this is done, put all posters in a heavy case, such as archival boxes or architect filing cabinets. Before putting the posters in the Mylar sleeve wipe off any dust and dirt, which can damage the poster during storage. Place them inside the sleeves and make sure that all edges are covered and will not be exposed to the archival box. Sealing them this way guards them from the infiltration of dust, especially if the posters are being stored under a bed or other furniture.

Another benefit for this type of storage is that each poster can be viewed without removing them from the protective covering. However, it can be cumbersome to find posters in the center or bottom of a large stack and possibly cause damage, which is why the backing board is important. As with any type of storage, keep them in a cool, dry environment and post a label on the box or file designating which posters are inside.

If the flat items are going to be stored standing up, they should be housed in a thick cardboard case that will not buckle. Excess space within the case should be padded to keep the poster immobile. It is, however, better to store them lying flat.

Storing Smaller Movie Materials

Lobby cards, window cards, movie stills, pressbooks, programs, heralds and folded posters should be placed in acid-free plastic sleeves on backing boards. These can easily be stored in filing cabinets or in lobby card storage boxes.

Glass slides should be wrapped individually in photo safe archival paper then placed in an archival sleeve. They should be placed vertically in metal drawers with dividers separating each one. These materials can be purchased through archival suppliers.

Posters kept in an architect filing cabinet. To further protect these posters it is suggested that the collector put the posters inside Mylar sleeves, which will prevent degrading during storage.

By J.C. Vaughn

Sean Connery. George Lazenby. Roger Moore. Timothy Dalton. Pierce Brosnan. Daniel Craig.

Bond. James Bond.

After more than five decades on the silver screen, it's nearly impossible to imagine a more ubiquitous introduction in cinema, and it didn't take long after the

character's creation for him to start moving in that direction.

Ian Fleming's secret agent 007 of Her Majesty's Secret Service first appeared in hardcover in the novel *Casino Royale* in 1953 and by 1954 the CBS television network had sensed enough potential to have it adapted as an episode of its anthology

From Russia With Love British Quad

Although the famous image of the "Bond pose" with the gun is correctly attributed to Robert McGinnis from **Thunderball**, artist Renato Fratini did a brilliant job depicting the attitude that Sean Connery brought to James Bond in his second outing as Ian Fleming's superspy in **From Russia with Love**. The wide format British quad poster gave Fratini room to highlight not only Bond, but Bond girl Daniela Bianchi and the other women in the film. In recent years the British quad has sold for $3,400-$5,675, Italian two-foglio for $1,080-$5,020, French one-panel $720-$3,110, set of eight lobby cards for $255-$1,435, six-sheet for $895-$1,315, style A one-sheet for $70-$910, and style B one-sheet for $90-$1,050.

series *Climax!*. That TV version of Bond,
which starred Barry Nelson, is just a foot-
note to those beyond the most serious 007
enthusiasts, and for several years the prop-
erty didn't go any further.

But the stage was set.

When producers Albert R. "Cubby"
Broccoli and Harry Saltzman cast Sean
Connery in the role of Bond for 1962's
Dr. No, they put both the character and the
actor on the map. The suave, sophisticated,
British secret agent with a duty to queen
and country, a passion for women, a wry
sense of humor, and a license to kill quickly became an institution for movie-goers.

Eventually Connery gave way to
George Lazenby, who gave way to
Connery again, who gave way to Roger
Moore, who gave way to Timothy Dalton,
who gave way to Pierce Brosnan, who

gave way to Daniel Craig. For more than
50 years, James Bond films have spawned
action, adventure, romance, gadgets, and
some truly collectible movie posters.

They've included superb artwork
by the likes of Robert McGinnis and
Bob Peak, great photo images such as
the lobby card of the Gert Frobe/Sean
Connery exchange from *Goldfinger* (Bond:
"Do you expect me to talk? Goldfinger:
"No, Mr. Bond, I expect you to die."), and
so much more. They've been the subjects
of books, including *James Bond: 50 Years
of Movie Posters*, which was released in
2012 along with the film *Skyfall*.

Given the franchise's globetrotting,
international flavor and long term success,
it's not surprising that there are many distinct and highly collectible variations of
posters from countries around the world,

One of the truly iconic teaser images from the entire film series is the 1974 U.S. "Christmas teaser" one-sheet from **The Man with the Golden Gun**, Roger Moore's second outing as Bond. While the film is set in exotic Asian locations such as Hong Kong, the poster focuses on the film's most distinctive prop, the Golden Gun itself. The poster depicts the assembly from a pen, cigarette lighter and a cuff link into the deadly tool of the assassin Francisco Scaramanga, who was played by Christopher Lee (who was actually a cousin of Bond creator Ian Fleming). The Style B one-sheet recently sold for $460-$1,315, British quad for $60-$835, six-sheet for $175-$575, three-sheet for $65-$455, insert for $50-$420, style A one-sheet for $25-$275, Christmas teaser for $65-$420.

but that's not to downplay the appeal of the U.S. versions, which have often had their own variations.

The 24 films in the series to date include *Dr. No* (1962, Sean Connery), *From Russia With Love* (1963, Sean Connery), *Goldfinger* (1964, Sean Connery), *Thunderball* (1965, Sean Connery), *You Only Live Twice* (1967, Sean Connery), *On Her Majesty's Secret Service* (1969, George Lazenby), *Diamonds Are Forever* (1971, Sean Connery), *Live and Let Die* (1973, Roger Moore), *The Man with the Golden Gun* (1974, Roger Moore), *The Spy Who Loved Me* (1977, Roger Moore), *Moonraker* (1979, Roger Moore), *For Your Eyes Only* (1981, Roger Moore), *Octopussy* (1983, Roger Moore), *A View to a Kill* (1985, Roger Moore), *The Living Daylights* (1987, Timothy Dalton), *License to Kill* (1989, Timothy Dalton), *GoldenEye* (1995, Pierce

Brosnan), *Tomorrow Never Dies* (1997, Pierce Brosnan), *The World is Not Enough* (1999, Pierce Brosnan), *Die Another Day* (2002, Pierce Brosnan), *Casino Royale* (2006, Daniel Craig), *Quantum of Solace* (2008, Daniel Craig), *Skyfall* (November 2012, Daniel Craig), and *Spectre* (November 2015, Daniel Craig).

Among the oddities, *Casino Royale* certainly has to top the list since it has actually had three incarnations. After the CBS television production in 1954, the film rights were held separately from the others. This resulted in the 1967 comedy spoof version which starred David Niven (reportedly Fleming's original choice to play Bond), Peter Sellers and Woody Allen, among others.

Given the post-World War II, Cold War flavor of the Fleming novel, it was impressive to many Bond fans how much of the

On **The Spy Who Loved Me** U.S. one-sheet, artist Bob Peak's powerful, evocative image showcases Roger Moore as James Bond and Barbara Bach as Soviet agent XXX (Major Anya Amasova) along with a nuclear submarine central to the plot of the 1977 film. It also features the modified Lotus Esprit Turbo underwater, one of the film's great gadget scenes. Unlike the other movies derived from the Ian Fleming novels, **The Spy Who Loved Me** used only the title, reportedly at Fleming's request. In recent years subway sold for $510-$1,910, six-sheet for $100-$465, 24-sheet for $395-$430, quad for $145-$425, banner for $20-345, one-sheet for $10-$240, and half-sheet for $45-$410.

The first release 1967 U.S. **Casino Royale** "Spanish/U.S." one-sheet has the famous Robert McGinnis art of the sexy girl with the title on it, as do many other editions from this film, but unlike the regular U.S. one-sheet this poster also has five inset images of Bond girls. The term "Spanish/U.S." means that it was printed in the U.S. for use in theaters with Spanish-speaking audiences. This version of Casino Royale was a comedy send-up starring David Niven, Peter Sellers, and Woody Allen, among others. The quad can sell for $335-$835, Japanese STB for $240-$775, style B one-sheet for $105-$540, style A one-sheet for $25-$510, three-sheet for $60-$220, and half-sheet for $40-$90

book's tone ended up in the film franchise reboot with Daniel Craig's debut in the role in 2006.

Also high on the oddity scale is *Never Say Never Again*, which saw Sean Connery reprise his role as 007 in a remake of *Thunderball*. This came about because Fleming, prior to the launch of a the film series, had collaborated with producer Kevin McClory and screenwriter Jack Whittingham on a series of plots for a possible Bond TV series. Fleming turned one of those plots into the novel *Thunderball*, but failed to credit McClory or Whittingham. In a protracted legal bat-

tle, McClory won the rights. After a drawn out process, the film was released in 1983.

McGinnis, who deservedly has his own chapter in this book, both with Frank McCarthy and on his own, worked on *Thunderball*, *You Only Live Twice*, *On Her Majesty's Secret Service*, *Diamonds Are Forever*, *Live and Let Die*, *The Man with the Golden Gun*, and the 1967 comedy version of *Casino Royale*.

*J.C. Vaughn is the Vice-President of Publishing for Gemstone Publishing. The first movie poster he ever purchased was Bob Peak's one-sheet for **The Spy Who Loved Me**.*

The exceedingly rare 40" x 60" poster with art by Gustaf Tenggren and animator Grim Natwick depicts Snow White, the dwarfs, the queen and her witch counterpart, the huntsman, and the prince in front of the castle. Above them is a collage of scenes from throughout the movie that timelines the beautiful story.

Heigh-Ho!

Gustaf Tenggren's Mark on
Snow White and the Seven Dwarfs

Artist Gustaf Tenggren had a short-lived tenure working for Disney, but the significance of his work left a defining impact on the company's legacy.

Tenggren's life began at a parish in Magra in Vastergotland, western Sweden in 1896. Both his father and grandfather were painters and decorators, which greatly influenced his career. Shortly after moving the family south to Gothenburg, his father moved to the U.S. to find work. Tenggren spent a lot of time with his grandfather, learning skills for his future occupation.

At 11 years old, Tenggren worked as a runner boy and an apprentice at a lithographer's shop. When his artistic talents emerged, he was encouraged to go to art school. He earned his first art school scholarship when he was just 13 and a

second followed 4 years later. His first illustration commissions came during his student days, while also painting decorations for the theater in town and taking portrait commissions. Beginning in 1918, he worked for the publishing company Åhlen & Åkerlund, illustrating a total of ten volumes of publications over the course of eight years.

During the summer of 1920 he moved to the U.S., first in Cleveland, Ohio and then onto New York City. He was working abroad for Åhlen & Åkerlund and found success in local jobs, until the Depression hit. Artistic work became much harder to find, so Tenggren ended up farming for five years.

He caught the break of a lifetime when he was offered a job at Disney in Los Angeles in 1935. It wasn't long

before Tenggren received the position of art director on *Snow White and the Seven Dwarfs*, the studio's first full-length film. Using the art and decorating skills he learned during his formative years, Tenggren spent almost three years painting artwork that helped the movie's layout artists.

Joe Gant and Albert Hurter had already designed Snow White, the Evil Queen, the Witch, and the Dwarfs. Tenggren was tasked with working on the forest and exterior scenes with the goal to produce the right mood for the scenes and backgrounds. Those paintings became major influences on significant backgrounds, including the queen's laboratory, the inside of the dwarfs' cottage, and scenes throughout the forest when Snow White was fleeing for her life from the huntsman.

In addition, he adapted the illustrations for the movie into painting for the posters, book illustrations, and advertising material.

The rare style C one-sheet is vividly colorful in shades of green, black, red, and blue. It plays on the scarier elements of the movie, with Snow White fleeing the huntsman in the forest while the trees eerily reach for her. The sides of the poster depict the dwarfs embodying each of their personalities brilliantly.

In recent years, the 40" x 60" has sold for $65,725, style B one-sheet for $6,250-$20,912, style C one-sheet for $15,812-$32,200, and the insert for $3,225-$10,350.

After the impact he had on *Snow White*, Tenggren was awarded several other assignments at Disney. Some of his other projects included creating art for *The Ugly Duckling*, *Hiawatha*, and *Fantasia*. He provided significant work on *Pinocchio*, designing the backgrounds, props, and clothing and was able to create complex imagery that produced a strong sense of depth. The last movie he worked on at Disney was *Bambi*, painting forest exteriors. However, his style wasn't in sync with the artwork of the movie, so he decided to leave the studio.

Following his departure from Disney in 1939, he illustrated children's books and started his own book projects called the Tenggren books, starting with *The Tenggren Mother Goose* and other folk tales and stories. He also worked on The Golden Press, producing picture books, including *The Poky Little Puppy*. He and his wife spent the later years of their life in Southport, Maine.

Film noir immediately conjures the vision of a man in trench coat and fedora, smoking cigarettes and drinking whiskey, when a mysterious, beautiful woman enters his office. His inner monologue tells him that this dame is dangerous, but she needs assistance because she's embroiled in a scheme that's spun out of control, or needs help leaving a no-good rabble rouser.

While this may be a common image, these movies are much more complicated than that. Noir is the subgenre of stylish Hollywood crime dramas of the '40s and '50s. The term was coined by French film critic Nino Frank, in 1946, when he recognized how many new movies had a darker look, in both style and content.

Many noir movies mirrored the tensions of the time period around World War II. Themes often relied heavily on paranoia, mistrust, loss, and fear, which could be felt throughout the battle weary country.

Since the U.S. was still reflecting on the terrible realities of the war, noir movies offered an outlet with hardened protagonists who were primarily antiheroes. They were cynical men, disillusioned by society, and woman that exuded sexuality, often to the detriment of male counterparts. Antiheroes were portrayed as hardboiled detectives, private investigators, war veterans, sometimes even gangsters, criminals, or lone wolf types. Most were driven by their pasts and their habit of repeating the same mistakes.

The movies had complex plotlines, filled with twists, turns, and shocking discoveries. Told in non-linear formats, noir movies utilized flashbacks to reveal crucial pieces to the mysterious puzzles. Foreboding music played in the background, witty dialogue was exchanged, and the main character often told the story in first person voiceover narration. The hardness of gangster movies, methodology of police procedurals, and haunting elements

On **The Maltese Falcon** six-sheet Spade appears in his fedora, glaring with gun pointed while Brigid leans casually on an ottoman. Recently the six-sheet sold for $191,200, Post-War French one-panel for $26,290, window card for $5,080-$16,730, one-sheet for $3,450-$14,340, half-sheet for $10,500, three-sheet for $4,950-$10,350, insert for $7,770-$9,560, and single lobby card for $650-$9,560.

of gothic romances could be found in many noir movies.

Visually, noir directors employed German expressionistic cinematography to dramatically draw attention to different pieces of the story. They filmed using low lighting and disorienting camera angles, made jarring cuts, and used gloomy composition. Ominous shadows, foggy streets, wet pavement, flashing neon signs, windows with venetian blinds, and billowing cigarette smoke are often found in film noir.

In 1941 *The Maltese Falcon* became the first film noir. Based on the novel by Dashiell Hammett, John Huston adapted the screenplay and directed this early gem. Humphrey Bogart starred as a private detective who takes a case that involves three eccentric adventurers, each of whom are trying to find a jewel encrusted statue of a falcon. It was nominated for three Oscars, including Best Picture.

Director Billy Wilder joined the subgenre with the 1944 suspense-filled *Double Indemnity*. Told primarily in flashbacks, Fred MacMurray played an insurance representative who is seduced by a provocative woman, played by Barbara Stanwyck, into a murder/insurance scheme. Based on the novel by James M. Cain, it was nominated for seven Academy Awards.

In 1946 *The Postman Always Rings Twice* became the third adaptation of Cain's book of the same name, though it was the first in English. John Garfield and Lana Turner starred as a drifter and a young woman who operates a diner with her husband. Once the pair start having an affair they hatch a plot to kill her husband. Whereas many movies would save the murder for the climax, this one takes place much sooner, putting the couple under the suspicious gaze of the local prosecutor.

Another noir hit that year was *The Big Sleep*, with married couple Bogart and Lauren Bacall. Directed by Howard Hawks, based on the Raymond Chandler novel, a private eye takes a job for a rich, retired general to resolve his daughter's gambling debts. Throughout the complex case, Detective Marlowe becomes entangled in murder and blackmail. The chemistry between Bogart and Bacall, a phrase that was practically one word during this era, sustains the love story subplot through

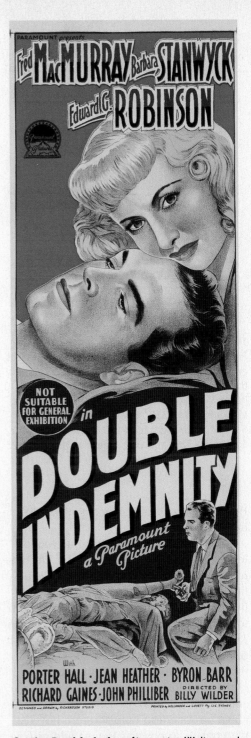

On the **Double Indemnity** poster Walter and Phyllis embrace while he holds a gun behind her back with an inset image of Barton looking on at the couple. The Australian daybill features the best art with the painted images lifted from the film of Phyllis pressing her cheek against Walter's head. The one-sheet can sell for for $1,840-$5,975, three-sheet for $2,185-$5,080, insert for $1,840-$4,063, half-sheet for $570-$2,630, Australian daybill for $775-$1,380, and single lobby card for $25-$775.

The Big Sleep poster displays a small image of Philip and Vivian embracing, leaning in for a kiss, encased in a fading red border. In recent years the French one-panel sold for $13,145-$21,510, Italian 2-foglio for $5,080-$13,145, three-sheet for $8,050-$11,350, Italian 4-folio for $5,975-$10,925, half-sheet for $120-$5,080, insert for $1,435-$4,780, and one-sheet for $875-$4,025.

The **Sunset Boulevard** style A one-sheet has a stark portrait of desperate Norma coated in red above an image of the leads embracing. A film strip literally ties the poster in the center. The style A one-sheet recently sold for $2,760-$20,910, Polish one-sheet for $7,770, half-sheet for $1,195-$6,570, French one-panel for $5,000, insert for $980-$3,830, and style B for $585-$2,150.

Bogart's taciturn confidence and Bacall's hypnotic gaze.

In *Out of the Past* a private detective leaves his profession for a simpler life running a gas station. But history catches up to him, and he's pulled back into that world by a client who had previously asked him to find his girlfriend. The 1947 film, starring Robert Mitchum and Jane Greer, used flashbacks to tell the convoluted story, making this a superb example of film noir.

In 1949 Joseph Cotten, Orson Welles, and Alida Valli starred in *The Third Man*, about an American pulp Western novelist who travels to postwar Vienna and discovers that a childhood friend has been killed. In the shadowy, Allied-occupied city he searches for the killer, despite the hindrances of local police, and makes a shocking discovery. Full of mystery and intrigue, the Carol Reed-directed film is considered one of the best movies of all time.

Later that year Jules Dassin directed the revenge tale *Thieves' Highway*. A.I. Bezzerides adapted the screenplay from his

novel about a war veteran who becomes a truck driver and learns that his father has lost his legs by the hands of an immoral produce dealer. Vowing to avenge his father, he takes on the corrupt businessman with the help of a prostitute and other truck drivers.

Huston had another hit with crime caper, *The Asphalt Jungle*, adapted from the W.R. Burnett novel. After being released from prison, a criminal mastermind organizes a major heist. Though the crime goes smoothly, after it's done, double crosses and paranoia quickly unravel the group. The ensemble cast in the 1950 movie included Sterling Hayden, Louis Calhern, Jean Hagen, James Whitmore, and Sam Jaffe. Marilyn Monroe had a small, but key role in the movie.

Sunset Boulevard with William Holden and Gloria Swanson was another hit that year, directed by Wilder. The story of murder begins when a mediocre writer pens a screenplay for a former silent film star clinging to relevancy in Hollywood. As the actress, Swanson played her with an increasingly

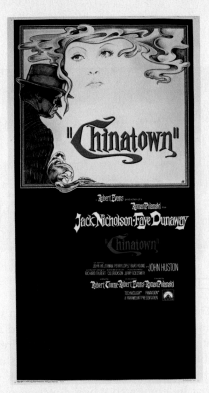

The **Kiss Me Deadly** poster features a sensational image of Mike kissing Velda with action scenes from the movie along the poster edges. The half-sheet can sell for $120-$835, one-sheet for $155-$775, six-sheet for $570, three-sheet for $420-$525, insert for $275-$480, title card for $20-$335, and set of eight lobby cards for $170-$260.

Chinatown has a very cool poster design with J.J. Gittes leaning in from the side of with the smoke from his cigarette billowing up to frame the ghostly face of Evelyn. In recent years the three-sheet sold for $60-$1,035, 40" x 60" for $60-$1,035, one-sheet for $75-$530, 30" x 40" for $115-$425, insert $60-$415, and set of 8 lobby cards for $50-$285.

unhinged desperation for stardom and fame. It was nominated for 11 Academy Awards.

The dizzyingly intricate *Kiss Me Deadly* was released in 1955. It starts simply enough, with a private eye of penny-ante divorce cases who comes upon a hitchhiker. Soon they are abducted by thugs and caught in a world of intrigue rapidly spinning out of control. As he investigates, the movie becomes centralized around a mysterious box containing "the great whatsit." The ensemble cast led by Ralph Meeker and Albert Dekker, includes the feature-film debuts of both Cloris Leachman and Maxine Cooper.

In 1958, Welles had triple duty as screenplay writer, director, and star in *Touch of Evil*. Loosely based on the novel, *Badge of Evil*, by Whit Masterson, the incredible cast features Charlton Heston, Janet Leigh, Joseph Calleia, Akim Tamiroff, Ray Collins, Marlene Dietrich, and Zsa Zsa Gabor. What begins with an explosion at the Mexican-American border escalates into kidnapping,

police corruption, and murder. *Touch of Evil* was one of the last entries in the subgenre of film noir.

In 1974 Jack Nicholson and Faye Dunaway starred in the neo-noir *Chinatown*. Similar to its predecessors, a private eye is hired to expose a married man's infidelities, but he learns that the situation is much more complicated, involving plenty of deceit, corruption, and murder. It uses elements of film noir from the '40s and '50s with updated themes and style.

For many years after film noir ended, movies and TV shows utilized elements and the style for inspiration, and sometimes comedic effect. The trademark plot twists and slights of hand, desperation, and femme fatales can be found in several movies of the past 40 years. Regardless of the storyline, film noir never left audiences bored or unentertained. We don't need a private eye to discover why they've stood the test of time.

Alfred Hitchcock, the Master of Suspense

Throughout his extensive career in the film industry, Alfred Hitchcock worked as a writer, producer, actor, editor, and crew member, but most importantly, he was a director. With a terrific eye for filmmaking that he employed while directing over 50 movies, what he truly excelled at was suspense.

Feelings of harsh treatment and being wrongfully accused were themes that ran throughout his work, which trace their roots back to his childhood. Born in London in 1899, Hitchcock described his childhood as lonely, due in part to being overweight. He was raised in strict Catholic fashion that involved some odd types of punishments. Hitchcock's father sent him to a police station with a note asking the officers to lock him up for ten minutes for misbehaving. His mother would make him stand at the foot of her bed for hours, which was alluded to in *Psycho*.

After finishing high school, Hitchcock went to St. Ignatius College then on to the University of London where he took art classes. He worked as a draftsman and advertising designer at Henley's cable company, then started writing short articles for an in-house publication. His earliest pieces were filled with themes of false imprisonment and endings that twisted in shocking ways. He started working in film in 1920 at the Famous Players-Lasky Company designing title cards for silent movies and as an assistant director.

His career as a director began in 1925.

The silent film, *The Pleasure Garden* is a romantic drama following two couples on the paths of long distance relationships with some dark, surprising twists. Though it was the first movie he directed,

The one-sheet for **The 39 Steps** features beautifully painted images of Robert Donat and Madeleine Carroll, with one showing them comfortably close while the other is the antithesis with them looking frightened and paranoid. The one-sheet can sell for $830-$18,000, three-sheet $10,220, title card $3,100, Swedish poster $630, and British quad $600.

it was the third to be released. The first Hitchcock directed release was *The Lodger*, a story about the London fog, based on the thriller novel by Marie Belloc Lowndes. The success of *The Lodger* prompted the film studio he was working with to release *The Pleasure Garden* and *The Mountain Eagle*. *The Lodger* was his first foray into thrillers, a subgenre he returned to in 1929 with *Blackmail*, his first talkie.

He began steadily making thrillers in 1934 with *The Man Who Knew Too Much*. Beginning to hone his skills, he established the pattern of deconstructing familial relationships in a story of suspense. One of his most celebrated British films is *The 39 Steps*, a chase thriller based on the novel by John Buchan about a man in London who tries to help a counterespionage agent, but ends up on the run trying to save himself and stop spies from stealing critical information. His last British film was *Jamaica Inn* based on the novel

by Daphne Du Maurier about a young woman who learns that she's living near a gang of criminals who cause shipwrecks for money. He directed several successful silent films and early talkies in England prior to going to Hollywood in 1939.

Many of his movies have reputations for their violence and complex psychological storylines. *Rebecca*, based on another celebrated novel by Du Maurier, tells the story of a young bride tormented by the maid who is obsessed with the husband's first wife. This was his first U.S. film and it earned an Oscar for Best Picture. His 1941 film *Suspicion*, about a woman who suspects her husband of being a murderer planning to make her his next victim, explores the foray of evil within a family. But, his movies show evil not just in physical violence but also through systemic and institutional torture. This was seen in *Notorious* in 1946, the bizarre love story that has an FBI agent put the woman he

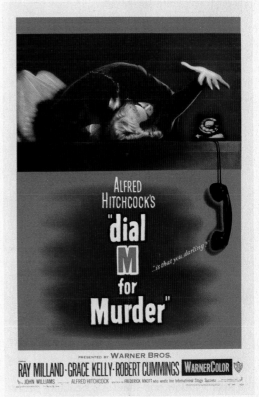

The **Notorious** one-sheet features a steamy image of Devlin and Alicia about to kiss, encircled by the outline of a key over a blue-brushed background. The French petite can sell for $11,950 one-sheet for $175-$8,365, insert for $1,095-$3,110, and half-sheet for $2,630.

The poster for **Dial M for Murder** is primarily a vibrant, deep shade of red with a struggling couple fighting on top of a table as the phone falls precariously. The one-sheet can sell for $1,725-$3,880, the 40" x 60" $3,880, three-sheet $1,780-$3,730, Italian 2P $3,080, set of 8 lobby cards $460-$1,610, and half-sheet $420-$1,195.

loves in the dangerous arms of a Nazi to learn about a spy ring.

From 1950 to 1960 Hitchcock produced his greatest work. He directed two excellent films in 1954, first with the sophisticated thriller *Dial M for Murder* – his only 3-D movie – about an ex-tennis player plotting to murder his wife, but when things don't go according to plan he has an excellent backup strategy. Then he directed one of his greatest hits, *Rear Window*, which turned viewers into voyeurs by watching a photographer who witnesses a murder. The following year he presented another brilliant thriller, *To Catch a Thief*, telling the story of a reformed jewel thief blamed for a new crime who must find the real thief, thereby proving his innocence. His 1958 film *Vertigo* explored the lost feminine identity seen in his films *Shadow of a Doubt* and

Notorious by pointing out the cause as a male proclivity. The 1959 film *North by Northwest* brought together the elements of a quintessential Hitchcock movie with clever shots, a dramatic score, subtle relationships, and crafted suspense. It should also be noted, that AMC's popular TV show *Mad Men* was influenced by *North by Northwest*.

His TV program *Alfred Hitchcock Presents*, which told unrelated stories of horror, crime, and thrillers aired from 1955 to 1961. The show reached more than his usual movie audiences, making Hitchcock a household name.

Perhaps his best remembered horror film was the 1960 hit *Psycho*. The iconic shower murder scene put the viewer in the killer's point of view. Along with Michael Powell's *Peeping Tom*, which was released in the United Kingdom a few

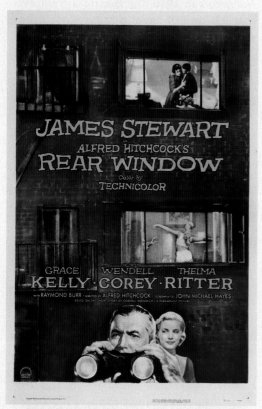

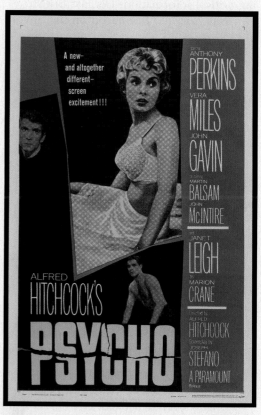

The **Rear Window** one-sheet is a beautiful poster of the building in shades of dark red with curious views into the two windows and James Stewart looking curiously from the bottom of the poster. In recent years the one-sheet has sold for $1,700-$9,560, three-sheet $2,600-$8,960, half-sheet style A $1,195-$4,180, half-sheet style B $1,150-$2,870, style Z one-sheet $3,880, Italian 2 –Foglio $3,345, and insert $900-$2,500.

The poster for **Psycho** has fragmented images as though it were slashed by Norman Bates' knife with a main scandalous image of Janet Leigh in her underwear peering cautiously over her shoulder. The one-sheet can sell for $570-$9,560, 40" x 60" $4,780, six-sheet $2,390, lobby card set of eight $300-$2,150, and half-sheet $420-$915.

months before *Psycho*, it was the first film to do so. The film also stunned viewers when the killer's identity was revealed. Adding to the skin crawling fear is the shrieking string orchestra score provided by Bernard Herrman.

His career began to wind down in the 1960s. His last big hit was the horror flick *The Birds* in 1963. Based on the novelette of the same name, Hitchcock directed another movie adaptation of a story by du Maurier. The environmental attack takes evil out of human hands and makes animals that aren't typically frightening into monsters.

Hitchcock directed over 50 films during his career from the early 1920s to the 1970s. The cameo appearances he made in his movies, the way he interacted in interviews, the style of his movie trailers, and his TV program *Alfred Hitchcock Presents* cemented his place as a cultural icon. Hitchcock could artistically dazzle, while frightening audiences, with his signature style.

While his movies are loved now, he didn't gain respect in the film industry until late in his career. Due to the stigma that the horror genre withstands, Hitchcock had been mostly considered

a talented craftsman of genre movies. Accolades for his work began in the late 1960s. He won the Irving G. Thalberg Memorial Award by the Academy Awards in 1968 and the Golden Globes' Cecil B. DeMille Award in 1972. He won the prestigious AFI Life Achievement Award in 1979, a year before his death. In 2012 the British Film Institute named his 1958 film *Vertigo* as the best movie ever in a poll that happens every 10 years. It was the first time in 50 years that a movie was chosen over *Citizen Kane*. Hitchcock truly was the Master of Suspense.

On **The Birds** poster, Melanie Daniels is cowering and screaming as the vicious animals attack her while Alfred Hitchcock stands off to the side, out of the action. A tagline at the top of the poster from Hitchcock states that it could be his "most terrifying motion picture." In recent years the 24-sheet has sold for $2,390, Canadian one-sheet $2,110, insert for $220-$1,955, one-sheet for $290-$1,450, six-sheet for $530-$1,135, and three-sheet for $690-$1,135.

Critic and Collector: Andrew Rawls

Movie fan and part-time film critic, Andrew Rawls, is a collector with a love of the medium. He collects and sells movie campaign materials with an eye for artwork, whether it's on posters, lobby cards, or movie stills.

Overstreet: How long have you been collecting movie posters?
Andrew Rawls (AR): For over fifteen years.

Overstreet: Why did you start collecting movie posters?
AR: For me it's always been about the films. I wanted something I could keep to remember films I enjoyed. What better way to do that than collect movie posters?

Overstreet: Are you a big fan of movies or do you just collect for the art? If so, what is it about movies that you love?
AR: As a part-time film critic I screen over six hundred movies a year. For me, films are an escape and they bring much needed joy and happiness to my life. If I didn't watch movies there's no way I'd be collecting posters.

Overstreet: What attracts you to collecting movie posters?
AR: For a collector of movie memorabilia there is no better feeling than when a film you

love was issued with great campaign materials – movie posters, lobby cards, stills, etc. For films such as Alfred Hitchcock's *Vertigo* from 1958 and Stanley Kubrick's *2001: A Space Odyssey* such is true.

Overstreet: Do you collect different movie poster sizes?
AR: On some titles the artwork is vastly superior in different formats. For example posters from *The Wizard of Oz* are rather lackluster whereas on the original and reissue lobby cards there are some great images. I also deal in original movie stills. These are photographs that often show key images or moments from the film. For example in Hitchcock's *North by Northwest* you have Cary Grant and the famous crop-duster scene which is pretty much the defining moment from the film. There are original stills out there with this image that are highly collectible and rare.

Overstreet: Do you collect other movie memorabilia?
AR: I also collect, buy and sell other original, theatrical materials such as lobby cards and original movie stills. I find in many cases the artwork from these

An epic drama of adventure and exploration

...taking you half a billion miles from Earth... further from home than any man in history. Destination: Jupiter.

MGM PRESENTS A STANLEY KUBRICK PRODUCTION

2001 a space odyssey

CINERAMA® Super Panavision™ and Metrocolor

is better than the movie posters issued. Pressbooks are also highly collectible because they were issued to theaters at the time a film was first released and show images of all the posters, advertisements and displays a theater could buy. Buying pressbooks is a great way to have a piece of the films' history without having to spend thousands of dollars on a poster.

Overstreet: Do you focus on a time period, genre, artist, or anything else?
AR: I'm primarily interested in movie memorabilia for films produced prior to 1980. However I do not limit my collect-

ing to one particular decade or period. Jonathon Glazer's 2013 *Under the Skin* is another example of a great film with a great movie poster. The poster design by Neil Kellerhouse is out of the norm, very unique and completely original.

Saul Bass, who designed many title sequences and film posters over his career, is my favorite poster artist. His perspective on the whole concept of graphic design using minimalistic style was so fresh and innovative there will never be another designer quite like him.

Overstreet: Is linen-backing a factor for you when it comes to purchasing posters?

AR: No. Most of the great movie posters from the last hundred years have been linen-backed in order to ensure they are around for years to come. Most collectors display their posters and linen-backing protects the poster from tearing or ripping over time. The key is to make sure the poster has been linen-backed by a high quality conservation expert. Often times a poster will appear rippled or lumpy because it was mounted incorrectly.

Overstreet: How do you store them?

AR: Posters should be stored with the utmost care so they don't deteriorate over time. Before a collector goes out and spends hundreds of dollars on Mylar sleeves and boards – which don't get me wrong are important – I would tell them to make sure the posters are in a good storage environment with low temperature and relative humidity. The biggest thing is humidity; if there is too much moisture in the environment a poster can become wavy over time.

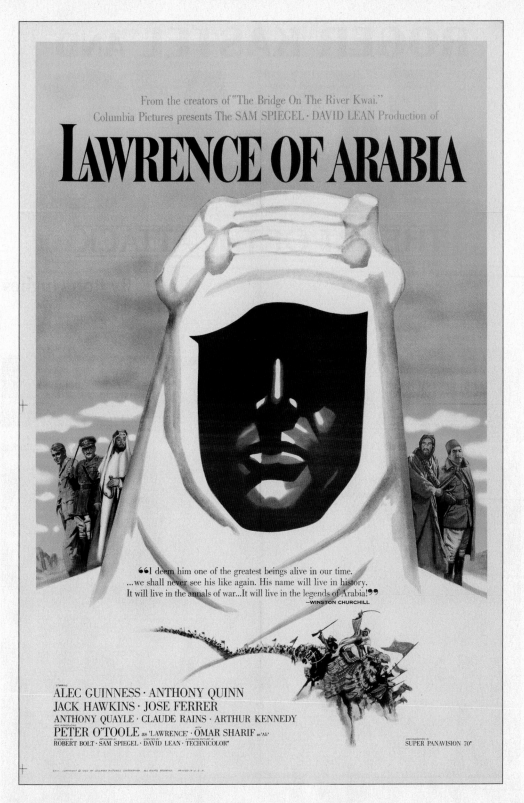

Overstreet: What advice would you give to someone new to the hobby to avoid overpaying or buying reprints that are claiming to be originals?

AR: Do some research, pick a budget and decide specifically what you want to focus on before jumping two feet in. There's lots of good information out there on valuation and don't be afraid to negotiate with what you feel is a fair asking price.

ROGER KASTEL AND
JAWS
THE ART OF THE ATTACK

By Rob Hughes

Article ©2015 Rob Hughes

"A hundred yards offshore, the fish sensed a change in the sea's rhythm... The vibrations were stronger now, and the fish recognized prey... The fish smelled her now, and the vibrations – erratic and sharp – signaled distress. The fish began to circle close to the surface. Its dorsal fin broke water, and its tail, thrashing back and forth, cut the glassy surface with a hiss. A series of tremors shook its body. For the first time, the woman felt fear, though she did not know why. Adrenaline shot through her trunk and limbs, generating a tingling heat and urging her to swim faster. She guessed that she was fifty yards from shore... The fish was about forty feet away from the woman, off to the side, when it turned suddenly to the left, dropped entirely below the surface, and, with two quick thrusts of its tail, was upon her."[1] This vivid description of Chrissie Watkins' fateful encounter with an unseen assailant from the murky depths of the Atlantic Ocean struck the very core of one of our most primal fears with the full force of the three-ton star of this thriller - that of being eaten alive! And thus, the cultural phenomenon was born, as *Jaws* ambushed an unsuspecting public, bit down with ferocious fervor and has never let go hence.

Jaws was written by author Peter Benchley (1940-2006), originally published by Doubleday as a hardcover (HC) edition in February 1974. The novel was an instant success, staying on the bestseller list for 44 weeks, ultimately selling a total of 125,000 copies. The book did not actually have a title until 20 minutes before it went to press. *Jaws* was chosen because, as Benchley stated, "...it's short; it fits on a jacket, and it may work."

For the cover of this first edition, Doubleday's design director, Alex Gottfried turned to artist Paul Bacon. Bacon drew a large shark head rising up from the bottom and Gottfried suggested that he add a swimmer above it, "to have a sense of disaster and a sense of scale." The subsequent cover art for the HC featured the classic layout design, yet a more stylistic and simplistic rendering to the opening scene, set against a jet-black background.[2]

And then came the time for the paperback version of the novel to be produced. The legendary publisher of Bantam Books, Oscar Dystel (who lived to the age of 101) bought the paperback rights to *Jaws* for the then-impressive sum of $575,000.[3] "Mr. Dystel's idea of the perfect book was one that combined a riveting story, a compelling cover and a hit movie,"[4] *The New York Times* said.

Bantam would hit the bullseye on all three. But, Dystel was not impressed with the minimalist art for the HC edition, so he turned to his ace artist, Roger Kastel, to create a much more inspired and impactful piece.

Kastel was a talented classically trained artist who had served in the Navy during the Korean War as a lithographer and a photographer.

"After the war, I wanted to get back into Frank J. Reilly's classes at the Art Students League of New York on West 57th Street in New York City, which I had attended for a little over a year before I went into the Navy. However, classes were jammed packed with students and I could not get in at first. He taught on Tuesdays and Thursdays, three hours in the morning and three hours in the afternoon. Reilly taught us from the ground up – how to draw and how to paint, from 'basic boot camp' all the way up to 'special forces' training,

Peter Bradford Benchley (1940 - 2006). Author of the novel **Jaws** and co-writer of the screenplay.

Roger Kastel, the artist who painted **Jaws** - one of the most famous images in Americana.

and everything in between. I still have my notes from these classes and would still be attending them to this day, had not Reilly died. Some of the more well known names that were my classmates are James Bama, Clark Hulings and Bob Schultz," Kastel said.

"When I graduated, I began painting western covers and doing drawings that my agent would solicit to the publishing companies for their various men's magazines," Kastel said.

"I did a good deal of art for *Good Housekeeping* (Hearst Corporation) and *Argosy* (Frank A. Munsey Company), and eventually ended up working exclusively for Bantam Books. I was sitting in Len Leone's (Bantam's art director) office one Friday when Oscar came in and said that he had a copy of *Jaws* that he wanted me to read and come up with a fresh idea for the new cover."

In the excellent article, "Real Hollywood Thriller: Who Stole Jaws" by Ben Marks, Kastel said, "[Oscar] wanted me to read the book to pick out a new part to illustrate. But, of course, the best part was the beginning, where Chrissie goes into the water nude."[5]

"I did a very rough concept sketch for Oscar and Len's approval. Len just told me, 'We want something more realistic and much stronger. Make the shark BIGGER! And, remember to leave room at the

top for type.' Otherwise, they gave me complete creative autonomy. But, before I could begin I needed to do some research. I went to the Museum of Natural History and asked, 'Do you have a shark exhibit?' The person told me that they did have one, but it was closed for cleaning," he said.

He was not deterred.

"It was lunchtime, so I went upstairs anyway, and there were all these different stuffed sharks, just laying on boards. I had my camera with me so I took a few pictures. The shark in my painting developed from there."[6] He further shared, "Now, I needed a model of a woman swimming. One day I was at the Bob Osonitch Studio, that did photography for artists, working with a very attractive model on a Christmas shoot for *Good Housekeeping Magazine*. I asked her if she might be agreeable to stay a bit longer to pose nude for the swimmer character I needed for my *Jaws* cover. She was, and laid down naked in the swimming position on a stool for me to photograph her."

Straightforward in design (based upon the original Doubleday HC edition), yet absolutely flawless in its execution, the cover painting that Kastel created for Bantam is a bonafide masterpiece. The scene depicts a beautiful nude woman, swimming across the surface of the aqua-blue ocean waters and glancing down at her impending doom as a gargantuan Great White Shark (looks like a 50-footer) methodically ascends from the icy depths, its massive maw full of sword-like teeth, hungry to devour his prey - every swimmer's nightmare incarnate! Infused with raw primal power, this painting perfectly surmised the menacing mood and grim direction of the novel like none other in one magnificent momentous moment. One simply could not lay their eyes upon such an inspired piece of artwork and not be compelled to read the story inside.

"The painting was approximately 20" x 30" in size, done in oil on illustration board – masonite with gesso. It took me between seven to ten days to complete. I did it sometime in the summer of 1974 and was paid $750," Kastel said.

The scene depicted on the cover contrasts with the actual scene in the book in that the Jaws cover image appears to be a daytime scene with a white sky background and bright water, while in the novel it took place at night

"I just felt that the painting should stand alone from the story itself. The shark and girl needed to be the center of interest – you can see exactly what's happening. The brighter image also works better with the type. I had to be conscious about leaving enough room at the top for the lettering. A darker nighttime scene would not have worked as well. I was not trying to be as literal as the novel," he said.

The first printing of the Bantam Books paperback edition of *Jaws* was published in January 1975. The response was instantaneous, with initially sales of 3.5 million copies, with another 6 million copies added when the motion picture debuted in June that year. Bantam

published 18 printings[7] with worldwide sales now estimated at about 20 million copies.[8] But the book was just the beginning of the mammoth promotion featuring Kastel's unforgettable cover art.

Before the novel had even been published, two astute film producers at Universal Pictures, Richard D. Zanuck and David Brown, had read the manuscript, loved it and decided to purchase the film rights for $150,000, plus an extra $25,000 for Benchley to write the screenplay.[9] The film would be directed by a young 27-year-old, up-and-coming Steven Spielberg, and starred Roy Scheider as Police Chief Martin Brody, Richard Dreyfuss in the role of oceanographer Matt Hooper and Robert Shaw as the grizzled shark-hunter Quint.[10] Benchley wrote the first three drafts of the screenplay, which was then revised by playwright Howard Sackler and writer/actor Carl Gottlieb.[11]

Under the direct guidance of Spielberg, Gottlieb scripted major revisions while principle photography was underway on

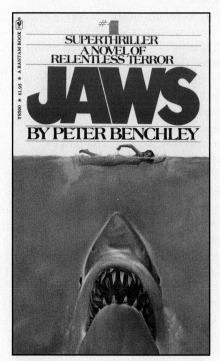

Jaws first edition paperback with Roger Kastel cover art (1975).

Roger Kastel paperback art was used for the iconic movie poster.

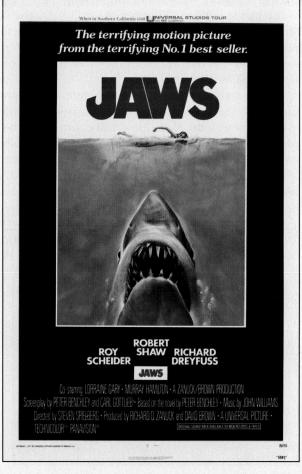

Martha's Vineyard, Massachusetts from May 2 to September 18, 1974.[12] The set was bombarded with problems from the very start, not the least of which was that the mechanical shark (that the crew had nicknamed "Bruce," after Spielberg's lawyer Bruce Ramer) kept malfunctioning due to the salt water corroding the shark's mechanical insides. Exasperated, Spielberg referred to the shark as, "The Great White Turd." The consequences of these myriad setbacks ballooned the original budget of $3.5 million (55 day shooting schedule) to over $11 million (more than 150 days of shooting schedule).[13] Nevertheless, Spielberg and his crew persevered and *Jaws* would soon prove to be an unprecedented sensation, busting the $100 million mark at the box office for the first time in history. It was well on its way to become the most successful motion picture of all time - a ranking that it would hold until the release of the original *Star Wars* (20th Century Fox) in 1977.

Jaws was the motion picture for which the phrase, "Summer Blockbuster" was coined. A feature story about the making of the movie entitled, "Summer of the Shark," made the cover of *Time*, with a powerfully dramatic painted cover by Bob Peak, known as the "Father of the Modern Hollywood Movie Poster."[14]

In the midst of this media whirlwind, but before the movie was actually released in theaters on June 20, 1975, a "full-court press" promotional blitz was already in full swing at Bantam and Universal.

"Len told me that Universal wanted to use my painting as the image for the movie poster," Kastel said.

At this point, Dystel decided to give the artwork rights away for free to Universal, obviously banking on the potential of immense increased paperback sales in tandem with the release of the motion picture alongside the one-sheet movie poster and other promotion associated with the film. This strategy proved very wise on Dystel's part, paying massive dividends with Bantam selling an additional six million copies of *Jaws* after the film's debut. However, the savvy Dystal overlooked one crucial area of the promotional juggernaut – merchandising – a mostly untapped field at the time.

Universal accepted Dystel's decision and exploited it to the utmost by showcasing Kastel's artwork on a seemingly endless barrage of movie tie-ins.

In addition to the paperback cover and the movie poster, Kastel's iconic *Jaws* art adorned T-shirts, socks, beach towels, toys (one of the most popular being *The Game of Jaws* by Ideal Toys), model kits, movie pressbooks, lobby card sets, lunch boxes, the album cover for the soundtrack by composer John Williams, a 500-piece movie poster puzzle (Milton Bradley), and Slurpee cups.

Several books about the making of the film were written, with *The Jaws Log* (Dell Publishing, 1975) by Gottlieb being the most respected (Gottlieb, by the way, portrayed the character of Meadows in the movie). This book is a wonderful eye-witness recollection of the principle photography events on Martha's Vineyard – the ups and downs, joys, challenges, frustrations and ultimate euphoric relief upon the location's final wrap - complete with rare photos, clever quotes and amusing anecdotes, presented with sublime seasoned commentary.[15]

The overall influence of the movie upon our society is simply immeasurable. In 1976, a San Diego, California based professional soccer team that played in the North American Soccer League (NASL) chose the Great White Shark as their icon, calling themselves the San Diego Jaws. A brand new comedy show called *Saturday Night Live* even

Director Steven Spielberg hams it up with his temperamental super-star, "Bruce" on location at Martha's Vineyard in 1974

got in on the act by creating the cute and clever spoof skit, "Land Shark" (1975) with Chevy Chase as the culprit. "Candy-Gram," anyone?

Jaws mania seemed to be everywhere, and yet, neither Bantam Books nor Roger Kastel saw a single dime of the astronomical action.

"I had never even heard of such a thing at the time. And, I never received any merchandising royalties for the use of my image," he said.

Not everyone was enamored with the artwork, though. Due to the nudity of the swimmer, the novel was actually banned in Boston, MA and St. Petersburg, FL.

"I thought I would never get another job in the industry. But, Bantam loved the controversial publicity, which actually boost the sales of the book quite a bit," he said.

Then came an odd request from Universal. The studio decided to take out a full color two-page spread, a "Coming Attraction" advertisement in *TV Guide,* which was scheduled to appear the week just prior to the release of the movie. The main hurdle was that the overall design of Kastel's original painting was a vertical composition, while the ad called for a

horizontal layout. "So, I was in Len's office and he tells me that Universal wanted me to add more water on each side of the image - to extend it out for the ad format. I just sat there a bit dumbfounded and said to Len, 'You gotta be kidding me? This is a joke, right?' Understand, this was a long time before computers and Photoshop and all these wonderful tools that make changes and adjustments to artwork much easier. What they were asking me to do I thought was ridiculous. I declined," Kastel said.

"So, I took the painting down to a photo lab in New York for them, and the lab used some sort of very complex technique to extend the water out on the right side of the art image. The lab basically took an area of the water and kept replicating it. I'm not exactly sure how they accomplished this, but I know it was an extremely difficult and very expensive process," he said.

This two-page spread ad appeared in *TV Guide Vol. 23 #24* (June 14, 1975) on the inside front cover and first page. The final result was rather impressive, but soon events took a turn toward the heartbreaking.

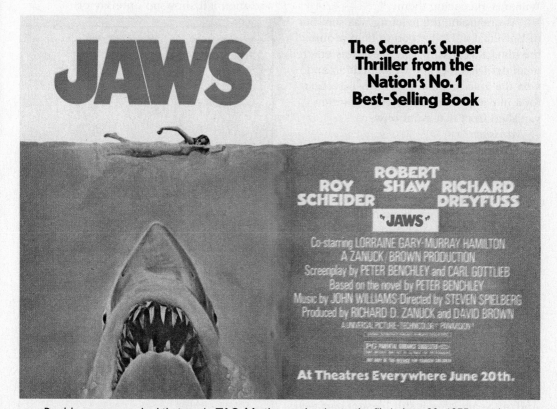

Double page spread ad that ran in **TV Guide** the week prior to the film's June 20, 1975 opening.

"As part of the book promotion tour, my painting was being showcased in the Society of Illustrators Show that was being held at the Museum of the City of New York. From there it toured all over the country," Kastel said. "I would often see mock-up *Jaws* movie posters hanging in lobbies." The Seiniger Advertising agency was entrusted to design the classic movie poster. This took them six full months to complete the job. Kastel continued, "The ad agency that worked on the movie poster made it sound as if [Paul] Bacon (the first edition HC cover artist) actually painted my piece."

During this pivotal period, Universal spent a $1.8 million in marketing, spearheaded by a then-unprecedented $700,000 on national TV spots. This included about two dozen 30-second trailers airing each night on the primetime networks from June 18 to June 20, 1975 – the opening day for *Jaws*. Universal and Bantam collaborated to come up with the classic *Jaws* title logo, agreeing to feature it both on the paperback as well as on all the subsequent advertisements for the movie. The key focus for this joint venture would be on Kastel's breathtaking art and John Williams' menacing theme.[16]

"At one point, the painting was sent out to Universal in Hollywood to help promote the film," Kastel said. "The piece was entered in an Art Directors Show competition and won the gold medal for Best Art Direction for a movie poster. The original painting vanished from that point onward."

Vanished?

"You have to understand that back in the 1960s and '70s, which was a very exciting time in my field, a lot of paintings were taken from the Bantam offices. It was not uncommon to not have my originals returned to me," Kastel said. "At the time, it was just another cover painting to me. No big deal, really. Oscar really felt bad about what happened though. He was still looking for the painting, trying to get it returned to me when he died." So, this turned out to be a double whammy for Kastel since, not only was he not being paid any royalties for the enormous amount of merchandising items featuring his art, but now his original was missing. And, 40 years later, it still has not surfaced.

Praise for Kastel's *Jaws* art is widespread and often deeply impassioned.

"I think Kastel's poster, like much of the best poster art of its era, tells the movie's story instantly, while making you want to learn more. The cool blue water situated opposite the blood red title just seals the deal,"[17] Tom Whalen, who has made a multitude of second generation or tribute movie posters for the publisher Mondo (based in Austin, Texas) said.

Wendell Minor, the artist who was first hired by Doubleday (before Bacon) to illustrate the cover for the first edition (HC) – a shot in which Amity is viewed through the open jaws of the shark, which was rejected – shared Whalen's enthusiastic opinion.

"Paul's jacket isn't bad, and it still holds up in a certain way, but it can't hold a candle to Roger's dramatic realism for the paperback and the movie poster. Whether Roger likes it or not, that's one of the great icons of American pop culture,"[18] he said.

As to the whereabouts of the original painting, Minor is adamant: "It was stolen. It's hanging in Hollywood somewhere. That's happened to me in the past, too, where a piece of artwork will disappear and then it'll show up on eBay or

something. That artwork would be quite valuable today."[19]

And what does Kastel think about all this?

"Either someone has it or it's lost in storage at Universal. They really should report it as stolen," he said. "When I'm at a convention and signing prints, people tell me stories about how they were afraid to go in the water when the book and movie came out, but that they really like the image. They might've been frightened at the time, but they aren't now. They love the shark. Hopefully, it will come back to me one day."[20]

Not that any of this deterred Kastel.

His *Jaws* artwork had caught the eye of a successful young writer/director named George Lucas, who was already knee-deep in principle photography on the highly-anticipated sequel to his mega-hit, *Star Wars*.

"Lucasfilm called me one Sunday afternoon and said that they were considering me for the next *Star Wars* movie poster and asked, 'Would I be interested?' I answered, 'Sure!' George had seen and was impressed with my *Jaws* piece and other paperback covers that I had done. They set up shop in an ad agency in Manhattan just for the movie. Six artists were invited and we were handed various movie stills. The one I liked the most was Luke on the Tauntaun. I was told that George wanted a romantic feel between Han Solo and Princess Leia. He really liked the *Gone with the Wind* (MGM, R-1968) movie poster."

That poster featured the now-classic image of Clark Gable holding Vivien Leigh in his arms, and on that Kastel would model his design.

"There were a lot of changes along the way while the movie was being shot. Lucas was giving suggestions and asking for various changes until I came up with what he was envisioning. I had never worked in the science fiction genre before, but this was a great opportunity for me and I was really excited about the project from the very start. There were many revisions along the way. I would complete the painting and an account executive would pick it up and fly it out to George in Hollywood or Europe – (two round trip tickets) one seat for the executive and one for the painting. George would make his notes and the executive would fly back to New York with the painting. I would use gesso to white out the areas that George wanted revised. There was only one painting - one painting with multiple revisions. I was floored when they called and told me that George decided to use my piece as the main movie poster image." That movie, of course, would be *The Empire Strikes Back*.

His other works of note would include the cover art for the novel *Hollywood Wives* (HarperCollins, 1983), written by Jackie Collins along with the cover painting to Nobel Prize winner and author John Steinbeck's epic work, *East of Eden* (Bantam Books, R-1976). Kastel also created two wonderful Doc Savage paintings for Bantam as well. One adorned the cover of a paperback novel and the other was used for the movie poster art for the film, *Doc Savage: The Man of Bronze* (Warner Brothers, 1975). "I used actor Steve Holland as the model for the body of Doc," Kastel said. "Holland was the actor who portrayed Flash Gordon in the TV series (Inter-Continental Film Productions, 1954-1955).[21] The face of Doc was modeled after actor Ron Ely," since Ely starred in the title role in the movie.

Kastel's remarkable career has spanned over six decades – an undeniable and timeless testament to his superb skill, vivid vision and versatility as an artist. He describes his own style as "realism." His images are most powerful and moving, leaving a lasting and indelible imprint upon the minds of those who have laid their eyes upon his works. *Jaws* would be considered his most famous work. Dramatic, bold and entirely engrossing, this piece evokes a mass myriad of strong emotions – intense passion, terrifying fear, extreme excitement and, above all, a sense of wonder. It is iconic, representing one of those ultra-rare pieces of fine art that transcends the genre to become a genuine example of true Americana.

"Some years back, I was painting in my studio when my grandson, Luke, walked in and asked me, 'Grandpa, did you ever paint a Mona Lisa?'" Kastel said. "I answered, 'No.' He said to me, 'Well, *Jaws* will just have to be your Mona Lisa.'"

End Notes:
#1 *JAWS* Chapter 1, pgs. 10-12 by Peter Benchley – R-2013 Ballantine Books, trade paperback edition.
#2 Wikipedia – JAWS (novel).
#3 Ibid.
#4 www.nytimes.com/2014/05/29/business/media/oscar-dystel-who-saved-bantam-books-dies-at-101.html?_r=0
#5 *Real Hollywood Thriller: Who Stole Jaws?* By Ben Marks - June 29, 2012. http://www.collectorsweekly.com/articles/real-hollywood-thriller-who-stole-Jaws/
#6 Ibid.
#7 20th-Century American Bestsellers. http://unsworth.unet.brandeis.edu/courses/bestsellers/search.cgi?title=Jaws
#8 Wikipedia – JAWS (novel).
#9 Ibid.
#10 Wikipedia – JAWS (film).
#11 *JAWS Memorabilia* by James Burrell. www.antique67.com/articles.php?article=124
#12 *JAWS Memories from Martha's Vineyard* – Expanded 2nd Edition by Matt Taylor. Titan Books, 2012.
#13 The JAWS Log - Expanded Edition by Carl Gottlieb, Chapter 5 page 53 and Chapter 5 Endnote #15.
#14 TIME magazine Vol. 105 #26 – June 23, 1975 pages 42-44, 49 -51.
#15 #11 *JAWS Memorabilia* by James Burrell.
#16 Wikipedia – JAWS (film).
#17 *Real Hollywood Thriller: Who Stole Jaws?* By Ben Marks - June 29, 2012.
#18 Ibid.
#19 Ibid.
#20 Ibid.
#21 IMDB – Flash Gordon TV series (1954-1955). http://www.imdb.com/title/tt0140738/combined

Susan Backlinie:
Filming the Iconic Opening Scene

In just three minutes Susan Backlinie became the most memorable image in *Jaws*. Backlinie portrayed Chrissie Watkins, a character with little screen time who set the film's tone and appeared on the legendary poster.

Backlinie swam competitively in high school, then professionally, before performing underwater plays in the "Weeki Wachee Water Show." She worked as a stuntwoman and trainer of exotic wild animals, such as lions and bears, performing stunts and training them to do simulated attacks – a dangerous job for anyone.

Backlinie interviewed with *Jaws* production executive, Bill Gilmore, in January 1974. Her character's pivotal scene was shot in June that year.

The actress said that at first, Spielberg was not thrilled about the producers' casting choice, because he originally wanted an actress from New York.

"I was kind of forced upon him by the producers, who told him that the role was just too dangerous for an actress without stunt work experience. Steven didn't know that I could act, so he was rather quiet and distant at first," Backlinie said. "But, after the first take he warmed up to me and we got along just fine."

The first attack scene began shooting on June 29, 1974 at Cow Bay. The scene was filmed "day for night," during the daylight hours with a dark filter on the camera lens. "When you're watching a movie, if the scene takes place at night and you can see details in the background, then it was shot 'day for night.' If the background is completely dark, then it was shot at night. I was really hoping that they were not going to film my attack scene during the night," Backlinie said. "You see, sharks roam around at night. They hunt at night. Feed at night. It's really not a good idea to be in the water at night."

For the attack itself, the crew was going to attach a tool to Backlinie, but opted for manpower because she felt unsafe. "I wore shorts that had cables attached to my hips that ran to pilings about 25-yards from shore, which in turn ran back to the beach. It operated like a pulley system, with the guys running back and forth on the beach, which jerked me this way and that in the water, as if I were in the jaws of the shark," she said. "I also wore fins because Steven wanted me as high as I could possibly get above the water, which proved difficult. I had to flail my arms back and forth, throw my head back and kick with all my strength to stay above the surface. This is what made the attack look so violent."

It was such a success that Spielberg spoofed Backlinie's classic *Jaws* scene in *1941* (Universal Pictures, 1979). "They put up the little white fence because that was so much a part of Jaws. And the water was freezing – under 50, I swear! – when I hit that water, I came running back to the beach," she said.

In the scene's comedic twist, instead of encountering the deadly shark, she grasped the periscope of a surfacing WWII Japanese submarine. One of the submariners appreciated her efforts, when he opened the hatch and discovered the beautiful (and naked) Backlinie hanging onto the periscope. With astonishment, he cried out – "Hollywood!" Yes, indeed.

Poster art for **Gentlemen Prefer Blondes** is among some of the greatest to feature Monroe. The one-sheet features a full length image of Russell and Monroe wearing sequined showgirl costumes in red and yellow with red gloves and top hats, and silver canes with the Eiffel Tower and scenes of French leisure in the background. The 40" x 60" extremely colorful poster has full length image of Russell and Monroe wearing sparkling showgirl outfits, long black gloves and top hats. In recent years, the one-sheet has sold for $280-$3,200, three-sheet $1,900-$2,100, six-sheet $1,700, 40" x 60" $3,200-$5,500, half-sheet $250, lobby card set $700-$950, British quad $700, Australian daybill $400-$650, insert $450, and pressbook $200.

Marilyn Monroe:
The Preferred Blonde

In the pantheon of actors who have entertained movie fans over the past 100 years, few have achieved the level of impact and recognition of Marilyn Monroe. In an industry overflowing with beautiful people, she stands out for her iconic look, bedroom eyes, and playful confidence. She could embody the delicate flower, the woman in charge, the silly flirt, or the femme fatale with ease and style.

Monroe was born Norma Jeane Mortensen on June 1, 1926 in Los Angeles, California. She never knew her father and her mother, Gladys, developed psychiatric problems while Monroe was very young. One of her earliest memories was of her mother trying to smother her with a pillow while she was laying in her crib. After her mother was committed to a mental institution, Monroe spent a good deal of her childhood in foster homes and an orphanage. While living in foster homes she was sexually assaulted at 11 years old. In 1937 family friends Grace and Doc Goddard took her in for a few years. But, in 1942 when Doc was transferred to the East Coast for work the couple couldn't afford to take Monroe with them and she returned to foster care.

Monroe dropped out of high school when she was 15 years old and married her boyfriend Jimmy Dougherty the next year. Dougherty was a merchant marine, so while he was sent to the South Pacific she worked in a munitions factory in Burbank, California. That was where she was discovered by photographer David Conover.

When Dougherty came back she was working successfully as a model and had changed her name to Marilyn Monroe to prepare for her acting career. Her goal was to become an actress of the caliber of Jean Harlow and Lana Turner. Separated by different life plans, their marriage fell apart leading to their divorce in 1946, the same year that she signed her first movie contract.

After adopting the name Marilyn Monroe, she dyed her hair the trademark blonde. Her career took off after she gained plenty of attention for her small part in John Huston's crime drama *The Asphalt Jungle* in 1950. That same year she played opposite Bette Davis in *All About Eve*, impressing audiences and critics alike with her performance.

She wasn't universally considered talented enough to carry starring roles, but Monroe proved that she had the skill to do so, winning honors and attracting large audiences for her movies. She proved her dramatic chops in 1953 while playing a young married woman who wanted to kill her husband with her lover in *Niagara*.

Next came a string of comedies and

musicals that showed off her comedic talent and lovely singing voice. She and fellow sex symbol Jane Russell scored big with their musical comedy *Gentlemen Prefer Blondes*. Not only did the movie feature two dynamic actresses of the day, it also boasted the film version of the song "Diamonds Are a Girl's Best Friend."

She followed that up with some of her biggest hits including the romantic comedy *How to Marry a Millionaire* with Betty Grable and Lauren Bacall and a supporting role in *There's No Business Like Show Business* in '54 with Ethel Merman and Donald O'Connor. In '55 she drove Tom Ewell crazy playing the buxom neighbor known simply as "The Girl" in *The Seven Year Itch*.

Despite her deep seated insecurities, her breathy voice was spellbinding and her curvy, hourglass figure turned heads around the world. Her pre-performance anxiety was so bad that she occasionally became physically ill and gained a reputation for showing up to film sets late, much to the chagrin of costars and the crew.

During her career she was signed to and released from several contracts with different film studios. She wanted to move on from playing the

The one-sheet for **How to Marry a Millionaire** shows Grable, Monroe, and Bacall lounging on the top of a brick wall in front of the New York City skyline. The image of the ladies is crisp, colorful, and sexy with the brick wall below them and the city behind them looking brushed, incomplete around the edges, keeping the focus on the ladies. The one-sheet can sell for $150-$2,250, 30" x 40" style Y $800, three-sheet $450, set of 8 lobby cards $575, half-sheet $250-$1,075, pressbook $50-$100, insert $215, and Australian daybill $350.

The Seven Year Itch three-sheet has a solid black background with large full length image of Monroe in the iconic white dress billowing from the subway grate while Tom Ewell in a much smaller stature looks on. The larger than life image of Monroe symbolizes the magnified level of temptation Ewell's character is going through in her presence. The one-sheet has a large close-up of Monroe waving with Ewell much smaller but full length. The little bit of her strapless top that is shown matches the color in the band around his hat, connecting the pair. The three-sheet has sold for $2,000-$5,000, 40" x 60" style Y $5,000, door panel $4,800, British double crown $3,800, one-sheet $650-$3,300, half-sheet $750-$2,600, lobby card set $1,000-$1,600, insert $300-$1,000, and Australian daybill $450.

happy-go-lucky dumb blonde roles, so she moved to New York City to study acting with Lee Strasberg at the Actors' Studio. Her next film was the dramedy *Bus Stop* in 1956, playing a saloon singer who is kidnapped by a thickheaded cowboy who became infatuated with her. She received significant praise for her performance as the bewildered singer.

She followed this up in romantic comedies with some of Hollywood's most beloved actors. In 1957, she starred opposite the great Laurence Olivier in

The Prince and the Showgirl. In this sexy romantic comedy she played an American showgirl who becomes entangled in political intrigue when the prince of Carpathia tries to woo her. Then she filmed the extremely popular comedy-musical *Some Like It Hot* with Jack Lemmon and Tony Curtis in 1959. Monroe played Sugar Kane, a singer with aspirations to marry a millionaire. Lemmon and Curtis posed as women in her band, on the run from gangsters after they witnessed the St. Valentine's Day Massacre. Her perfor-

mance in this movie earned her a Best Actress in a Comedy at the Golden Globe Awards.

Monroe was reunited with John Huston and joined by Clark Gable, Montgomery Clift, and Eli Wallach for *The Misfits* in 1961. The adventure drama was set in Nevada, where Monroe falls for Gable and a group of emotionally haggard cowboys for hard drinking and a jolting introduction to Western culture. It was her last feature length film.

She was filming *Something's Got to Give* in 1962 with Dean Martin, but was dismissed from the project for missing too many days of filming. An article printed in *The New York Times* at the time claimed that she was absent due to illness. Martin decided not to continue filming without her so the movie was shelved by the studio.

Off screen, she was also well known for stormy romantic relationships. She married Joe DiMaggio in 1954, though the marriage only lasted nine months, and she was then married to playwright Arthur Miller from 1956 to 1961. She was also romantically linked to Marlon Brando, Frank Sinatra, Yves Montand, and Elia Kazan. Off the silver screen, though still in the center of the spotlight, she famously sang "Happy Birthday, Mr. President" to John F. Kennedy at his birthday celebration on May 19, 1962. She was also rumored to have been involved with President Kennedy or his brother Robert around the time of her death.

Monroe died on August 5, 1962 at her home in Los Angeles when she was just

The poster for **The Prince and the Showgirl** shows a flirty, intimate image of Monroe and Olivier. He has one arm wrapped around her waist and the other is holding her hand while he kisses her shoulder. Monroe leans into him smiling as he kisses her while one strap of her dress falls from her shoulder. A medal is pinned to the bosom of her dress and below that is the tagline "Some countries have a medal for Everything." The six-sheet has sold for $3,300, three-sheet $700-$2,800, one-sheet $200-$1,200, Spanish one-sheet $2,600, lobby card set $1,500, and French grande/one-panel $900.

36 years old. An empty bottle of sleeping pills was found near her bed. There have been years of speculation that she was murdered, but the official cause of death was drug overdose. Strasberg delivered the eulogy at her funeral before a small group of friends and family. DiMaggio had red roses sent to her crypt for 20 years after her passing.

In addition to her acting chops and good looks, Monroe is remembered for her quick, witty sense of humor. One time when a reporter tried to shock her by asking what she wore to bed, she casually responded "Chanel Number 5." While filming *Some Like It Hot* costume designer Orry-Kelly was measuring her for her costume and pointed out that Tony Curtis had a nicer butt than she did. Monroe retorted by opening her shirt to show him her other assets, informing Orry-Kelly that Curtis couldn't compare to her breasts.

Monroe appeared in 33 films from 1947 through 1961. From bit parts in *Ladies of the Chorus* and *The Asphalt Jungle* to starring turns in *Niagara* and *Gentlemen Prefer Blondes*, she left an indelible mark on the film industry. Despite a difficult childhood she rose to become one of the biggest stars and a long lasting sex symbol with films grossing over $200 million during her career. Whether people are attracted to her beautiful face, curvaceous body, clever sense of humor, feminine mystique, or sexy persona, Marilyn Monroe is a mystery that will never be solved. One thing is for certain: gentlemen, and ladies, do prefer blondes.

At least this one.

The one-sheet for **Some Like It Hot** plays up the comedic tone of the film showing Curtis and Lemmon arm in arm while giving Monroe a boost. All three are making eye contact with the viewer, Monroe is smiling and winking, Curtis is subtle pouting his lips, and Lemmon is staring wide-eyed. In recent years, the one-sheet has sold for $350-$3,500, 30" x 40" style Z $4,900, 40" x 60" $2,700-$4,400, six-sheet $3,100, Italian four-foglio $3,100, lobby card set $1,000-$2,000, half-sheet $700-$1,500, and insert $650-$1,500.

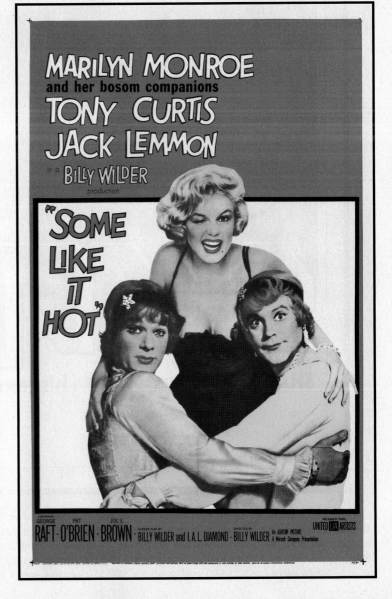

STARTS JULY 2 · DeMILLE and 72nd Street PLAYHOUSE

The mob wanted
Harlem back.
They got Shaft...
up to here.

SHAFT

SHAFT's his name. SHAFT's his game.

METRO-GOLDWYN-MAYER Presents "SHAFT" Starring RICHARD ROUNDTREE · Co-Starring MOSES GUNN
Screenplay by ERNEST TIDYMAN and JOHN D. F. BLACK · Based upon the novel by ERNEST TIDYMAN
Music by ISAAC HAYES · Produced by JOEL FREEMAN · Directed by GORDON PARKS·METROCOLOR

On the one-sheet for **Shaft,** he definitely looks like one bad mother. Swinging from a rope,
he's wearing shiny, black leather, firing his gun, and giving a grimace that will stop criminals cold.
In recent years the New York one-sheet advertising DeMille and 72nd Street Playhouse can sell for
$260, one-sheet for $20-$230, three-sheet for $70-$150, British quad for $45-$125, set of eight
lobby cards for $30-$80, half-sheet for $20-$70, and Japanese B2 for $20-$180.

BLAXPLOITATION: SYMBOLISM AND SATIRE

The 1970s saw a transition in filmmaking. Restrictions on content were loosening, young filmmakers were shirking the grand scale style of the '50s and '60s, traditional gender roles were swapped, Civil Rights and hippy stories were told, and drugs were featured onscreen. One of the most popular film styles to shake up the country during that decade was Blaxploitation. The subgenre of exploitation films was geared toward urban blacks, though they gained a wider audience across other races and ethnicities. Blaxploitation may have debuted in the '70s, but it traces its roots back to the '60s, during a time of racial turbulence.

In the mid-1960s actor Sidney Poitier and musician-producer Quincy Jones carved names for themselves in Hollywood. Poitier starred in films like *The Slender Thread, Guess Who's Coming to Dinner?*, and *In the Heat of the Night*. These films finally offered a broader range of characters for black actors, proving to white audiences that there was more depth and sophistication to the black experience than they usually saw on screen. He was often portrayed as a member of the middle class though, seen as tolerated by white society rather than accepted as an equal.

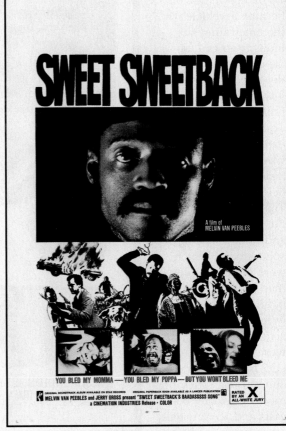

The poster for **Sweet Sweetback's Baadasssss Song** is set in four layers, almost strictly in black and white. The main image is a close-up of Sweetback's face, an expression that is no less than exhausted, set above a montage of gritty, violent images in black and white followed by three boxed images. The one-sheet has sold for $120-$900 in recent years.

During this time, Jones scored the soundtrack for the Sidney Pollack directed movie, *The Slender Thread*. Given the freedom to explore music outside of the traditional jazz score, Jones' style was quickly in high demand for Hollywood's big titles like *The Italian Job* and *The Heist*.

Despite the positive response to Poitier's films and Jones' soundtracks, many didn't feel that they portrayed the black experience or that their influence was producing enough of an impact. Race riots were breaking out all over the country over continued segregation, racism, and violence.

Blaxploitation became a vehicle for the entertainment industry to capitalize on expressions of these feelings through a variety of genres and funky soundtracks. Combining black and exploitation, the name was coined by NAACP head and ex-film publicist Junius Griffin. This type of film was the first to use soul and funk music in the soundtracks, which were more complex than most funk on the radio. Subtypes broadly focused on crime, action and martial arts, westerns, horror, comedy, nostalgia, drama, and musical. They portrayed primarily black casts and were usually set in poor neighborhoods. Poverty, ethnic slurs against white characters, and derogatory names were often part of the stories. Those set in the South usually dealt with slavery and the quest for freedom.

Mevlin Van Peebles' *Sweet Sweetback's Baadasssss Song* is widely credited with starting the subgenre in 1971. Focused on the energy of black power, similar to what was seen in urban neighborhoods of the late 1960s to early 1970s, the movie was an avant-garde interpretation of European modernism. The movie did well, despite only appearing in a few theaters throughout the country. With limited advertis-

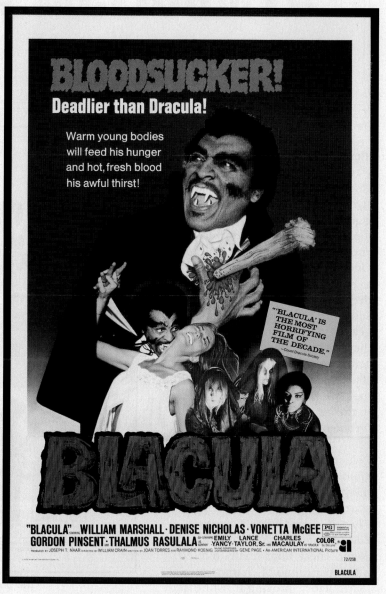

The **Blacula** one-sheet is just as campy as the movie with Blacula standing, mouth open, fangs bared while a stake plunges into his chest, giving it a three-dimensional look. The bottom half is a bit more frightening with Blacula biting a victim and a moody trio looks out at the viewer. The font of the title provides plenty of punch, appearing to be made of smeared blood. The 40" x 60" can sell for $385-$550, one-sheet for $20-$240, half-sheet for $20-$180, and set of eight lobby cards for $25-$110.

ing resources, Van Peebles released the soundtrack featuring Earth, Wind & Fire, which reached more theater goers and made Hollywood start paying attention.

Later that year, *Shaft* was released, presenting a mainstream successor to *Sweetback*. Both movies boasted similar themes, such as the protagonist's physical strength and virility, his sexual prowess, deeply rooted confidence, and ability to win every fight. Like *Sweetback*, *Shaft* also relied on the soundtrack to bolster ticket sales. Not only was the soundtrack loved by *Shaft* fans, it was a critical success. The

"Theme From Shaft" by Isaac Hayes won Best Original Song at the Academy Awards in 1972. His song combined with the way director Gordon Parks shot the opening scene showing soulful hero Shaft, played by Richard Roundtree, walking through New York City is an iconic moment in cinema history.

After a few establishing hits, Blaxploitation ventured out of urban action to feature blackness as a focal point in horror. In 1972 an African prince turned vampire by Dracula finds his way to Los Angeles in *Blacula*. William Marshall's performance as the titular character spawned the sequel *Scream Blacula Scream*, costarring the first lady of Blaxploitation, Pam Grier. A few years later *J.D's Revenge* took on horror in a grittier way, telling the story of a black law student possessed by the spirit of a revenge-seeking mobster.

The next wave of Blaxploitation films turned their attention to the ladies. *Coffy* in 1973 and *Foxy Brown* in 1974 starring Pam Grier and *Cleopatra Jones* in 1973 starring Tamara Dobson introduced audiences to the power of black women. In *Coffy* Grier took on the persona of a vigilante seeking revenge after her sister's life is ruined when she gets hooked on drugs. Grier's inspiring confidence led to another hit with *Foxy Brown* when she played a woman avenging her boyfriend's death. In *Cleopatra Jones* Dobson starred as a James Bond-like secret agent for the U.S. government tak-

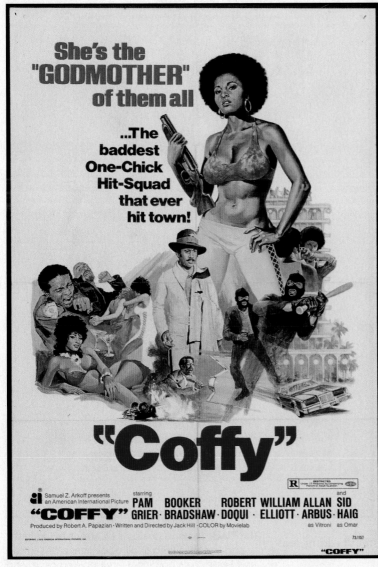

The **Coffy** one-sheet has a white background with gold brushed across the center of the image. A risqué image of Pam Grier dominates the poster in all her voluptuous glory, holding a gun. In recent years the one-sheet has sold for $50-$260, half-sheet for $70-$145, and set of eight lobby cards for $60-$205.

ing down drug trade and corrupt cops. Like most screen vixens, they were hyper-sexualized, yet also supremely aware of the battle between good and evil, fighting for justice in the thick of it.

Some considered the genre to be a symbol of black empowerment, with black writers and directors making movies about the black experience in the US. Others considered it to be perpetuating white stereotypes about black people, such as glorifying criminal and aggressive behavior. One such example was *Super Fly*, about a drug dealer in Harlem intent on making a last deal before leaving the business. Though the movie was intended to tell a story of the difficult life of a drug dealer, but for many it had the opposite effect, glamourizing the ghetto lifestyle as fancy clothes, fast cars, and bountiful cash.

The NAACP, Southern Christian Leadership Conference, and National Urban League joined to form the Coalition Against Blaxploitation. Their influence can be seen in the demise of the genre by the late 1970s, though some attribute the end to formulaic films losing audience interests. With Hollywood churning out as many movies as possible, their quality – particularly their message – was lost to a repetitive system lacking real substance.

Blaxploitation has had an impact on many prominent hip hop artists like Snoop Dogg, Big Daddy Kane, Ice-T, and Slick Rick who embraced the pimp persona driving luxury Cadillacs, depicting

women as objects or status symbols, and wearing flashy jewelry.

Newer films such as *I'm Gonna Git You Sucka*, *Austin Powers in Goldmember*, and *Undercover Brother* have featured comical versions of Blaxploitation characters while films like *Do the Right Thing*, *Boyz in the Hood*, *New Jack City*, and *Dead Presidents* offered elements of the genre without integrating some of the stereotypical behavior.

The **Black Samson** poster is all about being flashy and dazzling with a full body image of Samson and Leslie, he's holding a large golden cane, and a gold leash with a ferocious lion at the end of it. The poster is comically ostentatious with jewels glinting in the light with a chaotic city street behind them. The one-sheet can sell for $10-$200 and 30" x 40" for $15-$85.

In 1997 *Jackie Brown* paid homage to the era, telling a story about a flight attendant who becomes embroiled in a war between the police and an arms dealer, starring Blaxploitation icon Grier. Blaxploitation has also been featured in webcomics such as *World of Hurt* by Jay Potts that draws influence from *Shaft* and *Slaughter's Big Rip-Off*.

The argument over whether Blaxploitation helped the black movement or hindered it will never be resolved. Whether it's the later mediocre, formulaic movies or the clever earlier hits, though, Blaxploitation has left its mark on the film industry. It gave voice to a group of people who Hollywood had previously relegated to the sidelines and packed enough punch to make every movie fan pay attention.

The American international 40" x 60" poster for **Foxy Brown** was painted in warm colors with a central, large image of Pam Grier posing with gun. She is surrounded by smaller action images of men fighting with various weapons, Foxy fighting different women, and multi-colored images of Foxy in motion. The main one-sheet features a full body shot of Foxy Brown, both sexy and dangerous with a collage of images around her legs several of her kicking butt. In recent years the American international 40" x 60" sold for $490-$3,105 and one-sheet for $100-$660.

Jeff Potokar: Owning and Being a Part of Film History

Jeff Potokar works in the film industry and has been collecting movie posters for 30 years. Not only is he a fan of film, he also enjoys hunting for new pieces to add to his collection, particularly from the Golden Age of cinema.

Overstreet: How long have you been collecting movie posters?

Jeff Potokar (JP): I have been collecting since 1985, when I got posters through work that otherwise would have been thrown in the trash. I became a more serious collector in 2002.

Overstreet: Why did you start collecting movie posters?

JP: I always have loved film; even as a kid. Back then, I collected film magazines, namely *Famous Monsters of Filmland.*

I now work in film post production, have always loved the artistic beauty of posters and decided to one day collect and own additional small pieces of film history.

Overstreet: Are you a big fan of movies or do you just collect for the art? If so, what is it about movies that you love?

JP: I love films and also love art – fine art, etchings, etc. So this was a natural collecting avenue as I enjoy both art forms very much.

Overstreet: What attracts you to collecting movie posters?

JP: The hunt, the search, the research, the art of stone lithography – which I prefer, versus modern photo or digitally created imagery. Plus, I like material from the 1920s, '30s and '40s, especially and having something associated with these earlier films is very appealing.

Overstreet: What was the first movie poster that you collected?

JP: It was a "freebee" U.S. one-sheet, gotten from work – and destined for the trash – for *The Lost Boys*.

Overstreet: What is your favorite piece in your collection?

JP: I don't have a favorite as many are favorites for different reasons – it could be the director, the art, the actor/actress. But I am partial to a 1927 Belgian poster I have for the Lon Chaney Sr. film, called *Mr. Wu*.

Overstreet: What is the most valuable poster in your collection?

JP: I have not done a lot of research as far as value. I don't collect for investment, but for the love of the hobby and the imagery each contains.

Overstreet: Which posters do you want to add to your collection?

JP: Any Universal horror from the classic era of the 1930s, as well as Lon Chaney, Sr. material from the 1920s.

Overstreet: Do you collect different movie poster sizes?
JP: Yes. I collect posters from the U.S. as well as foreign posters. All are different sizes.

Overstreet: Do you collect other movie memorabilia?
JP: Yes. I also collect life masks, made of actors, which were and are used to design special FX make-ups.

Overstreet: Do you have a preference on what type of movie art you collect?

JP: I prefer to collect film posters, as well as window cards.

Overstreet: Do you focus on a time period, genre, artist, or anything else?
JP: I focus more on material that is from films pre-1945. I love the stone litho look and process. It was discontinued, as offset printing became the norm. I like drama, noir, horror and silent material, all from this period (1920s-1940s). If a poster or image grabs me, I may opt to buy it, even if not my usual focus.

Overstreet: How much does condition impact your decision to purchase a poster?
JP: Because I collect material that can be 70+ years old, a poster will often not be pristine as it has lived a life. Because of that, I'm happy and content to find material that may even be rarer, that is not a 10. Those often do not even exist and I can be happy with that.

Overstreet: Is linen-backing a factor for you when it comes to purchasing posters?
JP: No. I actually prefer my posters that are not linen-backed. If a poster needs backing, I would rather know its condition beforehand, and have it done myself, so I know exactly how much restoration has been done to a piece.

Overstreet: What about restoration?
JP: Restoration, for me, meaning conservation and preservation, and not making a poster look brand new, is very important. If a poster can be saved and preserved for future generations, I am all for it. For me, less is more, when it comes to restoration.

Overstreet: Do you consider resale value when purchasing posters?
JP: No, I don't. I don't buy to sell. Though if I choose to sell later on, the above question doesn't apply.

Overstreet: Where do you buy your posters?
JP: Sellers, eBay, Craigslist, and some well

known and respected dealers like eMovie-Poster – Bruce Hershenson.

Overstreet: How do you store them?
JP: Frames, in tubes and folded, and stored in acid free tissue paper.

Overstreet: Do you decorate with them?
JP: I have a few framed posters up on the walls. I also collect etchings so I'm careful to blend the right pieces to obtain the right look.

Overstreet: What advice would you give to someone new to the hobby to avoid overpaying or buying reprints that are claiming to be originals?
JP: Be diligent, ask questions, join poster forums like All Poster Forum, and do one's homework. If something is priced and looks too good to be true, it probably is. Research is so important. Do not buy randomly or just because. There are scammers out there and if one is careful, one can avoid being taken. And forums are always full of helpful people. Never be afraid to ask, or worry about sounding silly. It will pay off in the long run.

THE VALUE OF LINEN-BACKING

In any area of collecting, restoration is a tricky subject. While purists tend to believe that collectibles should be left in the best natural condition, others think that efforts to preserve and even improve the look of a piece is its own reward and can also increase monetary value. When it comes to movie posters, that discussion is focused around linen-backing.

Linen-backing is a conservation method used to preserve posters by mounting them, so that they can be stored and displayed without concern of causing damage that would devalue the poster. Pieces that are already damaged can be stabilized and improved by linen-backing, thereby restoring them to their earlier attractiveness. The process keeps the poster flat and smooth so that it can be handled easily, making it a popular method because posters are preserved better than non-linen-backed ones.

Movie posters are not issued to the public, so most pieces have been transported and displayed by non-collectors who may not consider preserving their integrity. Posters are displayed in theaters with some being reused when films are rereleased causing them to suffer small tears, creases, and pinholes. Most posters sold before the mid-1980s were issued folded, creating significant eyesores, particularly on darker colors.

The process of linen-backing involves mounting posters on acid free lining paper or rice paper and mounting the acid free paper onto a piece of stretched linen or canvas. When the process began real linen was most often used as it is an attractive fabric, soft and pliable. Most posters today, however, are linen-backed on cotton duck, a canvas material that is stiffer than linen and much cheaper, while linen is used more often on very rare pieces. It's also important to note that some people don't use the lining paper, skipping that step to save on the cost of mounting. Unfortunately, the poster does not stick to cloth as well as it does to the lining paper. Also, temperature and moisture changes can cause the poster paper to shrink forcing friction between the paper and the cloth which can lead to lines forming on the poster. The lining paper is important, because it acts as a buffer between the poster and the cloth.

Linen-backing can dramatically improve the collective appearance of the poster. Most defects are significantly improved when linen-backed. Fold lines can be flattened and tears can be repositioned to make them much less noticeable. Some restorers will use further restoration techniques, even fix color loss by using watercolor paints or colored pencils. There are restorers who will insert scrap poster pieces to fill in holes if a poster has a chunk missing.

It is the preferred archival method for conserving and/or restoring a poster. Linen-backed posters are more durable and easier to preserve and protect. They can be rolled for shipping and are easy to frame without worry of adding creases. It's a good process for older posters before they are framed and can increase the value. Linen-backing keeps the poster from sustaining any further damage during the handling and framing process.

There are many who buy and sell posters that believe unrestored posters achieve better results than restored/linen-backed posters. Others believe that rare posters with unsightly flaws can have their value increased by linen-backing and restoration. For rare posters without major flaws linen-backing can have virtually no effect and may slightly decrease the value. Many collectors with multiple pieces prefer the unrestored, non-linen-backed posters unless they are very rare posters. Linen-backing can obscure how much restoration has been done, making collectors nervous about the actual condition of the poster, and affect the price a poster can command. It also hides any backside markings that can be used to authenticate a poster.

It's important to note that once a poster is linen-backed it cannot be removed without causing damage. Consider whether you are a poster collector interested in the investment value of the piece or an art lover who wants it to look as good as it possibly can, regardless of monetary value. If you choose to linen-back, do the research to find an expert. Understand the process and techniques used on the poster and make sure the restorer uses only acid free materials and lining paper. Also, find out how much restoration they typically do and articulate how much you want done to the poster. When considering the process, linen-backing and restoration should be weighed separately. Collectors interested in protecting the value of their investment should research movie poster auction houses and dealers to compare prices of individual posters in similar condition that are linen-backed versus those that are not.

TOP 10 SALES AT HERITAGE AUCTIONS

Heritage Auctions is the world's largest movie poster auctioneer with annual sales routinely surpassing $7 million across three signature auctions and 52 weekly internet auctions. Heritage launched its Movie Poster category in 2001 under the leadership of Grey Smith, a recognized expert on film history and movie poster collecting; movie posters were among the auction house's first expansion into a category other than numismatics. During the years that followed, the category attracted some of the most famous collections ever assembled and now claims several world records including the most valuable movie poster ever sold at public auction, the most valuable movie poster insert ever sold at auction and the most valuable poster for *Frankenstein* ever sold.

London After Midnight (1927) one-sheet in very fine+ condition sold in November 2014 for $478,000.

King Kong (1933) style B linen-backed three-sheet in very fine+ condition sold in November 2012 for $388,375.

Frankenstein (1931) style C linen-backed three-sheet in fair/good condition sold in March 2015 for $358,500.

The Bride of Frankenstein (1935) style D linen-backed one-sheet in fine+ condition sold in November 2007 for $334,600.

The Black Cat (1934) style B one-sheet in near mint+ condition sold in November 2009 for $334,600.

Dracula (1931) style F linen-backed one-sheet in very fine condition sold in March 2009 for $310,700.

The Black Cat (1934) style D linen-backed one-sheet in very fine+ condition sold in March 2007 for $286,800.

Frankenstein (1931) insert in fine+ condition sold in July 2013 for $262,900.

Flying Down to Rio (1933) one-sheet in very fine/near mint condition sold in November 2008 for $239,000.

The Phantom of the Opera (1925) paper-backed one-sheet in fine/very fine condition sold in July 2014 for $203,150.

MOVIE POSTER DECORATING

By Eric Bradley

When Steve Wilkin displayed a discarded poster for the 1931 Universal horror classic *Frankenstein*, he picked the most accommodating spot in his house: his workshop. He found the poster in the late 1970s as a teen movie theater worker; his boss allowed him the rare privilege of crawling into the old theater's boarded-up projection booth where he uncovered the long-forgotten six-foot poster. No matter where he lived, the poster was on display.

"It's true - it did hang at the base of my second floor stairs," Wilkin said. "The building is a shop/barn that houses my work equipment and antique stuff display. I guess it's my man cave, so no high-end type of decoration."

Wilkin's claim his space was not home to anything "high-end" is ironic, since the movie poster that once hung in his shop

was none other than the only six-foot, three-sheet specimen known to exist. When he finally agreed to part with it, it brought $358,000 – a world record for the most valuable *Frankenstein* movie poster ever sold at public auction.

"I am now known as the 'Frankenstein Poster Guy' and often have to tell the tale at gatherings," he said. "I can truthfully say everyone loves the story!"

When it comes to decorating with movie posters, the collector has more than a century's worth of fangs, cleavage, exploding cars or moody helicopters racing over the swells of the South China Sea toward Vietnam. Let other people judge. We're talking about your *movie* here – not just your poster.

There is one simple fact to keep in mind before we jump into the hows and whys of covering your walls with screen gems: Movie posters were never created as "art." The movie poster, from its earliest history, is a piece of sales collateral designed to do one thing: sell tickets and get butts in theater seats. Posters are an investment for studios and the higher the investment the more the movie's marketing department expects a stronger return. It also shouldn't shock you to learn that

A-list actors have strict rules for studios to follow on how large their face or likeness should appear on a poster and the location and font size of the star's name. Nothing on a movie poster is there by accident. Now that we're all armed with that knowledge, it's easy to see why some posters are more valuable than others. It's like dominos – the more visually appealing the poster, the more tickets it sold, the more people saw the film, the more likely it was nominated for an award and became a classic of American cinema, and so on.

When you view movie posters in light of their original goal then maybe movie poster collectors have plenty in common with collectors of vintage advertising signs and the like. I bring up this point because when it comes to decorating with posters, generally speaking, the more outrageous the poster and generous the artistic treatment the larger the following and higher the price.

The true beauty of decorating with movie posters is the absolute freedom to represent who you really are, but only if you buy what you like. Movies, like music, touch a part of us few art forms ever reach. Maybe it's the subtle blend

of actors, lines, cinematography, and themes. Are you a wistful romantic at heart? There's more than enough posters of *Sleepless in Seattle, Love Actually* or *The Notebook* to be had for less than $50. Want to tell the world you see the world through the lens of a feminist? Posters for the few Hollywood films that adequately portray strong female characters and themes are few and far between – not surprising, since it has been reported that for every 15 or so male film directors there is but one female director. Posters for feminist films that challenge patriarchy and explore important gender politics have a strong following and are still accessible – French grande posters for the 1978 rerelease of *The Passion of Joan of Arc*, hailed as one of the most important feminist films of the 20th century, can be had for less than $50. Original one-sheets for the 1928 film sell at auction for $1,200 and up.

Bang for your Buck

Perhaps the most unique aspect of decorating with movie posters is the ability to get a lot of art and design for not a lot of money. Few movie poster categories stand out in this regard because of current collecting trends, number of collectors, and the amount of new posters coming to market. The best bargains are usually found where nobody else is looking:

Western Movie Posters – A personal favorite, posters for Western movies and shorts from the 1940s-1950s thunder with daring imagery, bold titles, and scenes of derring-do for less than $50. These posters offer all the excitement of their sci-fi and horror counterparts at a fraction of the price thanks, in part, to a generational quirk: the baby boomers who relished the films of Roy Rogers, Rex, King of Wild Horses, Tom Mix, and The Sons of the Pioneers, are in the process of selling their extensive collections to a public that does not carry the same fondness for cowboy and Indian flicks. These treasures can be had for less than $40, with truly amazing pieces available for a paltry $300 to $400 bucks.

Foreign Language – Posters made for the Polish market have a long and respected history for their innovative artistic design, but did you know you can snag Japanese, French, or Spanish examples of expensive U.S. classics for a fraction of the price?

Children's Films – It's safe to say that 99 percent of all posters made for children's movies sell for less than $100.

Musicals – With the exception of but a handful of scarce posters of which only a handful exist, posters for musicals can be found for less than $100, with exceptional Pre-War examples from the 1930s and classics such as *White Christmas* from 1954 available for less than $1,000 each.

Your movie poster decor can be as campy, hilarious, or as poignant as you want. It's all in your control and every choice projects a message about you in ways traditional art cannot. Decorating with movie posters instantly tells people your taste in movies, actors, eras, film genres, art direction, graphic design, typography, and much more. Perhaps, though, it also projects your relationship to an experience shared by millions of your fellow movie buffs. It's an experience that crosses generations, decades, race, age, and income. It all comes down to that important moment our hearts, budgets, and imaginations are all ready to shout: "Action!"

THE ART AND DESIGN OF SAUL BASS

FRANK SINATRA · ELEANOR PARKER · KIM NOVAK

THE MAN WITH THE GOLDEN ARM

A FILM BY OTTO PREMINGER

With Arnold Stang, Darren McGavin, Robert Strauss, John Conte, Doro Merande, George E. Stone, George Mathews, Leonid Kinskey, Emile Meyer, Shorty Rogers, Shelly Manne. Screenplay by Walter Newman & Lewis Meltzer, From the novel by Nelson Algren, Music by Elmer Bernstein, Produced & Directed by Otto Preminger, Released by United Artists

The central image on **The Man with the Golden Arm** poster is a fractured arm, symbolizing the destructive power of drugs. The film's stars appear as if they've been plastered onto the paper in black and white, surrounded by blocks of moody coloring. In recent years the one-sheet has sold for $660-$1,550, the three-sheet $2,480, half-sheet $130-$585, insert $180-$660, and the six-sheet $15,535.

In a career that spanned 40 years, Saul Bass worked with the likes Alfred Hitchcock, Martin Scorsese, Billy Wilder, Otto Preminger, and Stanley Kubrick, among others, creating memorable movie posters and title sequences.

Bass was born in 1920 in the Bronx, New York. He went to James Monroe High School, then was a part time student at the Art Students League in 1936 before taking night classes at Brooklyn College from 1944 to 1946.

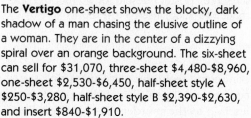

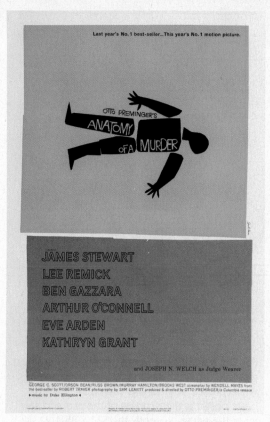

The **Vertigo** one-sheet shows the blocky, dark shadow of a man chasing the elusive outline of a woman. They are in the center of a dizzying spiral over an orange background. The six-sheet can sell for $31,070, three-sheet $4,480-$8,960, one-sheet $2,530-$6,450, half-sheet style A $250-$3,280, half-sheet style B $2,390-$2,630, and insert $840-$1,910.

The simplistic Anatomy of a Murder poster depicts the blocky shape of a body in disconnected pieces. The image succinctly illustrates the tone and premise of the film. The one-sheet can sell for $1,180-$2,950, silk screen poster $2,030, 30" x 40" $1,550, insert $70-$480, half-sheet style A $400, and half-sheet style B $90-$380.

He worked as a freelance commercial artist for advertising agencies, including Warner Bros., before leaving New York for Los Angeles. His career in Hollywood began when he designed print advertisements for *Champion*, *Death of a Salesman*, and *The Moon is Blue*. In 1954 he designed the poster for Otto Preminer's film *Carmen Jones*, impressing the director so much that he asked Bass to create the title sequence too. His next project was the title sequence for Billy Wilder's *The Seven Year Itch*.

Bass was one of the first designers to understand the impact a creative opening sequence could have on a film. In his sequence for *The Man with the Golden Arm*, he played on the film's subject matter of a musician's struggle with heroin addiction. The sequence featured strips of white across a field of black with the central image of an arm, mirroring the focal point relating to heroin addiction.

He developed on the sliced text that comes together and slides apart in the opening of *Psycho*, and the credits that race up and down that transitions into the angled shot of a skyscraper in *North by Northwest*.

Before Bass' work, title sequences were most often generic lists of the title, cast, and crew, often in the style of a playbill. It was common for the titles to be played on the curtains of a theater before opening them to the beginning of the movie. Breaking free of this tradition, Bass designed cut-out animation, mini-movie animation, and live action sequences. His title sequences became their own entertaining piece of the film.

THE MAGNIFICENT SEVEN · DIRECTED BY JOHN STURGES

For **The Magnificent Seven** poster, Bass created a simple design of seven red slashes across a white poster. What brings such power to the basic poster is the richness of the red and sterility of the white. Recently the 25" x 35-1/2" silk screen poster sold for $1,910-$5,080.

The Shining one-sheet is dominated by the title of the film in black, block lettering. Within the letters is a pointillist face, eyes ghastly wide and mouth set in pinched form. In recent years the silk screen poster has sold for $1,900, the one-sheet $40-$380, insert $40-$180.

Near the end of his career he worked with Martin Scorsese on *Goodfellas, Cape Fear, The Age of Innocence,* and *Casino,* and Steven Spielberg for *Schindler's List,* his last sequence. His influence can be seen on modern title sequences such as the animated titles for *Catch Me If You Can* and *Mad Men.*

His movie posters also broke away from traditions. Prior to his work most movie posters usually presented images of a key scene of the film or of the poising characters. Instead, Bass designed symbolic pieces depicting key elements and themes of the movie in a minimalistic style.

For *The Man with the Golden Arm* poster Bass created a crooked arm, symbolism the disjointed life of a heroin addict. For *Vertigo* the animated figure is sucked into the center of a dizzying vortex, capturing the anxiety and panic portrayed in the film. Another of his well-known posters was for *Anatomy of a Murder* depicting the animated figure of a body placed in the center, though each appendage is dis-connected from the torso mirroring the courtroom drama's dissection of the events leading to the murder. His work on *The Shining* features a ghostly close-up image of a face that could be emoting sheer terror or sinister intentions, a maddening point made throughout the movie.

In addition to the movie posters he designed posters for several film festivals, books, magazines, and album covers. He designed five posters for the Academy Award Presentations as well as the Student Academy Award for the Academy of Motion Picture Arts and Sciences. Bass also designed the jet stream logo for Continental Airlines in 1968, the United Airlines tulip logo in 1974, and AT&T's globe logo in 1983. Bass was a pioneer of the motion picture title sequences using revolutionizing animated film graphics and movie posters that utilize a minimalistic style. In an industry where bigger is always better, Bass managed to entice and amaze through the depth of symbolism.

Saul Bass passed away April 25, 1996.

The poster for **Schindler's List** is a set of barbed wire braided together down the center of the poster with the list punctured by one of the spikes. The one-sheet can sell for $1,195-$2,900.

QUENTIN TARANTINO, CULT HIT MAKER

Some directors develop followings. When they begin a new project their fans are ready to purchase tickets, no matter the storyline or the cast list. Through his pantheon of pop culture knowledge, whip cracking dialogue, shocking and often absurd violence, and ability to attract Hollywood's best actors and actresses, Quentin Tarantino has developed such a following. His movies may cover revenge, Westerns, historical reimagining, and Blaxploitation, but they all have one common thread. They are undeniably Tarantino.

He was an only child who instantly developed a love of movies and had a talent for storytelling. Raised by his mother Connie McHugh, he was born in 1963 in Knoxville, Tennessee. His father Tony Tarantino, left before Quentin was even born. Tarantino and his mother moved to California when he was four years old. Other than history, he did not enjoy school, so he spent his time reading comics and watching movies. He worked as a video store clerk, absorbing the artistic details of everything he watched, cultivating the ability to combine independent film style with tons of pop culture references and homages.

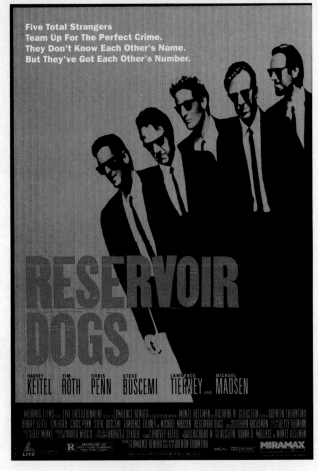

The **Reservoir Dogs** Cannes Festival poster shows a small image of the men entering a room with the only light coming through from behind them and beside the title of the film is a paw print in red. The one-sheet shows the five main characters in their suits and sunglasses looking cool and intimidating. In recent years the Cannes Festival poster has sold for $775, one-sheet $80-$450, Japanese B1 for $750, and British quad for $50-$300.

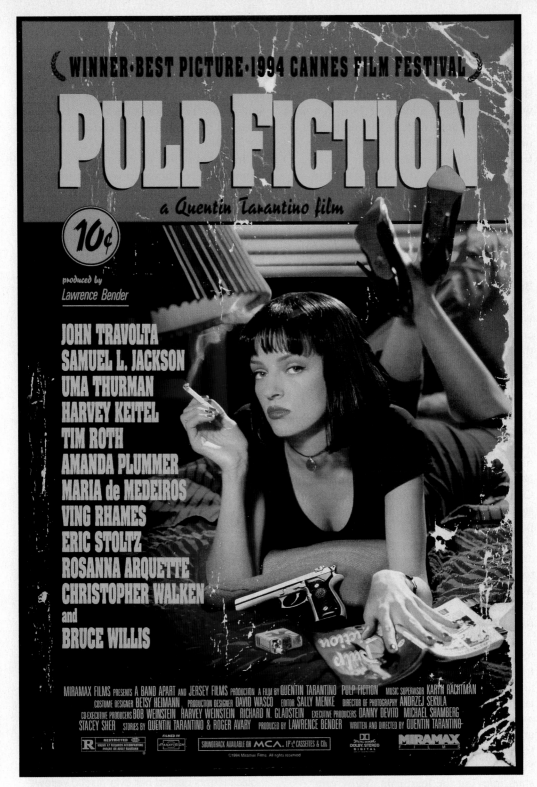

The advance one-sheet for **Pulp Fiction** looks like a beaten, battered paperback novel showing a sexy Mia Wallace lying on her stomach smoking a cigarette and reading. The other advance one-sheet shows Mia Wallace lying down reading without the background images of the room she's in and the one-sheet also features the cast and credits for the movie. The withdrawn advance one-sheet (after R.J. Reynolds threatened litigation because the cigarette package in front of Uma Thurman hadn't been approved by their manufacturer) can sell for $1,300-$2,270, advance one-sheet for $900-$1,800, other advance one-sheet for $80-$500, one-sheet for $35-$580, French one-panel for $60-$350, and British quad for $230.

Tarantino dropped out of school and took acting classes while working as an usher at an adult film theater. He left that job to work at Video Archives in Manhattan Beach, California. While working there he wrote screenplays, including *True Romance* and *Natural Born Killers*. During that time he also did a guest spot on *The Golden Girls* as an Elvis impersonator.

In 1990 he started working for the production company Cinetel. One of the producers there gave his *True Romance* script to director Tony Scott, who liked it and bought the rights. He was able to get the funding for his directorial debut, *Reservoir Dogs*, with producer Lawrence Bender. When the movie premiered at the Sundance Film Festival in 1992, audiences were blown away by the extremely violent crime thriller. Though it didn't do well in theaters, it became a cult hit internationally and on video. The next film he directed earned him an Oscar.

Pulp Fiction erupted on the scene in 1994. Filled with pop culture references and even more violence, the story followed several different storylines. Big name actors like John Travolta, Samuel L. Jackson, Bruce Willis, Uma Thurman, and Christopher Walken came together to tell stories of hitmen, a fledgling boxer, and a pair robbing a diner. It earned $108 million at the box office, making more than any other independent film in history, up to that point. *Pulp Fiction* received seven Academy Award nominations, winning Best Original Screenplay for Tarantino and Roger Avary.

His next two projects were led by tough female protagonists paying homage to beloved film subgenres. Three years after *Pulp Fiction*, Tarantino directed the crime thriller *Jackie Brown* about a stewardess who is caught smuggling money for an arms dealer. It was filmed as a tribute to Blaxploitation movies of the 1970s with Pam Grier, one of the subgenre's biggest stars, playing the lead role. Many critics considered it to be Tarantino's most mature project to date. He followed this by sharing his love for the subgenre of Kung Fu movies. While working on *Pulp Fiction* he and Thurman conceived the idea for a martial arts film that would be a tribute to his love of Kung Fu movies with

Kill Bill. The revenge story was about an assassin known as the Bride who plans to kill the people involved in the massacre of her wedding party. He wrote and shot so much for the movie that he needed to split it into two movies. *Kill Bill Vol. 1* was released in 2003 and *Kill Bill Vol. 2* came out in 2004.

In the mid-'90s he developed a filmmaking relationship with Robert Rodriguez. Tarantino wrote the script for *From Dusk Till Dawn* and Rodriguez directed it. Years later they worked together again on the double feature *Grindhouse*. The tribute to Grindhouse movies and theaters of the '70s, Tarantino wrote and directed *Death Proof* while Rodriguez wrote and directed *Planet Terror*. In Tarantino's *Death Proof* a psychotic stuntman uses his stunt car to murder young woman. Though the concept was intriguing, critics and audiences didn't

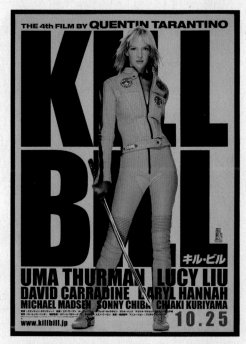

The **Kill Bill: Vol. 1** poster shows a full body image of the Bride wearing the yellow suit she sported in the movie with the title in large black letters behind her over a solid yellow background. The subway poster shows the lead characters known as the Deadly Viper Assassination Squad along with a member of the Crazy 88s. The advance one-sheet is split down the center by the Bride's sword over Japanese text. The Japanese B2 can sell for $500, subway poster $350, English 40 x 60 $250, and advance one-sheet $10-$185.

respond favorably to either movie, despite boasting casts that included Kurt Russell, Rosario Dawson, Bruce Willis, and Rose McGowan.

His next two projects were historical films. First was the revisionist look at World War II, *Inglourious Basterds*. Tarantino cast Hollywood heartthrob Brad Pitt to lead a group of Jewish-American soldiers on a quest to kill Hitler. Like many of his films, it got mixed reviews from audiences and critics, in part for revising events of the war, but the movie was nominated for eight Academy Awards. His next movie was the Western *Django Unchained* with Jamie Foxx as a freed slave trying to find his wife and Christoph Waltz as a bounty hunter. The movie earned Tarantino an Oscar for writing the screenplay.

As of the writing of this book, he is directing his post-Civil War film *The Hateful Eight* with Jackson, Russell, Jennifer Jason Leigh, Tim Roth, Demian Bichir, Walter Goggins, Bruce Dern, Michael Madsen, and Zoë Bell.

Tarantino may not be everyone's cup of tea, but like any cult movie director, his fans are fiercely loyal. Through careful study of many movie genres, deconstruction of the filmmaking process, and impressive ability to buck traditions, he has made incredibly interesting movies. His eclectic film style has been honed to a fine point making his movies undeniably Tarantino.

The **Death Proof** one-sheet in black, white, and red shows the death proof car speeding off the poster with the film's ladies silhouettes behind it on the horizon. The edges of the poster have a naturally worn look to them as though it'd been tacked onto quite a few walls. The **Grindhouse** double feature poster shows smaller images for **Planet Terror** and **Death Proof** with images of the films' stars underneath, paying homage to the exploitation films of the '60s and '70s. In recent years the one-sheet has sold for $50-$290, Japanese B1 for $20-$260, **Grindhouse** one-sheet for $20-$430, and **Grindhouse** vinyl banner for $180.

Several teasers were issued for **Inglourious Basterds**, each featuring two portraits of a single character, one full body in the foreground and one painted red in the background. Another teaser shows the handle of a rifle with the title etched into below a bloody hand. The one-sheet depicts the titular Basterds striding confidently with the vicious Col. Hans Landa and the films leading ladies Shosanna and Bridget von Hammersmark painted over a swatch of red. The teasers can sell for $20-$215, one-sheet for $35-$205, Japanese B1 for $50-$190, and British quad for $20-$115.

AUSTRALIAN DAYBILLS

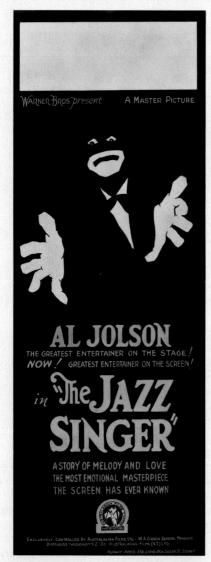

The mysterious, mostly black daybill for **The Jazz Singer** – which is known as the first movie musical – has blank space left at the top for theater information.

Movie poster sizes and artwork vary greatly around the world. Some are square shaped, while others are rectangular, some are traditionally landscape and others are usually portrait. In addition to sizes, they can also display different artwork from their original domestic poster counterparts. Australian daybills are among the most popular of international sizes.

Production of Australian daybills started during the early days of the 20th Century. The earliest versions measured 15" x 40", and were often denoted as long daybills. Two posters were usually printed on one sheet of paper using hand litho or stone litho processes. During this time period many daybills had a white border area at the top of the poster where theaters would add details about screenings, similar to U.S. window cards. Popular and highly respected artists of the period were Frank Tyler, Fred Powis, Tom Ferry, and Wynee Davies. Printers used in the early days of daybills included Hackett Offset, JNO Evans, Marchant, Matthews and Co, Offset Printers, Paper Products Litho, and Simmons.

Many of these early daybills were reissued through the '50s. But, since the dimensions changed, these reissues are easily spotted when compared to their original counterparts. Because of their age, these older daybills produced up until the early 1940s are very rare and hard to find.

Daybill sizes got leaner in the early '40s. During World War II most measured 10" x 30", reducing five inches from the width,

Boris Karloff imposingly looms over the daybill for **The Invisible Ray**, sending bolts of energy to the kissing couple below. This colorful piece is gorgeously eye catching for the fear and romance it displays. The top of the daybill offers space for theater show times.

This gorgeous daybill for **The Philadelphia Story** showcases the talented leads with small portraits, their names big and bold, and an inset image from the film with the credits below.

which allowed another daybill to be printed on a sheet of paper. This period of 10" x 30" daybills lasted approximately from 1941 to 1945. They were most often printed by Marchant, Simmons, and W.E. Smith. Marchant posters were the more popular

style, featuring photographic images that were retouched by artists.

Over the next 30 years daybills were made exclusively for Australian releases of films, though they were one of the variety of posters used in Australian movie the-

Romance flies on the **Roman Holiday** daybill with the leads just short of kissing while the bored Princess Ann is nestled in the background.

Cowboys rule on **The Man Who Shot Liberty Valance** daybill, featuring the scowling visages of the tough Tom Doniphon and Ransom Stoddard. This painted image has more punch than the photographic one, with room for the credits and inset images from the film.

The daybill for **In the Heat of the Night** manages to capture the titular theme with a moistly red image of the police investigating a body. The tagline boldly proclaims from the top of the piece with credits and title below.

aters. They were folded twice when issued and sold to movie theaters for 5¢ to 10¢.

At this point, daybills measured 13" x 30", similar to U.S. inserts. Like those printed during WWII, three daybills would be printed on one production sheet of paper. They were printed using the hand litho process, which gave them a rich texture and subtle tone that was found only in Australia. Up until the 1970s most daybills were printed as lithographs. In the '60s the posters were printed using American techniques to achieve a glossy finish. These daybills are sought after for their rarity and often unique artwork.

After WWII through the '60s, it was a common practice for daybills released to include a duotone version along with the color one. The duotones are often mistakenly referred to as reissues, despite the fact that they were usually released at the same time as the full color version.

Among the studios that produced daybills during the first half of the century was The Richardson Studio. It was founded by John Richardson in the early 1920s, beginning by producing artwork for silent films. At that time, posters produced by Richardson Studio had a tag at the bottom with "The poster produced by Richardson Studio" or "Drawn by Richardson Studio." Few have John Richardson's signature, making them extremely valuable and desired by collectors.

One of the most popular daybill producers in the '60s was Robert Burton Pty

The Empire Strikes Back daybill is one of the most sought after, depicting all seven leads while Darth Vader's mask dominates the top, the Millennium Falcon soars through the center, and the battle rages below.

The slim design of the daybill presents J and K of **Men in Black** as larger than life figures in a movie about policing extraterrestrials.

Ltd. Both W.E. Smith and The Richardson Studio had stopped making daybills by this point, opening plenty of opportunities for Burton. They used the previously popular hand litho process with old and archaic equipment, producing inconsistent and often basic art. The hand litho process at Burton included hand drawn and hand lettered images with a black litho crayon, placing the image directly on the plate. U.S. poster art or press book images were used for these daybills, drawn in shades of grey. They were printed using three or four colors, each on a separate plate. First,

the poster added the plate with the black and white image then through each color. After the process finished, the machine and plates were cleaned and no original art was saved.

Print runs were usually 3,000 copies in the '70s, bundled in groups of 20-25 daybills. Sizes varied from 13" by 30" to 13" by 26" from the mid-'60s to the 1980s. Currently they measure 26" x 30", are printed on thick glossy paper, and are much more durable than earlier versions. Daybills in general are highly sought after by collectors for their rarity.

SPORTS
WEATHER

METROPOLIS STAR

MONSTERS
HEROES
VILLAINS

SUPERHERO MOVIES SAVE THE DAY!

As of this book's publication, superhero movies are undoubtedly the most popular subgenre in film. A look at local theater listings will undoubtedly offer show times for at least one, and with the slate of films projected for the next five years, that's not likely to change.

Superhero movies are sterling examples of movie escapism. They offer exciting, sometimes intricate plots, ostentatious costumes, increasingly hard-to-believe action sequences, and – usually – good triumphing over evil. Typically with loyal fan bases built in through comics, radio, TV, and novels, superhero movies have a loyal following.

The first superhero movie, *The Mark of Zorro*, was released in 1920. Directed by Fred Niblo, it is based on the story "The Curse of Capistrano" by Johnston McCulley, published in *All-Story Weekly* in 1919. The silent movie stars Douglas Fairbanks as Don Diego Vega, a man who seems like a bumbling fool but is actually the courageous, suave Señor Zorro. The brave vigilante was featured in more Zorro movies, including *Don Q Son of Zorro* in 1925, *The Bold Caballero* in 1936 – which was the first Zorro movie with sound, *Zorro Rides Again* in 1937, *Zorro's Fighting Legion* in 1939, and *The Mark of Zorro* remake in 1940.

On the 1920 **The Mark of Zorro** poster, Zorro stands with his sword held loosely in his hand and a confident smile on his face, leaning causally on a barrel bearing his portrait. In recent years the one-sheet has sold for $17,250, set of eight lobby cards for $2,185, half-sheet for $600-$1,790, and title card for $660.

The Green Hornet was a black and white 13-chapter serial based on the *Green Hornet* radio show that also came out that year. Newspaper publisher Britt Reid takes on the guise of crime fighter Green Hornet, alongside his valet, Kato, to investigate and thwart criminals. While police consider Green Hornet and Kato to be criminals, the pair uncover several crime rackets by the Syndicate.

The 12-chapter *Adventures of Captain Marvel* serial, based on the Fawcett comic, was released the following year. When the Golden Scorpion is unearthed during an archeological expedition in Thailand, the potential for an atom smashing ray comes with it. At the same time, young radio operator Billy Batson encounters the wizard Shazam, who gives him the power to become Captain Marvel. With his newly imbued abilities, Captain Marvel fights to stop the Scorpion before he assembles the ray.

Captain America fought his way into superhero movies in 1944. In the 15-chapter serial, Captain America is District Attorney Grant Gardner, who fights the Scarab, a villain who poisons enemies and steals a device that can destroy buildings using sound vibrations. Captain America was the first Marvel character to appear outside of comics.

The Man of Steel flew to theaters for the first time in 1948's *Superman*. Two previous attempts had been made to bring Superman to the big screen before Columbia made this early superhero film. The 15-chapter black and white serial featured Kirk Alyn as Superman/Clark Kent and Noel Neill as Lois Lane. This first live-action Superman movie chronicled his journey to Earth, growing up as Clark, joining the *Daily Planet*, and fighting the Spider Lady as the superhero he was meant to be. The movie was a huge success, bolstering the careers of both leads. Alyn and Neill returned as Clark and

Gorgeously colorful, **The Green Hornet** poster depicts several images of the masked crimefighter. One close-up offers a detailed look at the mask while the others show him in several action scenes. The one-sheet can sell for $6,900, three-sheet for $4,480, chapter one-sheets for $660-$900, single lobby cards for $25-$770, sets of 8 lobby cards for $570, title card for $200-$385, and pressbook for $310.

Lois in 1950's *Atom Man vs. Superman*. Another black and white 15-chapter serial, Lex Luthor was introduced to the film series. Superman battles Luthor who uses a teleportation device and has taken on the new identity as Atom Man. He creates several weapons to threaten Metropolis with Superman trying to stop him every step of the way.

George Reeves donned the famous "S" on his chest for the first time in *Superman and the Mole-Men*. After under-

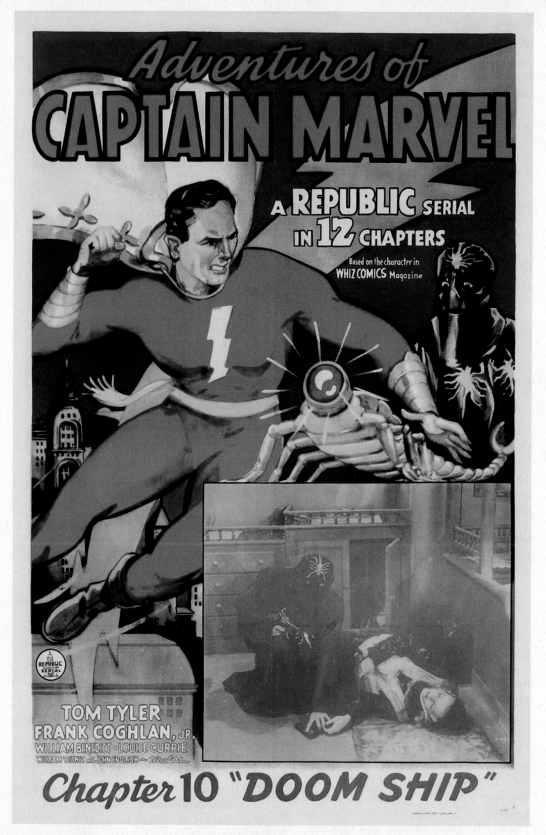

One-sheets produced for the different chapters of **Adventures of Captain Marvel** showcase Captain Marvel's strength and virility as he fights the Scorpion to protect humankind. The cloth banner can sell for $2,200-$6,570, one-sheet for $1,165-$5,750, six-sheet for $4,620, three-sheet for $4,040, and single lobby card for $80-$1,430.

ground dwellers come to the Earth's surface to explore, Superman is the only one who can prevent a tragedy when their appearances causes panic. The 1951 movie was the basis for the *Adventures of Superman* TV series.

Alyn returned to superhero movies in 1952 for *Blackhawk: Fearless Champion of Freedom*. Telling the story of the Blackhawks who flew together during WWII, the seven flyers work together after the war. In the serial, the group fights evil wherever it is, including a spy group bent on destroying democracy.

After nearly a decade without a superhero movie, the Caped Crusader "zonked" his way onto the scene. Based on the TV show, *Batman: The Movie* premiered in 1966, starring Adam West and Burt Ward as the Dynamic Duo. Many other cast members from the show were also in the movie, including Cesar Romero, Burgess Meredith, and Frank Gorshin as the Joker, Penguin, and Riddler, respectively. Lee Meriwether took on the guise of the villainess, temptress Catwoman. Batman and Robin fight the villains who want to hold the world for ransom by using an invention that instantly dehydrates people.

In 1978 *Superman: The Movie* broke new ground for superhero movies. Special effects

On the **Superman** three-sheet, the titular hero is larger than life, fighting the Spider Lady and thwarting crime wherever he finds it. Featuring multiple images, this colorful poster appears like its own comic book. The six-sheet can sell for $8,625-$15,535, three-sheet for $8,960-$18,400, chapter one-sheets for $1,285-$2,870, and lobby card for $95-$345.

The 1966 **Batman** one-sheet features photographic images of Batman, Robin, Catwoman, the Joker, the Riddler, and Penguin, surrounded by animated scenes of defeated henchmen dangling off of several surfaces. The bold credits below announce the cast, most of whom are on the TV show. In recent years the Japanese STB has sold for $1,315-$2,390, lobby card set for $560-$955, 40" x 60" for $750, French grande for $320-$655, one-sheet for $120-$625, three-sheet for $280-$405, and insert for $205-$355.

were finally able to feasibly portray the comic book action on screen, leading to dazzling stunts, including Superman flying, running with super-speed, and the crumbling San Andreas Fault. It followed Clark Kent/Kal-El/Superman from Krypton to Earth, awkward adolescent to reporter with a secret identity fighting the nefarious Lex Luthor. With Christopher Reeve as the super-powered alien and Margot Kidder as Lois Lane, it made over $300 million worldwide and spawned three sequels.

Swamp Thing took audiences to a darker place in 1982, in the horror/sci-fi movie helmed by popular horror director Wes

Craven. A research scientist is turned into a monster made from swamp plants after a violent incident with a special chemical. The "beauty and the beast" story takes on classic monster movie elements by posing the monster as the misunderstood hero and the regular people as the villains.

In 1984 the first major superheroine movie was released. *Supergirl*, a spinoff of 1978's *Superman*, told the story of Superman's cousin Kara Zor-El, initially living in a Kryptonian city. Helen Slater starred as Kara, who travels to Earth in hopes of retrieving a powerful orb from her home planet. While discovering her

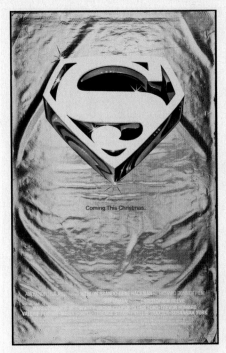

The 1978 **Superman** one-sheet shows an image of clouds, dark on the edges, yet brighter in the center where a red, yellow, and blue blur flies across the sky. The six-sheet can sell for $135-$700, three-sheet for $40-$580, mylar symbol advance for $45-$510, mylar title advance for $50-$475, set of lobby cards for $30-$420, insert for $35-$225, and one-sheet for $10-$145.

powers and trying to fit in as an average person, she fights a power hungry witch to regain the orb.

Two years later Marvel's *Howard the Duck* made a splash. Howard, the sarcastic, talking duck must stop an alien invader. Starring Lea Thompson, with Ed Gale as the body and Chip Zien as the voice of Howard, the notoriously bad movie has become a cult classic.

Batman's next incarnation came in 1989. Tim Burton directed *Batman* with a mix of superhero action and his signature panache and moody style. He created controversy by casting comedic actor Michael Keaton as Bruce Wayne/Batman and the intense Jack Nicholson as the frightening Joker. The gamble paid off and audiences drove the movie to over $400 million at the box office. *Batman Returns* in '91 continued the wonderful chemistry of Burton and Keaton, adding in the delightful

Michelle Pfeiffer as Selina Kyle/Catwoman and Danny DeVito as Oswald Cobblepot/Penguin.

Next up, the *Teenage Mutant Ninja Turtles* made their radical debut in theaters. Comics and cartoon characters, the Ninja Turtles try to help the citizens of New York City, keep themselves hidden from the public eye, and eat as much pizza as possible. A crime wave leads them to the Foot Clan and Shredder, who has ties to their leader, Splinter. At this point, the 1990 movie was the third highest grossing superhero movie of all time, behind *Superman* in '78 and *Batman* in '89.

Batman: Mask of Phantasm, the animated movie based on *Batman: The Animated Series*, was released in 1993. The stylish movie told an expanded story similar to the show, but reaching beyond the usual fight between Batman and the Joker to include the mysterious figure, the

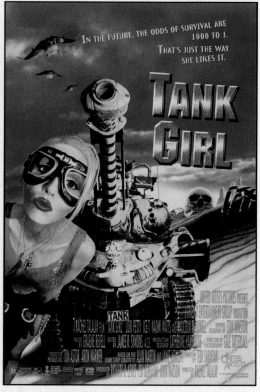

The 1990 **Teenage Mutant Ninja Turtles** one-sheet is a look at New York skyscrapers from the ground up. The Ninja Turtles are peaking from the sewer with just a portion of their faces shown, displaying their trademark masks. The one-sheet usually sells for $10-$90.

Comically skewed, the brightly colored **Tank Girl** one-sheet displays a close-up of Tank Girl in neon tanktop and goggles with her trusty tank behind her. A skeleton climbs the sand in the background under an ocean-blue sky. A set of lobby cards can sell for $15-$60, teaser for $10-$40, and one-sheet for $10-$25.

Phantasm. It is often considered the best animated Batman movie.

The year 1994 saw the release of several superhero movies, both silly and serious. Using fantasy style, *The Crow* told a revenge story of a musician who is killed, but is able to come back from the dead to avenge his murdered fiancée. Tragically, part of why it's remembered is because the lead actor, Brandon Lee, was killed by a defective blank that was fired while filming.

On the lighter side, *The Mask* made Jim Carrey into a superhero. This vibrantly colorful comedy is about a modest banker who becomes a superhero after finding a mysterious mask that gives him magical powers. Not only did this silly superhero flick feature a zoot-suited Carrey, it was also Cameron Diaz's first movie.

In *Blankman*, Damon Wayans and David Alan Grier starred as average (or

under-average) guys trying to fight crime. A simple minded inventor, Blankman – a comic book fan – tries to create a bullet-proof costume to fight crime.

Another wacky superhero movie from this time period was *Tank Girl*, in 1995. In a post-apocalyptic British world, the antihero Tank Girl and her cohorts fight a giant corporation in water starved Australia.

Judge Dredd also came out that year. In a dystopian future, Judge Dredd is a police officer with the powers of a judge who is convicted for a crime that he didn't commit. Sylvester Stallone starred as the wrongly-accused Dredd with Diane Lane playing Judge Hershey.

In 1998, *Blade* became the first film licensed by Marvel Studios. Different than most superhero movies, it's more of a horror flick than a comic book movie, with

The Incredibles one-sheet represents everything the movie is: brightly colorful, chaotic story, and hilarious action. Mr. Incredible stands proudly in the center while his family and Frozone battle Syndrome and his giant robot. Beneath the explosions and mayhem, the Parr family enjoy moments of domestic bliss. The one-sheet can sell for $25-$130.

Blade as a half-mortal, half-vampire bent on slaying as many vampires as possible. Wesley Snipes is stylish and intimidating as the sword-wielding hero.

X-Men tells the story of an evolving world with some people exhibiting superhuman powers, labeling them as mutants. The 2000 movie combined Bryan Singer, a director known for dramas, and serious actors like Patrick Stewart and Ian McKellen. It also introduced Hugh Jackman to U.S. audiences. This precursor to Marvel's team-based superhero films has plenty of mutants on the side of good and bad with layers of moral ambiguity.

Unbreakable, an early hit for M. Night Shyamalan in 2000, is an intellectual superhero movie. Samuel L. Jackson plays Elijah Price: a frail, easily injured man who believes his antithesis – a nearly indestructible man – must exist. He finds him in David Dunn, played by Bruce Willis. The movie is clever and filled with the type of plot twists that established Shyamalan's reputation.

Spider-Man first spun his web on film in 2002. Impressive special effects sent Spider-Man soaring through New York City to battle the Green Goblin, navigate the changes in his physical make-up, and swoon over M.J. The post-9/11 movie had audiences rooting passionately for the Web-slinger to protect the wounded city. It was the first movie that made $100 million in its opening weekend.

The Powerpuff Girls Movie also hit theaters that year. A prequel to the TV show, it tells the origin story of the Powerpuff Girls and how they became the protectors of Townsville. The fun, high energy movie was an entertaining adventure for the tiny heroines.

The supernatural superhero movie *Hellboy* was released in 2004. A demonic beast works to keep the world safe from paranormal activities as part of the Bureau of Paranormal Research and Defense, commonly known as the BPRD. It featured the artistic direction of Guillermo del Toro, the likeable brute aspects of Ron Perlman, and the physicality of nonhuman character actor Doug Jones.

Pixar jumped into the superhero sub-genre with the animated adventure *The Incredibles*. The 2004 hit followed a super-powered family trying to live normal lives in suburbia. Heartfelt and funny, yet also exciting, it fit into much of what makes a great superhero movie: cool powers, rising above the odds, a flashy villain, and plenty of action.

A year later, *Batman Begins* began a new superhero movie trend. Christopher Nolan, the director of the enigmatic *Memento*, achieved popularity and respect from a new movie fandom. His Gotham was darker and dirtier than Batman's last outing, in the neon-soaked *Batman & Robin*. Christian Bale gave Batman a growl and audiences a new appreciation for what Bruce Wayne endured to become the Batman.

Another intellectually stimulating super-hero movie arrived with *V for Vendetta*. Released in 2006, it's set in a future Britain. Oppressed by tyranny, a masked freedom fighter known as V plans to overthrow the establishment. A young woman joins him in the fight after he teaches her to see things his way. The script, based on the comic by Alan Moore, was adapted by Andy and Lana Wachowski of *The Matrix* fame.

The Marvel Cinematic Universe began with *Iron Man* in 2008. Robert Downey, Jr., a man with his own complicated public persona, starred as Tony Stark, the egotis-tical playboy inventor who would become a superhero. Adding Gwyneth Paltrow as the meticulous Pepper Potts, who puts up with Tony's shenanigans, to Downey's ability to play a loveable jerk, his bicker-ing with J.A.R.V.I.S. and a robot arm gave the movie a comical tone.

The second contemporary Marvel install-ment, *The Incredible Hulk*, was released a month later. Led by Edward Norton, Liv Tyler, Tim Roth, and William Hurt, *The Incredible Hulk* skipped the origin story. Bruce Banner is trying to find a cure to end his alter ego and become a normal man, but he must be the Hulk to battle a soldier who has become an abomination.

Just a few weeks later, *The Dark Knight* came to theaters. Nolan's second

Batman movie is considered by many to be his best. The story is better than the first, plus audiences get to see two legend-ary villains, high-tech gadgets straight out of a Bond movie, and a more introspective Bruce Wayne. The clear reason this movie made over $1 billion at the box office – the first superhero movie to do so – was Heath Ledger. Some audiences went out of morbid curiosity to see the actor who had died months before the movie's release. Others went because Ledger embodied the Joker as a brilliant lunatic that had people mesmerized from the voiceover in the first teaser, to the maniacal laughter as he swung upside down from a tower at the end of the movie.

"Who watches the Watchmen?" The question was asked in 2009's *Watchmen*. Based on one of the best graphic novels of all time, written by Moore, it was directed by Zack Snyder. He used panels from the comic to establish shots in the movie, deftly providing connective tissue to the source material. The intellectual superhero movie takes a different look at the masked lot as well as their perspective on the peo-ple they protect.

Things were much less serious a year later in *Kick-Ass*. Part comedy, part action movie, *Kick-Ass* explored what would happen if regular people, who don't have billions of dollars, become superheroes. More bloody than the usual superhero movie, it also features a foul-mouthed little girl beating up men three times her size and making it look like it's just another day on the playground.

The god of thunder joined the new world of Marvel with *Thor* in 2011. To make a god accessible to audiences, he is stripped of his power, cast out of his beau-tiful home, and dropped onto Earth where he must earn respect without his trusty hammer and impressive battle garb. Chris Hemsworth's massive size, the regal way he carries himself, and his confident demeanor combined to make him the perfect Thor. As his brother Loki, Tom Hiddleston took a role that could have been a petulant whiner and turned him into a delightfully devilish villain audiences loved in this, its sequel, and in *The Avengers*.

X-Men: First Class provided a fresh start for the mutants in 2011. After a

Many posters were printed for **The Dark Knight**, mostly teasers, and the Joker ruled popularity both with theaters and with collectors. The most popular teaser, style A, shows a blurry, translucent image of the Joker who looks like he is writing "Why so serious?" on the poster, followed by a grotesque smile. The international style E one-sheet is a gray, black, and blue look at Batman standing before a crumbling building with the Bat symbol lighting up the skyscraper in fiery orange. In recent years the Japanese B1 has sold for $20-$700, teaser style A/"Why so serious?" style for $60-$540, advance style H/Batman playing cards for $30-$270, style E one-sheet for $30-$125, and advance style B/graffiti for $35-$120.

The **Captain America: The First Avenger** shield style one-sheet features a profile shot of sweaty, dirty Captain America, jaw set in a battle ready stance, with his shield dominating the bottom half of the poster. The cast style one-sheet shows Captain America standing proudly front and center, surrounded by Peggy Carter, Bucky Barnes, and the rest of the cast, and Red Skull looming in the background. In recent years the special "War Bonds" poster has sold for $85-$315, shield style one-sheet for $20-$50, and cast style one-sheet for $25-$35.

messy, disappointing *X-Men: The Last Stand*, which saw several popular characters get killed, 20th Century Fox went back to the drawing board. Set in the '60s, young versions of Charles Xavier/Professor X, Eric Lensherr/Magneto, Raven/Mystique, and others begin what will become lifelong battles. After seeing the power they would yield in the future, this more basic look at the heroes and villains depicts their growth and struggle with a great story.

The star spangled man with a plan reentered superhero movies with *Captain America: The First Avenger* later that year. True blue patriotic Steve Rogers wants to join the fight in World War II, but his scrawny build keeps him from suiting up. He is recruited for a program that turns him into a super soldier to face Nazis and Hydra. As Cap, Chris Evans dropped the swagger he displayed in many of his movies to play an honorable, humble soldier.

In 2012 *The Avengers* became, and remains, the highest grossing superhero movie of all time with $1.5 billion world-wide. Directed by geek god Joss Whedon, it is filled with his brand of pop culture references as everyday speak. The building blocks of Marvel movies that began in 2008 with *Iron Man* and *The Incredible Hulk*, followed by *Thor* and *Captain America: The First Avenger* came to fruition. Six heroes, all of whom had been featured onscreen in some capacity, joined together, battled each other, and fought an alien race led by Thor's brother Loki.

After the Avengers saved New York, it was time for *The Amazing Spider-Man*. Another superhero rebooted after a disappointing predecessor, this origin story saw Peter Parker/Spider-Man back to being a skinny teenager, this time fighting science experiment gone wrong, the Lizard. The off-screen relationship between leads Andrew Garfield and Emma Stone, who portrays Gwen Stacy sustained the romantic subplot.

Superman reemerged for the second time in the 2000s in *Man of Steel*. Henry Cavill stepped in as Clark Kent/Kal-El in the 2013 movie, which felt heavier and more serious, akin to a Batman movie. One aspect in this movie not usually seen in superhero flicks, is the obvious carnage that occurs during fighting between Superman and General Zod. This laid the groundwork for the upcoming *Batman v Superman: Dawn of Justice.*

The **Guardians of the Galaxy** poster is busy, utter chaos with the five leads in the middle of a fight shooting space age weaponry and slicing with daggers. The background is, naturally, set in space with various craft flying at them. The teaser takes the opposite approach with the quintet casually posing with assorted weaponry with a much calmer looking sky behind them. The bus stop can sell for $210, IMAX 13" x 19" for $80, one-sheet for $70, and teaser for $20-$70.

Many bets were made on the success or failure of 2014's *Guardians of the Galaxy*. If *The Avengers* are world-saving larger-than-life heroes, than *Guardians of the Galaxy* are their hard partying, boisterous cousins who still managed to save the day by improvisation and sheer gumption. Bolstered by a great vintage soundtrack and gorgeous special effects, it made audiences love a roguish space pirate, vindictive daughter, metaphor incompetent tough guy, feisty gun-toting raccoon creature, and a goofy tree-being.

In 2015 the Avengers returned for *Avengers: Age of Ultron*. Fans excitedly supported the sequel with a frightening robotic villain, and new Avengers in the ever expanding world of Marvel movies. Hawkeye, who so far had seen the least amount of screen time, was given an emotionally anchoring subplot.

Released during the summer of 2015, *Ant-Man*, stars guy next door actor Paul Rudd who becomes a superhero in a suit that shrinks him to the size of ants. Like *Iron Man* and *Guardians of the Galaxy*, this Marvel superhero movie blends comedy and action with exciting stunts and plenty of comic relief, though it focused the action in a way that made it more of a heist film than a typical hero flick.

In modern filmmaking, superhero movies are the closest studios come to a sure thing. There are still some that fail, or at the very least only break even budget-wise, but the gamble is still worth it, given the enormous amounts of money some make. Even when one of the films in this genre is a box office dud, superhero movies show no signs of slowing down.

Deadpool, Batman v Superman: Dawn of Justice, Captain America: Civil War, X-Men: Apocalypse, Teenage Mutant Ninja Turtles: Half Shell, Suicide Squad, Gambit, and *Doctor Strange* are all set for 2016. Plans for 2017 to 2020 include sequels for Wolverine, Guardians of the Galaxy, the Fantastic Four, Spider-Man, Thor, and the Avengers. New stories include the Power Rangers, Wonder Woman, the Justice League, the Flash, Black Panther, Aquaman, Captain Marvel, Shazam, Inhumans, Cyborg, and the Green Lantern Corps.

Live-action or animated, dramatic or comedic, superhero movies represent nearly 100 years of cinematic adventures. We are enchanted by their powers, enamored with their courage, and excited by their successes. Superhero movies have saved many audiences from an otherwise boring day.

Terminator 2: Judgment Day
signed by Linda Hamilton and
Robert Patrick.

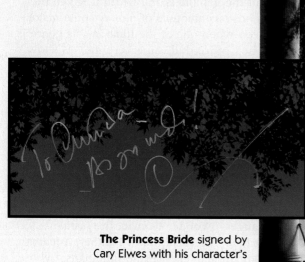

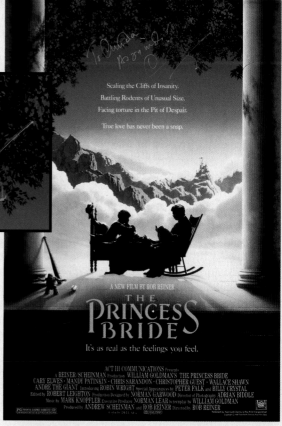

The Princess Bride signed by
Cary Elwes with his character's
trademark quote, "As you wish."

COLLECTING
Autographed
MOVIE POSTERS

In most cases, movie poster collectors are movie fans, and many of them consider owning posters as a means of extending their connection with the films they love. Taking it a step further, collecting *autographed* movie posters can amplify that enjoyment, and in some cases enhance it further by meeting film stars, directors, and writers.

Collecting autographed posters is a facet of the hobby that leads to an assortment of opinions. Some believe that autographs deface a poster, therefore making it less valuable, while others see autographs as cachet, improving the stature of a poster.

The value of posters are bolstered by autographs when they are signed by a celebrity or artist who is particularly noteworthy or by several members of a cast. Because increased value is no guarantee, those who collect autographed posters may appreciate owning a piece that was touched by their favorite celebrity or they may enjoy it for the experience of attending events where they meet the person who is signing.

The Fan Experience

I've been a movie lover my entire life. Not in the way that everyone enjoys movies, but as a fan who will research the movie to learn about the director's vision, how the actors achieved certain emotional responses, how special effects were accomplished, which lines were ad-libbed, who wrote it and what else has he or she written.

As a movie buff, my movie poster collection is focused on my favorite movies, rather than ones with the best artwork or those with high resale value. I collect them because I love film and for years now I've been collecting with the goal of having them autographed.

Pop culture, comics, and horror conventions are great places to get posters signed. These days most conventions host dozens of celebrity guests from TV, film, comics, and videogames. I have a list of cons that I enjoy going to, so I will routinely check their guest lists for months in advance. This gives me time to find a new poster to have signed by a guest I want to meet if I don't already have it.

Meeting a celebrity that was in a movie I enjoy enhances the experience of watching that movie. They'll answer questions about the project and tell you fun behind the scenes tidbits. They'll share how they were motivated for certain scenes and tell stories about costars.

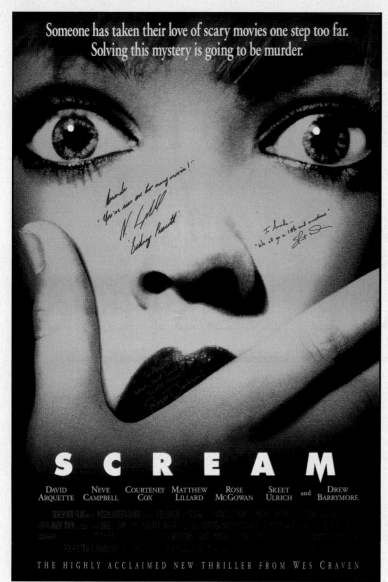

Someone has taken their love of scary movies one step too far.
Solving this mystery is going to be murder.

S C R E A M

DAVID
ARQUETTE
NEVE
CAMPBELL
COURTENEY
COX
MATTHEW
LILLARD
ROSE
McGOWAN
SKEET
ULRICH
and
DREW
BARRYMORE

THE HIGHLY ACCLAIMED NEW THRILLER FROM WES CRAVEN

Scream poster signed by Neve Campbell, Skeet Ulrich, and Roger Jackson.

him sign that poster. This experience was markedly different, with him gently ribbing me. When I said that it was a great movie he sternly looked up and said, "It's the best movie." When I stammered and nodded, he smirked jovially.

At a few events I got to meet three stars of *The Boondock Saints*, a cult hit from 1999. In the movie Sean Patrick Flanery, Norman Reedus, and David Della Rocco play gruff, foul-mouthed Bostonians who drink a lot of beer, smoke plenty of cigarettes, and kill mobsters. When I met the trio they were as charmingly rough around the edges as their characters. It was delightfully amusing. This experience is also fun because I have bragging rights for meeting Reedus before Daryl Dixon-*The Walking Dead* fever swept the nation.

When I met Cary Elwes, I asked if he'd write "As you wish" on my *The Princess Bride* poster, to which he replied, "Absolutely not," while he'd already started writing it. We talked about the sword fight scene between him and Mandy Patinkin (as Inigo Montoya) and about filming with a broken toe. When I told him that I enjoyed his performance in *Saw*, a look of sur-

I gravitate toward movies with strong female leads, who take charge, protect others, and set aside the damsel in distress stereotype that many women are still cast in. To that end, one of my favorite movies is *Terminator 2: Judgment Day*, starring Linda Hamilton as the indomitable Sarah Connor. When I met her and asked her to sign my T2 poster, I thanked her for the resilience she displayed in that movie and told her that I found it inspiring. Her response was so sweet and gracious. I saw her the next morning before the convention opened and she hugged me, kissed me on the cheek, remembered my name and held a conversation with me before heading inside for the day. A few months later I was fortunate enough to meet Robert Patrick and have

Halloween poster signed by writer-director John Carpenter with Michael Myers actors Dick Warlock, George P. Wilbur, Don Shanks, Chris Durand, Brad Loree, and Tyler Mane.

prise crossed his face and then he very graciously said "Thank you." Considering I've watched him in *The Princess Bride* since I was a small child, this moment truly stands out as a favorite moment of my convention experiences.

Meeting cast members of *Scream* was another immense highlight. Neve Campbell was friendly and talkative, Skeet Ulrich was relaxed and affable, and Roger Jackson (who voiced Ghostface) used that famous voice to simultaneously make me smile and run a chill down my spine. Each in turn wrote a quote from the movie to accompany their signatures.

Our *Halloween* poster is the best piece in our autographed poster collection. It has been signed by John Carpenter (director, co-writer), and six men who have played Michael Myers: Dick Warlock (*Halloween II*), George P. Wilbur (*Halloween 4: The Return of Michael Myers, Halloween: The Curse of Michael Myers*), Don Shanks (*Halloween 5: The Revenge of Michael Myers*), Chris Durand (*Halloween H20*), Brad Loree (*Halloween: Resurrection*), and Tyler Mane (Rob Zombie's *Halloween, Halloween II*). They may be names that many are unfamiliar with, but collectively these men have done stunts in many of Hollywood's biggest movies from *The Green*

Berets to *Die Hard* to *X-Men* to *Captain America: The Winter Soldier* and hundreds more. Plus, horror actors get into meeting fans. I can say I've been chocked (for photos) by Michael Myers and Jason Voorhees and growled at by Freddy Krueger, yet lived to tell the tale!

These experiences make the posters so much more valuable to me. Not only am I looking at artwork for my favorite movies, but I'm remembering meeting the people who signed them and what our conversations entailed. And that's pretty great.

Collecting Pre-Autographed Posters

When collecting posters, lobby cards, and stills that are already autographed, verifying authenticity is the most important part of the process. The most important part. Unfortunately, anyone can start a website

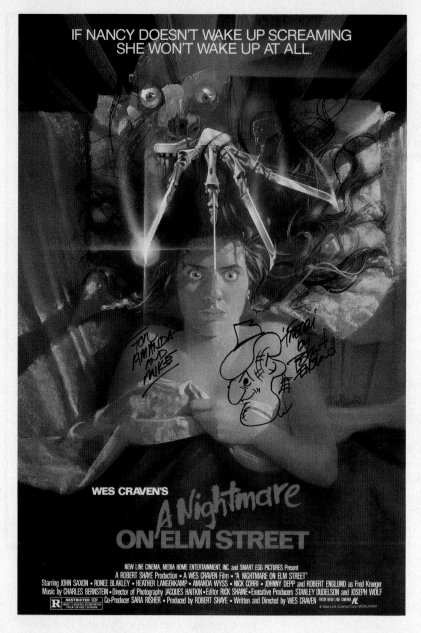

IF NANCY DOESN'T WAKE UP SCREAMING
SHE WON'T WAKE UP AT ALL.

WES CRAVEN'S

A Nightmare
ON ELM STREET

NEW LINE CINEMA, MEDIA HOME ENTERTAINMENT, INC. and SMART EGG PICTURES Present
A ROBERT SHAYE Production • A WES CRAVEN Film • "A NIGHTMARE ON ELM STREET"
Starring JOHN SAXON • RONEE BLAKLEY • HEATHER LANGENKAMP • AMANDA WYSS • NICK CORRI • Johnny Depp and ROBERT ENGLUND as Fred Krueger
Music by CHARLES BERNSTEIN • Director of Photography JACQUES HAITKIN • Editor RICK SHAINE • Executive Producers STANLEY DUDELSON and JOSEPH WOLF
Co-Producer SARA RISHER • Produced by ROBERT SHAYE • Written and Directed by WES CRAVEN FROM NEW LINE CINEMA
© New Line Cinema Corp. MCMLXXXIV

Robert Englund kept slipping into Freddy voice when he signed our **A Nightmare on Elm** Street poster. He also drew a sketch of Freddy beside his signature.

Hake's Americana & Collectibles said. "Any signed item we offer must come with the proper paperwork from a third party so the bidder can bid with piece of mind. That keeps our opinion as an auction house out of it and avoids conflict of interest."

Organizations such as Professional Sports Authenticator (PSA/DNA) and James Spence Authentication (JSA) are dedicated to authenticating autographs by studying and compiling examples. Once verified, these agencies will give the autographed item a letter or certificate of authenticity – commonly called a LOA or COA.

"All that matters on autographs is provenance," Bruce Hershenson, founder of eMoviePoster said. "Is there a direct connection to the person who signed it, and if so, how is it proven?" He went on to point out that there are unscrupulous people who will offer authentication without being part of a trustworthy organization.

Another helpful tool when it

or join sales platforms, like eBay, and claim that their autographs are authentic. Doing just a brief search, I found what look like fake versions of signatures I have, but also some that could be real. Buying from a website or seller that is unfamiliar is a gamble.

For peace of mind, only buy autographed posters from reputable dealers and auction houses. Places like Hake's Americana & Collectibles, eMoviePoster, Heritage Auctions, and CineMasterpieces are safe for purchasing autographed posters because they have items authenticated and verify provenance.

"We send to a reputable third party authenticator," Alex Winter, president of

THE STAR WARS SAGA CONTINUES

STAR WARS THE EMPIRE STRIKES BACK

MARK HAMILL · HARRISON FORD · CARRIE FISHER
BILLY DEE WILLIAMS · ANTHONY DANIELS
as C-3PO
Co-starring DAVID PROWSE · KENNY BAKER · PETER MAYHEW · FRANK OZ
as Darth Vader   as R2-D2   as Chewbacca   as Yoda
Directed by IRVIN KERSHNER   Produced by GARY KURTZ
Screenplay by LEIGH BRACKETT and LAWRENCE KASDAN   Story by GEORGE LUCAS
Executive Producer GEORGE LUCAS   Music by JOHN WILLIAMS
PG PARENTAL GUIDANCE SUGGESTED   DOLBY STEREO   ORIGINAL SOUNDTRACK ON RSO RECORDS
SOME MATERIAL MAY NOT BE SUITABLE FOR CHILDREN
A Lucasfilm Ltd. Production — A Twentieth-Century Fox Release

The Empire Strikes Back "Gone with the Wind" style is a beautiful poster, but does not autograph well. In certain lighting it's hard to distinguish where Peter Mayhew's signature is located. By the credits, Billy Dee Williams' signature is more noticeable, but can still get lost in the art.

comes to collecting pre-signed autographed posters are poster forums. These online message boards, like All Poster Forum and The Vintage Movie Posters Forum are filled with collectors and dealers willing and ready to share their knowledge and experiences. If an autographed item hasn't been verified by an authentication agency, forum members can assist by offering guidance and sometimes examples of the autograph in question for comparison. No, it is not a foolproof method, but it can be very helpful.

Having Your Posters Autographed

One of the easiest ways for collectors who want the fan experience of meeting the people signing their posters is to go to con-

ventions. Though dominated by certain types of guests – comics, anime, horror, nostalgia – celebrities from any genre can show up at local cons.

There are a few things to consider before heading out to the con with your poster. First, study the artwork. Is it the kind of poster that will make a signature pop or might the signature get lost in the art? Take a look at *The Empire Strikes Back* one-sheet accompanying this article. The "Gone with the Wind" style poster has gorgeous art by Roger Kastel, but the signatures get lost in the shades of color. Specifically Peter Mayhew's signature beside the figure of Chewbacca is hard to see, particularly in certain light. After spending the money on the poster and the signature, this can be very disappointing, so make sure the poster will sign well.

Next, consider carrying a pen. If the poster will be signed by multiple people, this can build uniformity on the poster. This is also helpful depending on the colors of the poster and how certain pen ink will appear once signed.

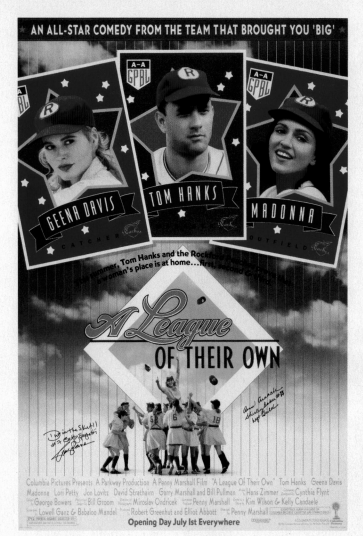

A League of Their Own poster signed by Ann Cusack and Tracy Reiner. The actresses provided personal flair by adding their character names, their jersey numbers, and their positions on the field.

Collectors who are thinking about resale value in the future shouldn't have the autographs personalized. People will still buy these posters, depending on the rarity of the signature, but they are much more likely to sell if not personalized.

Some celebrities, however, will not sign without personalizing for this very reason. Particularly if one person has a stack of posters to be signed without personalizing. It's fairly easy to find out which celebrities won't sign without personalizing by searching their names with convention appearances, checking forums, convention message boards, and social media pages.

Once the poster is signed, have it authenticated as soon as possible, if resale is a factor.

Most convention pages also list what celebrities charge for autographs. It's important to know how much they will charge to ensure that enough money has been set aside for these signatures. If the convention doesn't have that information listed, it can usually be found by web searches of the celebrity and convention appearances.

Do not roll or fold the poster immediately after it has been signed. Give it a minute to dry, especially if the person signed with a paint pen. Examine the autograph area to make sure the person didn't accidentally leave any smudges from food or beverage debris. Unfortunately, this does happen. If something was transferred onto the poster use a paper towel to clean the soiled area and do not roll or fold if it is wet. If the stain persists, the ink in that area may need restored.

With the amount of money tied to collecting autographed posters, keep it protected during the event. Carry rolled posters in an acid-free plastic sleeve, then inside either a 3-ply thick cardboard or hard plastic tube. If using cardboard, do not use the kind with a snap seal because it can damage the ends of the poster. Use one with cap that can easily be removed and replaced. The cardboard tubes are thinner and less cumbersome, however, plastic tubes generally come with a strap that can be worn, leaving hands free.

For folded posters, carry them in an acid-free Mylar sleeve then in some kind of binder or book that will protect them from damage during the rest of the con.

Blade Runner signed by Harrison Ford, Rutger Hauer, Ridley Scott, Syd Mead, Sean Young, Edward James Olmos, Daryl Hannah, Joe Turkel, Joanna Cassidy, and James Hong.

COLLECTING BLADE RUNNER AUTOGRAPHS
By Michael Solof

I bought my *Blade Runner* poster from a reputable auction house with verified signatures by Harrison Ford and Rutger Hauer.

I then took this to the San Diego Comic Con in 2007 when the 25th anniversary of the movie was being held and got the signatures of Ridley Scott, Syd Mead (conceptual artist), Sean Young, Edward James Olmos, Daryl Hannah, Joe Turkel, Joanna Cassidy, and James Hong.

It was my first time dealing with getting anything signed and the cast were all lined up behind about ten, 8-foot long tables in the signing area. I walked up to James Hong, spoke with him for a few moments and unfolded the poster for him to sign, which he happily did. Then he said the words I didn't quite expect: "That'll be $60.00." Gulp!

Luckily I tend to travel with a chunk of cash to cover any large impulse purchases – but this was unexpected. That continued as each cast member said words to the effect of "That'll be $60" on down the line. When I got down to Ridley Scott, I was down to my last $20. He was nice enough to take pity on my predicament and sign my poster for that amount. Whew!

Since that time I have gotten in touch with William Sanderson, who was very nice to correspond with, and who has offered to also sign the poster. But, I'd have to send it to where he lives across the country. I haven't built up the courage yet to do that. Someday.

It was recently appraised at, well, let's just say a nice chunk of change. I don't plan to sell it though, since it's my favorite movie. But you can bet that when I do, I'll be saying to the buyer, "That'll be a heck of a lot more than $60 bucks!"

FLOURISH AND COLOR:

THE ART OF BOB PEAK

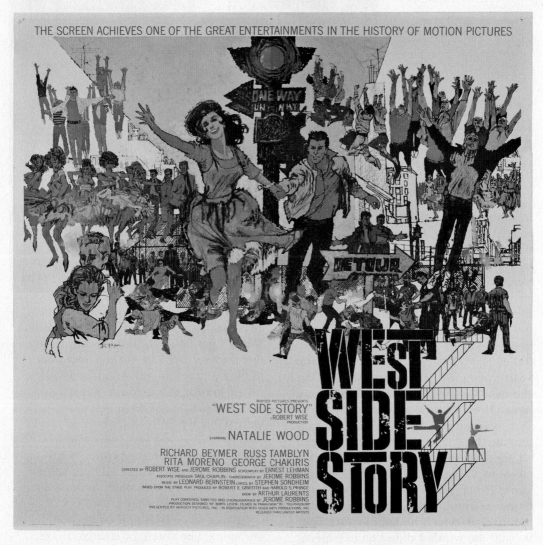

The colorful **West Side Story** poster shows Maria and Tony in the center, splitting images of their families and friends in high energy poses. The British quad used the same art, but boiled down the colors to yellow and red with green and blue on the main image. In recent years the six-sheet has sold for $2,600 and the British quad for $540.

The **My Fair Lady** poster is primarily pink, featuring several images of Eliza and Professor Higgins, around a portrait of the pair. The one-sheet can sell for $50-$1,010, six-sheet for $180-$750, three-sheet for $130-$660, and half-sheet for $310.

about the impact of layout, illustration, and lettering, while working in all three departments. Before finishing college he served a stint in the military during the Korean War. When he returned to the U.S. he transferred to the prestigious Art Center College of Design in Los Angeles and graduated in 1951 with honors.

Peak moved to New York in 1953 to work for The Alexander E. Chaite Studios, one of the few illustration groups that worked for the publishing industry. Concerned that his art was derivative of his artistic influences, he reinvented his style, using more expressiveness and saturated color. While some discouraged the new style, it earned him a meeting with Old Hickory Bourbon Liquor. He got an ad campaign for Old Hickory in '55, to the surprise of more established artists. Peak also got a personal art agent and after that job offers came fast.

Peak's work appeared in national magazines and high profile advertising. He worked on ads for Pepsi, Chrysler, and Trans World Airlines, and magazines like *Cosmopolitan*, *Redbook*, *Ladies' Home Journal*, and *Esquire*. His art appeared in many industries, including fashion, automotive design, travel, sports, music, and fine art. His talent for creating trends, innovative use of color, and flamboyant style led to movie posters.

The first movie poster assignment Peak landed was for *West Side Story* in 1960, which also employed artist Saul Bass. Peak's poster sets Maria and Tony in the center, running toward their hopeful future, though an ominous traffic light divides the pair with a warning One Way sign. Their family and friends are split on

Bob Peak's movie posters are fine art representations of films. The imaginative, prolific artist has the skill to create diverse, intricate pieces that embody the tone and style of each movie. His posters feature complicated illustrations in montage format. It's no mystery why he has been dubbed the father of the modern movie poster.

From a young age Peak knew he wanted to be an artist. He was born in Denver, Colorado in 1927, then grew up in Kansas. His mother worked for the greeting card giant, Hallmark, utilizing her calligraphy skills, which undoubtedly influenced Peak. When he was 7 years old, Peak was given brushes and paint in a beginner's art supplies set and within two years he was drawing impressive portraits for such a young artist.

After graduating high school he studied at Wichita State University, majoring in geology with a minor in art. During college he worked part-time in the in-house art department of printing company, McCormick-Armstrong. There he learned

The poster for **Camelot** depicts profiles and dancing images of
King Arthur and Guenevere as the focal point of the poster with
scenes from the movie painted around them. Recently the 40" x 60"
sold for $130-$300, three-sheet for $65-$215, six-sheet for $35-
$130, one-sheet for $40-$65, and French one-panel for $20-60.

The **Apocalypse Now** poster depicts close-ups of warrior-like Kurtz and Willard, both looking battle weary. It is mostly red and black, reflecting the bleakness of war. The six-sheet can sell for $210-$450, advance one-sheet for $25-$410, three-sheet for $80-$335, insert for $20-$245, and one-sheet for $20-$230.

each side, caught in fights and theatrical dance numbers. The characters are drawn in solid colors, mostly in warm tones of yellow, orange, and pink.

In 1964 he was commissioned to create the poster for *My Fair Lady*. Embodying the style of this musical, the poster is a delightfully pink collage with a white portrait of Eliza Doolittle and Professor Henry Higgins dominating the center. Other images feature many dancing couples, extravagant ballrooms, crowded streets, and snippets of their lessons together. It's gorgeously glamorous, and elegantly feminine, counteracting the misogyny displayed by Higgins throughout the movie.

A few years later in 1967, Peak drew the poster for the fantasy-period piece, *Camelot*. It is focused on two images of Arthur and Guenevere: a joyful look at the couple dancing and profiles of their faces. Guenevere's hair and dress flow in tendrils around the poster, symbolizing the way she enchants Arthur. Surrounding the couple are images from the movie, chronicling their adventures in beautiful renaissance style.

In 1979 Peak created what is largely

considered his greatest movie poster. On the *Apocalypse Now* poster, the wet, ghoulish face of Colonel Kurtz is the central image in front of a blazing sun. A line of helicopters crosses the top of the poster, segmenting Kurtz's head with the battle-worn face of Captain Willard, and streams of light trail off the bridge below them. The whole poster is blanketed in red, reflecting the heat and grit of war.

Peak created another gorgeous poster that year for *Star Trek: The Motion Picture*. Close-ups of series leads Captain Kirk and Mr. Spock with Ilia appear in a rainbow that streaks up the middle of the poster, like beams of energy and light from their transporter. Naturally, this is set over the black sky of space, blanketed by stars. The Enterprise soars across the bottom of the poster leaving a blue light trail just above the title which glows with multi-colored energy.

In 1981 he went back to creating a period inspired poster for *Excalibur*. Battle and romance combine in a collage that brings together swords and sorcery, romance and violence. Excalibur is in the center, glistening silver and glowing with energy and at the top Merlin peaks out from behind a waves of green as swordsmen fight below.

Peak provided art for several *Star Trek* posters and in 1984 he produced some of his best work for *Star Trek III: The Search for Spock*. A large portrait of Spock's impassive face dominates the center of the poster. Beams of light emanate from him –

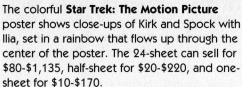

The colorful **Star Trek: The Motion Picture** poster shows close-ups of Kirk and Spock with Ilia, set in a rainbow that flows up through the center of the poster. The 24-sheet can sell for $80-$1,135, half-sheet for $20-$220, and one-sheet for $10-$170.

On the **Star Trek III: The Search for Spock** poster Mr. Spock's face is painted larger in shades of red and blue with light streaming from him. Captain Kirk and his crew are painted in smaller stature at the bottom with the Enterprise battling at the top. The one-sheet can sell for $15-$130, Australian daybill for $20-$90, British quad for $10-$50, and German A1 for $25-$40.

half blue, cold like his logical Vulcan side and half red, emotional like his human side. The Enterprise does battle at the top of the poster with a determined Captain Kirk and his team at the bottom in search of Spock.

His other poster work can be seen on *Birdman of Alcatraz, The Manchurian Candidate, Fistful Of Dollars, Modesty Blaise, In Like Flint, Thoroughly Modern Millie, Kaleidoscope, Funny Girl, The Spy Who Loved Me, Enter The Dragon, Harry and Tonto, For Love of Ivy, There Was a Crooked Man, The Great Waltz, Islands in the Stream, Every Which Way But Loose, The Wiz, Something Wicked This Way Comes, Hair, The Black Stallion,* and *Rollerball.*

Peak always had several projects in the works between posters, magazines, and advertising art. In '64 he went on an ibex

hunting expedition with Shah of Iran for *Sports Illustrated*. He designed 30 stamps for the 1984 Summer Olympics in Los Angeles and the 1984 Winter Olympics in Sarajevo, Yugoslavia. He also drew 45 covers for *Time Magazine*, including a popular portrait of Mother Teresa.

Peak was named Artist of the Year by the Artists Guild of New York in '61, elected to the Society of Illustrators Hall of Fame in '77, and was given the Key Art Lifetime Achievement Award by *The Hollywood Reporter* in '92.

During his working life, Peak created art for over 100 posters. Though his use of bold color became his signature, with each poster he was able to distinguish the style and tone of the movie. Those flamboyant flourishes have made his art highly coveted by movie poster collectors.

On the **Excalibur** poster the famed sword is nestled into the middle of the poster, surrounded by images of passion and violence. In recent years, the one-sheet sold for $20-$140, 40" x 60" for $25-$110, 30" x 40" for $60-$110, and insert for $20-$95.

STAR WARS
A NEW
(AND LASTING) HOPE

We love underdogs. It doesn't matter your favorite genre, whether it's action adventure, romantic comedy, science fiction, drama, or horror, everyone loves an underdog. In the mid-1970s movie fans were treated to an iconic underdog story. A little known director had an idea for a science fiction tale about a group of rebels fighting an empire. He put together an ensemble cast, some known, some new to the industry, and added innovative special effects to a little film he called *Star Wars*. Audiences definitely cheered for these underdogs, and almost 40 years later, they still haven't stopped.

Star Wars was created by George Lucas, a man with two passions. Before his love of film came his love of fast cars. As a child, he aspired to be a race car driver, but after surviving a near fatal car accident in high school he changed his mind. His appreciation of cinematography and clever camera tricks began while attending community college. It bloomed into career aspirations when he transferred to the University of Southern California's filmmaking school. His film career began in the mid-1960s, working in the sound department, as a camera operator, production assistant, cinematographer, and editor.

Though his first feature film, *THX-1138*, was considered a flop by its studio, his second one, *American Graffiti*, did quite well. The teen movie about a group of friends spending a final night together after graduation was released in 1973. Boasting the young talents of Ron Howard, Richard Dreyfuss, Candy Clark, and a kid named Harrison Ford, it was filled with nostalgia,

COMING
TO
YOUR
GALAXY
THIS
SUMMER.

STAR WARS

GEORGE LUCAS THE MAN WHO BROUGHT YOU AMERICAN GRAFFITI, NOW BRINGS YOU AN ADVENTURE AS BIG AS THE COSMOS ITSELF: STAR WARS THE STORY OF A BOY, A GIRL, AND A UNIVERSE ITS A SPECTACLE LIGHT YEARS AHEAD OF ITS TIME. FROM 20TH CENTURY-FOX.

The first and second advance posters were similar to each other. The first advance is more reflective with metallic chrome finish and the second had a duller finish. The other difference is the variance in the letter "W". The first advance is considered much more valuable than the second due to the rarity of the finish and different font of the "W", though advance style B is more familiar to the public. It's somewhat basic but the tagline sells it, having become one of the most recognizable of all time with "Coming to your galaxy this summer." The advance style A can sell for $210-$2,150 and advance style B for $155-$1,135.

love of beautiful cars, and music. Co-written and directed by Lucas, it earned five Academy Award nominations, including Best Director, Best Picture, and Best Original Screenplay.

Lucas wanted his next project to be the modern equivalent of a Saturday morning children's program, combining fairy tale elements with fantasy and adventure, set in space. It evolved into the feature length *Star Wars*, which eventually became titled *Star Wars: Episode IV – A New Hope*, which he wrote and directed.

When it was released in 1977, the movie mesmerized audiences with its unique blend of special effects, characters – both human and droid – and exotic settings. The story began 19 years after the formation of the evil Empire with the galaxy in a state of turmoil as a rebel faction tried to fight back. The Empire was ruled by a vicious emperor and overseen by his number one apprentice, Darth Vader (David Prowse, voiced by James Earl Jones). Princess Leia (Carrie Fisher) was among the rebels trying to save the galaxy through subterfuge and cunning. Luke Skywalker (Mark Hamill) was a young farmer bucking to be free, and who began training in the ways of the Force by Jedi Obi-Wan Kenobi (Alec Guinness), and Han Solo (Ford) was a smuggler scoundrel who reluctantly joined the fight with his Wookie

Almost since the beginning, **Star Wars** collectibles have become a constant fixture in the collecting landscape from comics and books to figures and props to cards and posters. Promotion for each film relied heavily on the incredible artwork provided by some of the best contemporary movie poster artists. The first promotional poster for **A New Hope** was drawn by Howard Chaykin in a comic book style, depicting the main trio of Luke, Leia, and Han with the epic villain Darth Vader. It introduces viewers to the idea that this will be an adventure, as well as science fiction, printed by 20th Century Fox in 1976. The poster was unveiled at the World Science Fiction Convention in Kansas City in a very limited print run, measuring much smaller than the one-sheet at 20" x 29". The promotional poster can sell for $1,015-$2,630.

The style A one-sheet is the one most associated with the film with art by Tom Jung. Luke is clearly portrayed as the hero with an elevated position over Leia, shirt ripped open, and light coming from his lightsaber that splits the image. Jung may not have known about where the story would go because it also makes early allusion to a possible love interest between the two considering their flowing clothing and visible skin, akin to images on romance novels. The style A one-sheet often sells for $100-$2,025.

co-pilot, Chewbacca (Peter Mayhew).

During its initial release, *Star Wars* earned over $307 million.

In 1980, the story continued in *The Empire Strikes Back* with Luke journeying to the planet Dagobah to be trained by Jedi Master Yoda. Leia and Han fled the Imperial forces after an attack on their rebel base and ended up on the Cloud City of Bespin with Han's former friend Lando Calrissian (Billy Dee Williams), where Darth Vader had set a trap for young Luke. Despite warnings from Yoda and the now-ghostly Obi-Wan to stay on Dagobah, Luke took the bait and left to save his friends, while promis-

ing to return and finish his training. During a dramatic duel that cost Luke his hand, Darth Vader dropped the ultimate movie bombshell, revealing to young Luke that he is his father, Anakin Skywalker. Directed by Irvin Kershner, with story by Lucas and screenplay by Leigh Brackett and Lawrence Kasdan, the worldwide box office total beyond $530 million.

The third episode of the trilogy came out in 1983, directed by Richard Marquand, written by Kasdan and Lucas. *Return of the Jedi* saw the Empire working on a more powerful Death Star while the Rebels planned their most ambitious attack. Before joining

The style C one-sheet is arguably the least familiar, though it depicts all of the principle characters. Tom Chantrell provided the artwork, contrasting colors of blue and black with red and orange. It cements Han, Luke, and Leia as the main characters, with Darth Vader in the background set between Luke and Leia. Style C was intended for British release and depicted Chewbacca, R2-D2, C-3PO, Obi-Wan Kenobi, and Grand Moff Tarkin for the first time. The style C one-sheet sells for $200-$2,370.

The style D, also known as the circus poster, was a collaboration between two artists. Charles White, III was commissioned to draw the poster for the 1978 summer rerelease of **Star Wars**. He invited Drew Struzan to contribute to the portraiture while he worked on other aspects. The poster has a 1930s and '40s style from concept to font. Luke and Leia are the main image with smaller ones of Han, C-3PO, R2-D2, and Chewbacca. Because there was not enough room to include the necessary credits, White and Struzan made the main image smaller than the poster size and drew Obi-Wan looking on from the side, making it appear to be hanging from a wooden board, giving the circus appearance. The style D "circus" one-sheet can reach $65-$1,135

The rarest of the posters is the one that commemorated the first anniversary of the release. The simple poster depicts a large birthday cake surrounded by the original toy figures. Few were printed making them difficult to find, and highly coveted by collectors. The 1978 Happy Birthday one-sheet recently sold for $700-$3,150.

The style A (usually known as the "**Gone with the Wind**" style) one-sheet was painted by Roger Kastel. It is the most popular of the **Empire** posters, depicting an image of Han and Leia embracing with their impassioned love affair paralleling Rhett Butler and Scarlett O'Hara. The comparison between **Gone with the Wind** and **Empire** is the vivid color, the heat of Georgia versus the coolness of space and Luke on his Tauntaun replaces the man on horseback in the **Gone with the Wind** poster. There was some controversy over the poster's lack in depicting new character Lando Calrissian. It was pulled from distribution, most likely based on this fact. The style A "**Gone with the Wind**" one-sheet recently sold for $70-$1,135.

The style B one-sheet by Jung presents Darth Vader as the major figure with Leia, Han, and Lando on one side, and two images of Luke on the other. Stormtroopers appear to run through the poster and fighters fly from Darth Vader's cape. The style B one-sheet can sell for $20-$975.

the fight, Luke learned that Leia was his twin sister and shared the news with her on the Forest Moon of Endor. After the fighting ended she put a nervous Han at ease that her love for Luke was familial and the pair began their relationship in earnest. When faced with killing his son or the Emperor (Ian McDiarmid), Darth Vader chose to save his son at the last minute, costing him his life. The Empire fell at the hands of the Rebels, led by a young farmer, princess, scruffy looking nerf herder, a Wookie, an old smoothie, and a couple of droids. The final piece in Lucas' first trilogy made over $570 million.

By the late 1990s special effects technology had made significant leaps forward and Lucas decided it was time to continue his *Star Wars* saga with the prequel trilogy. Released in 1999, written and directed by

Struzan provided the art for the **Return of the Jedi** advance, originally titled **Revenge of the Jedi**. The poster was pulled because it was pointed out that the Jedi did not take revenge, hence the title did not make sense. Few made it to theaters. Between 8,000 to 9,000 were printed and George Lucas sold them to fans through his fan club. It only took three days to sell all of them. The other interesting fact about this poster was that it had three fold lines instead of the usual four. Adding to the fun of collectability, some were printed with a release date and some weren't. Based on being pulled and the title change, it makes it the most sought after poster for the series. The advance undated one-sheet can sell for $435-$2,150 and advance dated one-sheet for $190-$1,790.

The replacement style A has art by Tim Reamer, depicting a pair of hands holding a lightsaber with the Death Star in the background. The poster is primarily black with electric blue coming off of the lightsaber as it swings upward. In recent years the replacement style A has sold for $15-$85.

The style B is more eye-catching, showing a collage of good and evil characters. With artwork by Kazuhiko Sano it's the one most associated with the movie. Leia, Han, and Luke are in the center with Leia in the iconic gold bikini, Han firing a blaster, and Luke ready to swing his lightsaber. The abhorrent Jabba the Hutt and his minions are on one side while Lando and Wicket on the other. Darth Vader looms from the top. The style B one-sheet can sell for $30-$510.

Lucas, *The Phantom Menace* began with Darth Vader as a child and young Jedi Obi-Wan Kenobi (Ewan McGregor). Jedi Master Qui-Gon Jinn (Liam Neeson) saw the potential in young Anakin Skywalker (Jake Lloyd) while Queen Amidala (Natalie Portman) led the people of Naboo against invasion.

The movie made $1 billion worldwide, but fans were divided regarding the movie's success. Many longtime Star Wars fans felt that it was bogged down by politics, they didn't connect with some new characters, and the tone was more like a family film. This critique is due in part to the immense pressure older fans put on the new movie, with 16 years' worth of love and loyalty. Younger fans, or those new to the series, loved Darth Maul, from his weapon to his striking appearance and physicality. They also found Jar Jar Binks – a character often disliked by older fans – to be funny.

Special effects were also a point of disagreement. No one could argue that the new effects had no boundaries, prompting huge battles, gleaming new ships, and impressive creatures, but some fans preferred the practical effects of the original over the computer effects of the new.

In 2002 *Attack of the Clones* picked up ten years later with Anakin (Hayden Christensen) training to be a Jedi, taught by Obi-Wan while Padmé Amidala had become a senator of the Galactic Republic.

The Phantom Menace advance poster, created by Ellen Lee, depicts the boy Anakin Skywalker with the shadow of Darth Vader. The small initial print run sold out in less than 2 weeks and over 60,000 were printed to fill backorders. In recent years the advance style one-sheet sold for $10-$180.

The follow-up regular one-sheet was created by Struzan displaying a montage of the new characters. It shows the very menacing Darth Maul in the background with Anakin front and center. The two suns of Tatooine shine through the center of the poster with Queen Amidala appearing regally and Qui-Gon Jinn looking forward wisely. The one-sheet can sell for $20-$120.

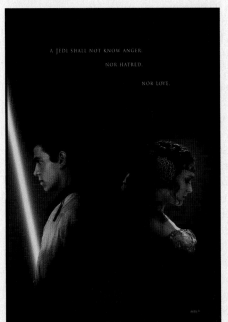

The advanced style one-sheet for **Attack of the Clones** shows Anakin and Padmé, backs to each other with the doomed romantic tagline "A Jedi shall not know anger. Nor hatred. Nor love." Created by Struzan, Padmé has taken on a softer appearance for her new role as romantic lead. In recent years the advance one-sheet sold for $10-$70.

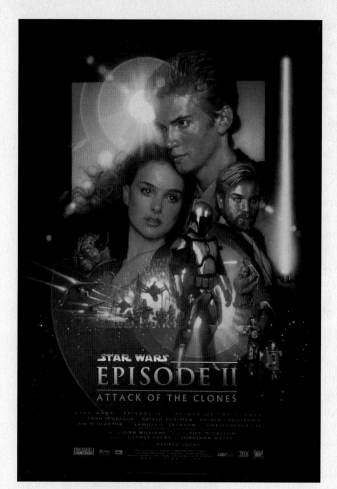

The one-sheet was designed by Struzan, depicting Padmé leaning into Anakin with his chin tucked against her forehead. Standing in the foreground is bounty hunter Jango Fett, the father of the notorious Boba Fett. No villain has previously appeared in the foreground making it clear that this character has significance. The one-sheet can sell for $10-85.

Obi-Wan traced the location of an assassin to a remote region of the galaxy where a clone army had been building, using the DNA of Bounty Hunter Jango Fett (Temuera Morrison). Anakin swore to protect Padmé and the pair fell in love on the beautiful planet of Naboo. Visions of his mother in distress prompted Anakin to go home to learn that she had been kidnapped. He found her in time for her death and he subsequently slaughtered a party of Tusken Raiders, well on his way to the Dark Side. It ended with the Jedi in aggressive negotiations with Count Dooku and the separatists. Lucas directed this one and co-wrote it with Jonathan Hales. *Attack of the Clones* reached over $649 million at the box office worldwide.

Lucas wrote and directed the final installment of his second trilogy. *Revenge of the Sith* was released in 2005 with the Jedi leading the clone army in a battle against the Separatists. Supreme Chancellor Palpatine continued his political maneuvers to gain more power while whispering into the con-

tinuously receptive ear of Anakin Skywalker. After having a vision that Padmé would die in childbirth he made the ultimate choice, pledging himself to the Emperor and his burgeoning Galactic Empire. As the Jedi were being exterminated across the galaxy, Master Yoda and a few others were forced into hiding. Upon discovering Anakin's betrayal, Obi-Wan battled his former Padawan, leaving Anakin for dead, but he was saved by the Emperor and becomes Darth Vader, while Padmé gave birth to twins. *Revenge of the Sith* totaled almost $849 million at the box office worldwide

On October 30, 2012, it was announced that The Walt Disney Company had acquired Lucasfilm for $4 billion, making George Lucas, with 40 million Disney shares, the company's second-largest non-institutional shareholder, following the trust of Steve Jobs, the late Apple co-founder. In the time since, Disney has announced a full slate of new Star Wars film projects and expansions to both Disneyland and Walt Disney World.

Star Wars long ago became a global sensation, expanding into multiple forms of media, accumulating generations of passionate fans, and generating myriad collectibles. In the build-up to the December 2015 release of Episode VII, we've been reminded that it can bring down the house with a screen shot, a line, or a few notes of the score.

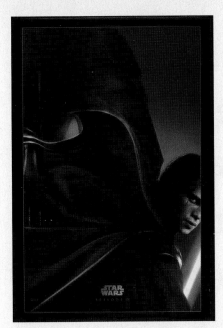

The advance style A for **Revenge of the Sith** displays Anakin at the edge of the poster with the cape turning into Vader's helmet. The way the cape takes up the dominate portion of the poster clearly states that Vader is more consuming than Anakin. It is so big it dwarfs him, flowing off of his back depicting the fluidity of his transformation into the Sith lord. The advance one-sheet can sell for $10-$205.

Struzan painted the regular one-sheet, Padmé is no longer leaning on Anakin, she looks diplomatic and he looks troubled. The foreground image is the battle between Anakin and Obi-Wan. Yoda and Mace Windu are also in action, the emperor appears on his first theatrical one-sheet poster, and Darth Vader looms over Anakin. Recently the one-sheet sold for $10-$100.

Homage was paid to **A New Hope** with a style D circus poster by Matt Busch. Almost a mirror image, it has a similar color scheme, Anakin and Padmé replace Luke and Leia, General Grievous in place of Vader, Yoda takes the place of Han and R2-D2 with C-3PO replace the jawas. A younger Obi-Wan is seen along the side where his older counterpart appears on the original. The style D Fan Club "circus" one-sheet sells for $95-$285.

From Research
to Purchase:
David Lieberman &
CineMasterpieces.com

*David Lieberman has been buying and selling movie posters for
over 30 years. He is the owner and founder of CineMasterpieces,
a website that offers highly sought after original movie posters through
fixed price sales. The website also provides helpful editorials, tips,
and features about many facets of movie poster collecting.*

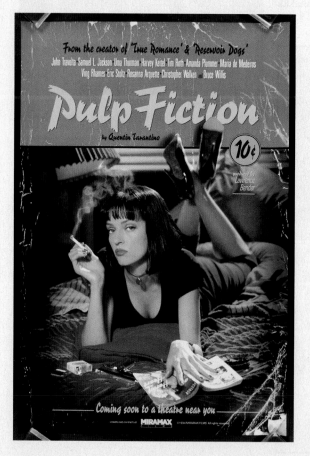

Overstreet: How long have you been
collecting movie posters?
David Lieberman (DL): Over 30
years.

Overstreet: Do you collect other
types of movie memorabilia?
DL: Not really. I've bought a few
props over the years but I mainly
stick to posters.

Overstreet: Do you collect from certain series or genres?
DL: I've always liked *Star Wars*,
James Bond, and horror. I do have
several Italian and French posters
hanging in my house.

Overstreet: Are there any you wanted that got away?
DL: If it got away that means I didn't
want it bad enough!

Overstreet: CineMasterpieces.com
provides a lot of information about
movie posters. What is your goal in
doing that?

DL: A few reasons: 1. To help novice collectors. We constantly get communication from collectors telling us how much they appreciate the information we provide.
2. It saves us time. The more information we provide on the site means less time for us answering questions by phone or by email. 3. It helps to increase business.

Overstreet: Your website offers collectors the chance to visit your office. Do you ever host gallery style events?
DL: No. We are not a retail store. We do have an office and can meet with potential clients by appointment only.

Overstreet: You sell posters on eBay. Many collectors are leery about using auction websites like that. How do you foster trust with collectors on eBay?
DL: We describe the condition of our posters accurately and take close-up photos so a buyer knows exactly what he or she is getting. We also have a no questions asked return policy. Also, our feedback rating is outstanding and we are a top rated seller. Less than 1% of eBay sellers achieve top rated seller status.

Overstreet: How do you determine pricing for the posters on CineMasterpieces.com?
DL: We look at what a poster has sold for at auction and then we look at other dealer websites and try to be competitive.

Overstreet: As stated on your website, you rarely sell autographed items. Why is that?
DL: The market is flooded with fake autographs. Many of them even have fake certificates of authenticity. We are not autograph experts so we won't list an item unless it comes with a COA from a reputable company like PSA or we are certain of the signature by some other means.

Overstreet: From an artistic standpoint, many people prefer painted posters to photographic ones. Can you name some of the photographic posters that achieve high prices and share why?
DL: *Pulp Fiction* recalled "Lucky Strikes" one-sheet – rarer than the regular release one sheet. It was recalled because it has a "Lucky Strikes" cigarette pack on it and they did not have authorization to use it on the poster.

They'll never get caught.
They're on a mission from God.

JOHN BELUSHI   DAN AYKROYD
THE BLUES BROTHERS

JAMES BROWN · CAB CALLOWAY · RAY CHARLES · CARRIE FISHER · ARETHA FRANKLIN · HENRY GIBSON
THE BLUES BROTHERS BAND
Written by DAN AYKROYD and JOHN LANDIS · Produced by ROBERT K. WEISS · Directed by JOHN LANDIS
Executive Producer BERNIE BRILLSTEIN
Original Soundtrack Recording on ATLANTIC Records and Tapes.   Read the JOVE BOOK   A UNIVERSAL PICTURE

The Matrix international one-sheet – very rare.

Halloween Australian one-sheet – very rare and it is one of only a few original posters to feature the villain Michael Myers.

The Blues Brothers subway two-sheet – very rare and it is the largest and best looking original poster from the film.

L.A. Confidential Canadian/international one-sheet – very rare with only a few copies known to have been sold publicly.

Overstreet: Do you think restoration increases or decreases poster value?
DL: If it is an old very valuable poster and it had significant defects like tape, tears, and missing pieces then restoration can definitely increase its value. If the poster was already in great shape and then it is restored/linen-backed then depending on the poster it can either increase its value or not increase it at all. Only in rare cases can restoration decrease a posters value.

For example: If someone took a mint rolled international double sided one sheet for *The Matrix* and had it linen-backed.

Overstreet: How do you spot reprints among original posters?

DL: We are asked this question every day – sometimes several times a day.

Depending on the poster and what year it is from, here are just some of the things we look for:

What is the exact size in inches? Where did it come from? Does it come from a questionable source? Does it come from a known seller of fakes and reproductions? There are plenty of seemingly trustworthy sellers on eBay and other sites that for years have been successfully passing off fake posters as originals to new collectors. Is it folded or rolled? If it is from the 1970s-'80s, does it have a GAU logo?

Is there an NSS number on the front? Just because a poster has an NSS number on the front does not automatically make it an "original." When a poster is copied/reproduced, the NSS number is often reproduced as well in order make it look more authentic. Is there an NSS stamp on the back?

Does it "look" and "feel" right? Does it smell right? What kind of paper is it? Matte, flat, glossy, regular paper, cardstock? Is the print quality acceptable (blurry or sharp)? Is it stone or offset lithography? Is it a popular title with known reproductions? Are there known reprints or reproductions of it? Is the artwork slightly cropped?

Does it say Portal Publications on the bottom border? If it does, *it is a reproduction* with no real value.

Is it "minty white"? Does it look like it was printed yesterday? Could it possibly be an original "rerelease" poster?

Is it single or double sided? Just because a poster is double sided does not make it authentic. There are plenty of double sided "fakes"" for titles such as *Spider-Man*, *The Matrix*, *The Dark Knight*, as well as many others.

Every now and then we come across an old movie poster in great shape that seems too good to be true. One that is very old, unused, and in near pristine condition. Yes, there are Near Mint unused vintage original movie posters. If you look at other collectibles, there are coins, baseball cards and comic books that have survived for over 50 years in Near Mint condition. It doesn't happen often, but it does happen.

Overstreet: Are there any niches within movie posters that you can see growing in popularity and/or producing high sales? **DL:** Classic horror and science fiction

have always been collectible and probably always will be. Star Wars is incredibly popular, and now with the new films being announced a whole new audience is interested in vintage posters from the original trilogy.

Overstreet: What advice would you give to someone who wants to start collecting movie posters, but is doing so on a budget? **DL:** eBay and other online auction sites are a great place to start. Look for auctions that have gone unnoticed. You can sometimes get a real bargain. You also can get burned with a fake or a reproduction, but as long as you don't spend too much money and are willing to chalk it up as a learning experience you will be ok.

Overstreet: How about advice for someone with more money to invest in movie posters? **DL:** I would not really suggest "investing" in movie posters. However I do think one should always buy the best of the best if they can. The best condition and the rarest items usually perform well over time.

Before Movie Trailers: There Were Lobby Cards

Movie trailers have gained a status so lofty that they can make or break a film's success. Show us a trailer that follows one scene for two minutes or only focuses on the resurgence of one actor/actress without presenting a synopsis of the actual story and we won't be interested. But, if we see a well planned trailer that offers flashes of the action, snippets of witty dialogue, explosions (literal or romantic), and a baseline for what the movie is actually about, and we are hooked.

Trailers became popularly used in the 1930s. Long before they achieved their current significance, theaters needed other ways to entice movie fans into their houses. They did so with artwork.

Lobby cards were one of many options theaters used to intrigue viewers. Introduced in November 1914, as suggested by the name, they were designed for display in a theater's lobby. They are smaller than posters, usually measuring 11" by 14" set in landscape format and printed on card stock, a sturdier alternative to paper. Lobby cards were typically issued in sets of eight, though occasionally some were released in sets as small as four and up to twenty cards. Each card features a different scene or collection of images from the film briefly summarizing the movie with captions.

A set of lobby cards begins with the title card, which specifically identifies the primary cast, lists the credits, and presents

the general premise of the film. Title cards stood out because of their artwork, similar to one-sheets, which didn't appear on the scene cards that followed. For many collectors the title cards are akin to smaller posters, selling for significantly more than regular scene cards.

The rest of the set, with imagery from the film, teased the action without spoiling it. The early lobby cards didn't feature photographs, just details about the movie. During the silent film era cards were often black and white or duotone stills. By the 1920s studios punched up their appeal by creating hand-tinted full color lobby cards displaying vivid pictures that brought the film's characters to life.

Unfortunately, they are no longer used in U.S. theaters and are not produced very often. Studios ceased production of cards in the 1980s in the U.S., though card sets were still produced for international releases.

Collectability of lobby cards is greatly influenced by the use of color and scenes they depict. Cards that offer close-ups of movie monsters or primary cast members as well as cards showcasing crucial scenes are favorites among collectors. They are more successful than cards with distant images of the stars or a "dead" card which does not feature the cast at all or shows an insignificant scene.

Of course the film's popularity is a key. Examples of highly coveted lobby cards include the "Letters of Transit" card from *Casablanca*, Norman Bates and the house from *Psycho*, the Marilyn Monroe card for *The Asphalt Jungle*, the crop duster scene from *North by Northwest*, and Orson Welles at the podium in *Citizen Kane*. Each of these examples captures the essence of the film, similar to good movie trailers. Cards can be worth as little as a few dollars for dead cards or those from less popular films, and up to $25,000 for a card from *Dracula* or *Frankenstein*.

Lobby cards show in-depth looks at movies by chronicling the story on eight different cards. Whether they offer the basics in film credits or exhibit colorful images of the stars of the Golden Age, lobby cards are beautiful representations of cinema history.

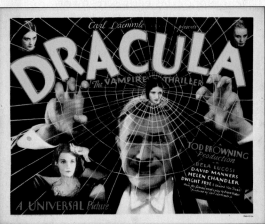

JAMES CAMERON, KING OF THE BLOCKBUSTER WORLD

Big budget, special effects driven movies have become commonplace in the landscape of American cinema. Theater shaking explosions, adrenaline fueled chase scenes, imagination bending effects, and dazzling choreography fill action flicks, science fiction hits, and thrillers bringing in movie audiences by the droves. Yet, few directors can present a strong, grounding emotional story while compiling enough fresh action to produce a blockbuster. On the short list of directors who can is James Cameron.

Cameron has been a movie lover since childhood. He was born in Ontario, Canada in 1954, then his family moved to California, the land of movies, in 1971. He studied physics at California State University, but after graduating he decided to pursue a career as a filmmaker rather than in science. He became a truck driver to help support his early screenwriting projects when his first break came at Roger Corman Studios. He worked as a model maker then became an art director for *Battle Beyond the Stars* in 1980. Utilizing his impressive skills, Cameron quickly moved up the ladder to second unit director and production designer. He made his directorial and screenwriting debut with *Piranha II: The Spawning* filmed in 1981 then released in 1983.

The Terminator one-sheet depicts a close image of Arnold Schwarzenegger in a leather jacket and black sunglasses. His jacket is open to reveal the center of his muscular chest, a serial number reads across one lens of his sunglasses, and he's holding a giant hand gun. In recent years the one-sheet has sold for $10-$400, Australian daybill for $10-$175, Japanese B2 for $20-$50, British quad for $100-$200, Czech one for $100-$300, Polish One for $275, and lobby card set of eight for $250.

In 1984 he directed *Terminator*, his first of several giant hits. Cameron and Gale Anne Hurd co-wrote the script for *Terminator*, then he directed the film and she produced it. The movie opens in post-apocalyptic 2029 as humankind, led by John Connor, fights the machines who incited a nuclear holocaust. A machine known as a terminator goes back in time to 1984 in order to kill Sarah Connor, the mother of the man who will lead humanity in the fight against the machines. The science fiction action-thriller earned both critical and audience praise.

The same year *The Terminator* was released he signed on to direct *Aliens*, the sequel to Ridley Scott's sci-fi scare fest *Alien*. Cameron was an excellent choice to helm the project pairing the director who favored tough heroines with Ripley, the consummate survivor. A few years later he wrote and directed *The Abyss* about a crew

on an oil rig attempting to rescue the team on a sunken submarine. Though the movie boasts good performances by the cast, it did not fare well with audiences.

The disappointment from *The Abyss* was quickly overshadowed by the success of *Terminator 2: Judgement Day* in 1991. *T2* was a huge hit filled with action, an intriguing story, revolutionary special effects, and a buff Linda Hamilton as Sarah Connor, who had become a formidable action heroine. His next mega action hit came in 1994 with *True Lies*, reuniting him with Arnold Schwarzenegger and Bill Paxton, also starring Jamie Lee Curtis and Tom Arnold. Unlike his earlier action films, *True Lies* successfully melded action and comedy with every character constantly telling lies of varying degree and grandeur.

The next film he wrote and directed crashed into theaters in 1997 and held the box office record for highest grossing film

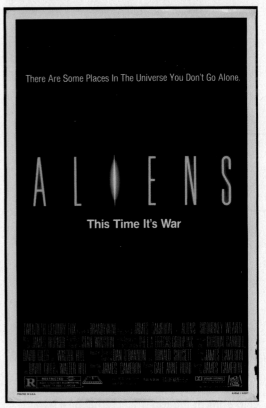

The **Aliens** Ripley style A one-sheet represents an early look at a woman as action hero with Ripley carrying Newt in one arm and a giant gun in the other, surrounded by eggs that are splitting open to emit a green glow. The English double crown takes a similar approach showing Ripley in the exciting scene when she's revealed to be in the giant mechanized suit. The other one-sheet appears more like a teaser. It is solid black with the credits and tagline in white text and the title in glowing, thin blue letters complete with an "I" that appears to be a door opening. The title one-sheet for $10-$375, Ripley style A one-sheet can sell for $40-$330, British double crown for $125, Polish large for $200, and Japanese B1 for $115.

for 12 years. *Titanic* was a difficult project on many fronts, particularly in its astronomical budget, mishaps on set, and problems filming the actual wreckage of the Titanic rotting on the ocean floor. Starring Kate Winslet and Leonardo DiCaprio the movie combined a sweeping historic epic with the intoxicating, tragically doomed, relationship of Rose and Jack. The film was nominated for a record tying 14 Oscar nominations and took home 11 trophies, including Best Director for Cameron and Best Picture.

Cameron took a long break from big budget films over the course of the next decade. He co-created the *Dark Angel* TV series, then worked on several underwater documentaries, including *Ghost of the Abyss* in 2003 and *Aliens of the Deep* in 2005.

He reentered the feature film foray in 2009 with his second movie to hold the record for highest grossing film of all time, surpassing *Titanic*. *Avatar* boasted amazing state of the art technology and revolutionary 3-D filming. Not only did it jump off the screen in entrancing 3-D, the world of *Avatar* featured some of the most imaginative creatures to appear on film in vibrant, gorgeous colors. The movie grossed about $2 billion in North America and $6 billion worldwide.

The touchstone of Cameron's career has been his ability to balance dazzling special effects sequences with a great story. He had a significant impact on action films in the 1980s and 1990s and has helmed some of the highest grossing films of all time filled with technical advancements. He will – definitely – be back.

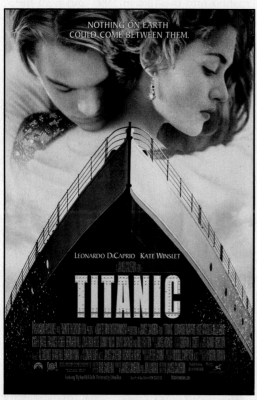

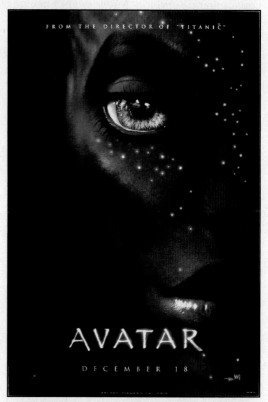

On the **Titanic** style A one-sheet, the boat dominates the poster with Jack and Rose embracing at the top. The international style B shows them dancing forehead to forehead with a streamlined image of the Titanic rushing onward at the bottom of the poster. The style A one-sheet can sell for $15-$130, international style B one-sheet for $20-$150, "I'm Flying, Jack" version for $10-$80, 2012 rerelease style C for $340, and teaser one-sheet for $100.

The **Avatar** one-sheet teaser style A comprises a close-up of half of Neytiri's blue face cast in some midnight blue shadow accentuating the shimmering freckles on her face, her yellow-green eye is a shocking contrast to the blue. The one-sheet shows Neytiri and Jake, in human form, faces side by side above an image of Jake in Na'vi form riding a mountain banshee. In recent years the one-sheet teaser style A has sold for $10-$2,870, one-sheet for $10-$60, teaser style G 2010 rerelease for $20-$50.

Charlie Stevens: Movie Poster Collecting and Community

Charlie Stevens, a movie poster aficionado and blogger, enjoys collecting for the connection to his favorite films. Not only has his hobby created friendships around the world, he uses the knowledge he's acquired to help the collecting community.

Overstreet: How long have you been collecting movie posters?
Charlie Stevens (CS): Since 1998 or so – 17 years.

Overstreet: Why did you start collecting movie posters?
CS: I fell in love with movies and wanted something to connect to the film.

Overstreet: Are you a big fan of movies or do you just collect for the art? If so, what is it about movies that you love?
CS: I'm a big fan of movies and especially certain actors and actresses. I have purchased a few posters just for the art but the bulk of my collection is centered on specific films and/or actors and actresses. Clint Eastwood, Audrey Hepburn, and Elizabeth Taylor being the bulk of my collection. What I love about mov-

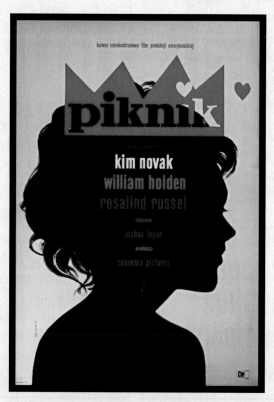

ies is they simply allow you to escape for a short period of time and often allow you to question yourself about the world, relationships, and the future.

Overstreet: What attracts you to collecting movie posters?
CS: They are a part of the films production, part of the history of making the film. For example Bill Gold, who also designed *Casablanca*, worked on pretty much every poster for Eastwood starting with *Dirty Harry* up to *Mystic River*. They are wonderfully full of color, they are delicate, and an immediate visual cue to recall the film. Think about pretty much any classic poster: *Dial M for Murder* with the hanging phone, *Unforgiven* with William Munny holding his pistol behind his back – I mean sure, he ended up killing the antagonist with

a shotgun, but the poster immediately makes you recall the film.

I think also the people who really collect posters are very close, it is a very small world. You make friends all over the world. I live in Houston and my buddy in Argentina just sent me a *Butterfield 8* poster because he knows I like Liz Taylor and my friend in Australia just sent me the poster from a well-known Australian film call *Red Dog* because I was an immediate fan. I can tell you many more of these stories. We all take care of each other.

Overstreet: What was the first movie poster that you collected?
CS: I can't recall the exact one. It was either *Great Expectation* (1998) - the art portrait of Gwyneth Paltrow by Francesco Clemente (the real artist who made all of Finn's work) or the poster from *Rushmore*, Wes Anderson's follow-up to *Bottle Rocket*. Funny thing is I had no real sense of them being investments and hung them up straight away with push pins in my room. I never thought I would end up having thousands of posters – just thinking these two were so cool to have over my desk. Something to look at while I did my homework.

Overstreet: What is your favorite piece in your collection?
CS: There are too many to name. The first one that comes to mind straight away is the Polish poster for *Picnic*. I fell in love with this one straight away. Never thought I would find it and after searching for many years found it from a very small seller in Poland that sold out of a coffee shop, the way I understand. I paid an arm and a leg but have never regretting buying it. The art is by Waldemar Swierzy.

Overstreet: What is the most valuable poster in your collection?
CS: Probably a tie between my *Breakfast at Tiffany's* U.S. one-sheet and my *Dial M for Murder* U.S. three-sheet. Both range from $4,000 to $8,000 depending on the auction and/or retailer.

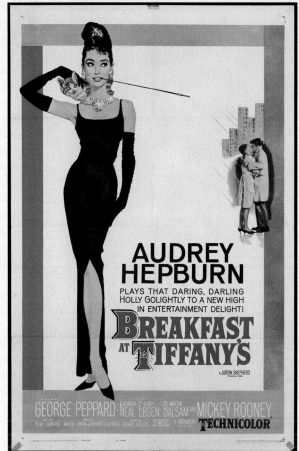

Overstreet: Which posters do you want to add to your collection?
CS: I need a few more Audrey Hepburn U.S. one-sheets to finish off a set of them, namely *Roman Holiday*. I need a first release *Rear Window* to go with my *Dial M for Murder* three-sheet and *To Catch a Thief* six-sheet. And I've been pining for a *War of the Worlds* U.S. one-sheet. But I never have the discipline to save up. I go a year or so in between bouts of discipline, buying less valuable posters and then I'll quit for six months and save up for a big one.

Overstreet: Do you collect different movie poster sizes?
CS: I pretty much have every kind from every country.

Overstreet: Do you collect other movie memorabilia?
CS: I like photo stills. Photo stills are really fun because you will see a classic image on Tumblr or Facebook and wonder where it came from. Then you find the original

Overstreet: Do you focus on a time period, genre, artist, or anything else?
CS: Movies and actor/actresses.

Overstreet: How much does condition impact your decision to purchase a poster?
CS: Some. For modern posters with clay based ink, the posters have to be pretty darn close to perfect. I can be satisfied with some edge wear because I know that it's from a theater attendant taking it out of the frame, but if a modern poster has issues in the middle part of the poster I typically stay away. Breaking of the clay based ink reveal white creases. For older posters as long as most of the art is still there I can be satisfied. I also restore posters, so anything that I can fix, I will buy.

You should also be aware of the standard grading scales. Some use their own but the Jon Warren guide is heavily referenced.

Overstreet: Is linen-backing a factor for you when it comes to purchasing posters?
CS: Linen-backing is a hot topic for me. I started an entire website dedicated to investigating the practice and what collectors should know. I had a bad experience with a restorer and decided to learn the art/science on my own. It is basically chemistry. I even introduced a restoration scale on my blog. (*Editor's Note*: To read this article on Charlie's blog go to pulpfixin.com and search for "Emerging Necessity of a Conservation, Support, and Restoration Scale.")

The bottom line is that a collector will never really know what they are buying and what has been covered up with a linen-backed poster. Even the best and most well educated collectors and sellers can be fooled. One example I recently posted on movieposterworks.com was about what you don't know about your restored poster. One of my friend's posters got wet from a roof leak and I am helping him by relining a couple of his linen-backed posters. Just looking at it there appeared to be minimal airbrush work and it looked great.

still and you pump out hundreds of dollars to have it. My favorite is this Liz Taylor from *A Place in the Sun* – her eyes in this photo are just beyond compare. Where else are you going to find this in a vintage format?

Overstreet: Do you have a preference on what type of movie art you collect?
CS: Not really. I don't typically collect for the art. Some collectors will buy posters of movies they have never seen. I am guilty in buying some posters of films with actors/actresses that I love and haven't gotten around to seeing all their films. Some buy based on artist – I know one guy that is a huge Bob Peak fan – *Superman* and *Apocalypse Now*, etc. Drew Struzan – *Star Wars* and even Saul Bass – *Anatomy of a Murder*, *Vertigo*. But I personally very rarely buy just for the art.

Once I pulled off the support the restorer didn't even bother to remove much of the tape residue, electing to cover it with acrylic, permanent paint. The acrylic doesn't wash away and made the impregnated parts of the poster hard to work with. The acid in the paper had yellowed it and once that acid had been removed, with a good de-acidification wash, the paint and the paper no longer matched.

Overstreet: What about restoration?
CS: I recently wrote a blog post on this. There has been much conversation on the differences between conservation vs. restoration. (*Editor's Note*: To read this article on Charlie's blog go to pulpfixin.com and search for "Conservation vs. Restoration.")

Overstreet: Do you consider resale value when purchasing posters?
CS: Sure, it's hard not to. You want to buy a poster for less than you could possibly sell it for at some point. Preferable 20% or more below auction values because consignment fees typically range from 20% to 50% depending on the final hammer price. But then some posters, I don't waste any time trying to find a lower price.

Overstreet: Where do you buy your posters?
CS: Everywhere they are sold. I like eBay because you can find better deals if you are educated enough to avoid the fakes. In 17 years I can count on one hand the number of fakes I've purchased thinking they were original. You just have to be smart. If the deal is too good to be true it probably is.

Overstreet: How do you store them?
CS: Flat files mainly – I have 35 drawers full. I place a poster and then have either acid free paper or poly bags in between them. I also keep a bunch rolled in boxes designed specifically for movie posters.

Overstreet: Do you decorate with them?
CS: Sure. If I am willing to take a break from buying and purchase frames. I have probably 30 up at any one time.

10054-2/29

Overstreet: What advice would you give to someone new to the hobby to avoid overpaying or buying reprints that are claiming to be originals?
CS: Buy from a reputable dealer. Join a forum and ask as many questions as you can. I started out on All Poster Forum asking for help in identifying if a *Pulp Fiction* poster was authentic and then later started my own forum with two of my poster buddies: www.vintagemoviepostersforum.com. Poster collectors love to help other collectors. Like any group, it takes a commitment and thick skin for longevity – but we never shy from fast and free help. Overpaying is also a subject of contention. Is it overpaying if you were willing to spend the money? Posters are valued differently by different collectors. Some people will spend thousands on James Bond posters, I wouldn't pay much more than what I had in my pocket other than to potentially flip it to another collector. The best advice is to buy what you like from a reputable dealer, based on what you can afford, enjoy them, and don't worry about the rest. I underline "you," because many new collectors seem to think there is this standard set of posters every collector should have – I've seen it time and time again. Just buy what you love, not what you think other people will like.

SCRIPTS
TO SODA CANS:
COLLECTING MOVIE MEMORABILIA

Movie memorabilia covers a vast landscape of collectibles in addition to movie posters. There are one-of-a-kind or rare pieces that were part of the film, items issued in limited quantities, and mass produced collectibles available at neighborhood stores and conventions.

Similar to movie posters, other paper and related items are rich with collecting possibilities. First and foremost are scripts. They can be early drafts filled with notations and highlighting, final scripts worn down at the edges and creased at the center from use, or pristine collectible copies that were barely, if ever, used.

There are logistical collectibles, such as production binders with unit breakdowns, shooting schedules, call sheets, and contact lists. This category also has pitch folders for special effects, makeup, and costuming that were presented to directors and producers for approval. Collectors can buy actual storyboards that mapped out the movies or blueprints and concept designs used to create set pieces and customized vehicles. Even filming location displays, expense reports, as well as parking passes and dashboard cards used during filming

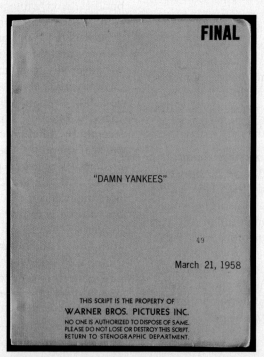

can be purchased.

There are also plenty of larger, three-dimensional pieces to be bought and displayed. Whether it's a period piece or contemporary, movies have cool costumes that can be collected once filming is done. Similarly, collectors can buy puppets and masks that were used during filming, or makeup and model tests, sculpts, maquettes (scale models), and busts that inspired final projects. Set pieces and props can cover everything from couches and motorcycles to pocket watches and production sticker sets.

Pieces used by the crew during the filming are also available to collectors. Some sought after material includes clapperboards, which are the black and white boards that are clapped together in front of the camera before the director yells, "Action!" to begin a new take. This also includes on-set photos and reference images, film cells, technical equipment like viewfinders and light testers, as well as chairs and chairback signs designating seats for the director, cast, and other crew members.

After filming has wrapped the movie process isn't complete and neither is the collecting jour-

ney. Some studios will give keepsakes, such as wine with specialty labels, to cast and crew members. Other event items include wrap party invitations, premiere invitations, programs, and keepsakes, and junket press passes and swag bags. And let's not forget awards. Sometimes awards, from small film festivals all the way up to the Oscars, find their way into auctions.

For collectors who may not have the funds to afford these rare and one of a kind items, there is a wealth of mass produced collectibles that can be found in department stores, comic book shops, toy stores, book stores, in auctions, and at conventions. These include clothing, lunch-

boxes, school supplies, toys, action figures, character busts, playsets, costumes, mugs and pint glasses, soundtracks, and much more.

Film series like Star Wars, James Bond, Harry Potter, and the Hunger Games are rife with collectibles like lightsabers, atta-ché cases filled with spy goodies, wizard wands, and mockingjay pins. For big budget franchises anything is possible from premiums at fast food restaurants to ice cube trays shaped like characters and chess sets pitting good characters against the evil ones. With so many collecting opportunities, movie fans will never want to say, "That's a wrap!"

THE MUSIC OF THE MOVIES: COLLECTING SOUNDTRACKS

Movie memorabilia collecting covers a broad spectrum. Just within movie posters there are different sizes with different artwork, international versions, down to pressbooks and glass slides. Outside of posters, people collect costumes from films, props, make-up test pieces, and models. One area that appeals to both film and music fans, is movie soundtracks.

Some of the most memorable and beloved movies have soundtracks so rich and symbolic that they take on their own character, setting the scene, and sometimes even stealing it. In addition to being auditory artistry, soundtracks display interesting artwork. Many use cover art that matches the movie poster while others feature original artwork made specifically for the soundtrack.

Alex Winter, President of Hake's Americana & Collectibles and a lifelong music aficionado, collects movie soundtracks as an extension of his record album collection. After getting a turntable in 1985, he learned a deep appreciation for the sound quality, preferring records to other music platforms. Though he took a detour into CDs throughout the '90s, when production of records nearly ceased, since 2000 and the resurgence of vinyl, he has reembraced his preference for music in that format.

In 1980, he bought his first piece of recorded music, AC/DC's *Back in Black* on cassette, and then in 1985, he began collecting records and soundtracks, based on his then-current taste in music.

Now his purchases are based on several factors,

including the stars in the movie, attractiveness of the album cover art, and the music itself. A fan of going to conventions, he also includes in his decision-making process the potential of having them autographed.

Winter has two favorite soundtracks in his collection. The first is from the movie *Easy Rider*. Up until the 1950s soundtracks were comprised of classical music or songs composed specifically for the soundtrack. *Easy Rider* was one of the pioneering soundtracks filled with contemporary music, including some songs that were already commercial hits, instead of a score or show tunes. *Easy Rider* helped soundtracks "become box office business," Winter said. In addition to the historical significance, he likes the movie and music – particularly Jimi Hendrix. He even has a copy signed by Peter Fonda, who co-wrote and starred in the movie.

His other favorite comes from the boxing documentary *Jack Johnson*, which chronicled the rise of the first African-American to become world heavyweight champion. This one is a favorite because it is filled with music by jazz legend Miles Davis.

Winter also collects soundtracks based on their art and packaging. He likes album covers that feature art by cartoonist and poster artist Jack Davis. When it comes to packaging, he prefers die-cut covers, generally interesting packaging, and records that are visually stimulating. As an example, Winter mentioned the soundtrack for *X-Men: Days of Future Past*. There is a numbered edition of

2,000 copies, gold stamped on the back in sequential order, with one clear vinyl and one blue vinyl. Though not strictly a fan of the movie series, he appreciates the artistic appeal of the album and its coveted, limited edition run.

His interest in covers and packaging means that he doesn't necessarily listen to some of the soundtracks regularly. He collects more for the angle of being an interesting and attractive product.

"It could be a soundtrack I've never heard, it could be a movie I've never seen, a movie I never want to see, but I could buy it because of the soundtrack cover art," Winter said.

Since he started collecting records, he has amassed quite a collection and many are signed. The most valuable record in his collection is his Miles Davis *Sketches of Spain* Spanish first pressing, signed by Davis, remarqued with a sketch of him playing the trumpet. His most valuable soundtrack records are *Willy Wonka & the Chocolate Factory* signed by the cast, *Hellraiser 2* signed by the cast, and the documentary *Turn On, Tune In, Drop Out* rare promotional pressing, which he describes as "visually very cool."

For many years, even after the arrival of CDs, soundtrack LPs for movies that bombed at the box office was a thriving niche. Since so many copies ended up in the cut-out bins, it was relatively hard to find good copies. There are still some strong performers in this area of collecting, he said.

Records across the board are popular

amongst music lovers and collectors. A soundtrack for popular movies and those known for their music – such as *Footloose* – are available everywhere, he said. But other soundtracks issued for 1980s movies can be difficult to find and expensive, particularly for obscure movies or those not known for their soundtracks, such as *Swamp Thing* and *Hellraiser 2*.

A decade later, soundtracks were still issued on vinyl, but became few and far between. Even a small pressing of a soundtrack during that time period can cost hundreds of dollars. They can be found, but often appeared in cut-out bins. This means that the soundtracks are often close out copies and the jackets will be hole-punched, have cut-outs, or clipped corners. Being a self-described "condition freak," makes Winter shy away from those copies.

The thriving market for record collecting

has caught the attention of studios and distributors, and now they are reissuing soundtracks and records. Like rereleased movie posters, this gives collectors the chance to purchase coveted pieces for scarce, hard to find, or even non-existent records of soundtracks. Hardcore collectors want that first pressing, rather than a reissued new one, he said, but he also notes that reissues can display new and differently stylized artwork.

"On the flipside there are great re-pressings being done on colored vinyl with totally different artwork for records that were so hard to find they had to repress it or in some cases it never came out on vinyl and it's getting a first time pressing now. Soundtracks are still very big in many ways," he said.

He has been getting records signed for as long as he's been collecting them. At first it was primarily the musicians. But flash forward to going to conventions with friends, and that has changed. He was taking DVDs to conventions and sometimes bought photos there to have them signed.

"Why did I just do that instead of getting records signed?" he thought after a few conventions.

This way, he gets the autographs he wants and the soundtracks can go into his record collection. Now he pulls something from his collection or buys a new record before conventions for that purpose. He gets anyone associated with the movie, including actors, directors, composers, soundtrack

cover artists, etc. to sign his records. For him it's a chance to have a collection that's different from the standard 8" x 10" photos most people get at conventions.

While his goal is not to have all of his soundtracks signed, he hopes to get many signed based on availability and appearances. For him, the enjoyment of having records signed is a combination of different aspects, such as if he likes the movie and the soundtrack or just the art. It's also fun for him because actors and actresses are often surprised to be signing the soundtracks.

"The reaction I get when I get an album signed by someone who is not a musician is incredible. Many times they've never signed it before or very infrequently," he said.

A prize piece in his autographed collection is *The Walking Dead* soundtrack. With a gatefold cover, he is having cast members sign all over it, on the front, back, inside, the inner sleeves, and insert poster. So far, almost everyone who has signed it had not seen the record before. Cast members who signed his *Walking Dead* soundtrack include Scott Wilson, Emily Kinney, Michael Rooker, Chandler Riggs, Sarah Wayne Callies, Jon Bernthal, Chad L. Coleman, Lawrence Gilliard, Jr., Josh McDermitt, Alanna Masterson, Seth Gilliam, Denise Crosby, Addy Miller, Jeff Kober, and Adrian Kali Turner. Given the show's large – and ever growing – cast, he plans to continue adding more names to this prized soundtrack.

One of his favorite *Walking Dead* experiences was meeting McDermitt, who was excited to discuss music with him. The pair even bonded over their appreciation of Miles Davis and jazz. As Winter described it, he thought it was a refreshing experience, giving McDermitt a chance to talk about something different, rather than answer questions he's often asked.

The soundtrack for *The Evil Dead* tops the list of records he'd like to acquire someday. Though he has seen the soundtrack, it is difficult to find in high grade. Because he prefers quality and presentation over volume, Winter would rather wait 10 years to get that one good copy rather than continuously upgrade. He would love to have a high grade copy of *The Evil Dead* to get signed by Bruce Campbell and other cast members, who frequently attend horror and comic conventions.

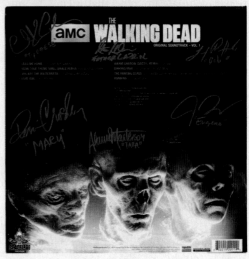

Not only does he enjoy talking music with the people who sign his records, Winter said he also likes finding hidden gems in a variety of ways. One of his favorite spots is Iko's, a music trade shop in York, Pennsylvania. For 25 years he has been frequenting the establishment, developing a friendship with the owner. He makes weekly visits to the store where the owner saves things he thinks Winter will want. The store only deals in trading high grade pieces, giving him piece of mind that the quality will be of the highest caliber.

In addition to Iko's, he also attends records shows where thousands of albums are available for consumption. He also purchases some online, though he is very particular because he believes records should be bought in person.

"Record collectors in general prefer to see a record in person. That way they can inspect the jacket, inner sleeve and inserts and the surface of the record itself. Defects do not always show up in photos, so buying online this way can be an issue. Much also has to do with the pressing and its unique identifying marks, which is also something that is best confirmed by an in-person inspection," he said.

With such a vast collection, Winter displays some of his soundtracks and other records, both at work and at home.

Displayed records are all placed in 12" x 12" frames. On his office wall are the soundtracks for *Hellraiser 2*, *Willy Wonka & the Chocolate Factory*, *A Clockwork Orange*, and *Freddy's Greatest Hits* with music from the *Nightmare on Elm Street* franchise – all signed by various cast members. At home he displays soundtracks for *Easy Rider*, *Ultraman*, *Children of the Corn*, *Weird Science*, and *Godzilla*.

His many other records are stored safely in wood cases of 12" x 12" cubicles. Each record is standing upright, the correct way to store records, as Winter describes it. This will keep records from warping due to excessive weight of other records when incorrectly stacked horizontally.

The soundtrack portion of his collection

is only a part of his larger music collection. He also collects other movie memorabilia, such as posters and promotional items. His Blaxploitation memorabilia is among his favorite movie collectibles, as those films truly embraced the use of great music by the likes of James Brown, Isaac Hayes, Curtis Mayfield, and many others. His music collection includes posters, autographs, promotional material, anything that relates to any band or album he likes is fair game, and pinback buttons which is a small sidebar of his collection. As far as the records go, it is about 90% LPs with a nice selection of 45 and 78 rpm singles as well as picture discs.

In total, Winter's music collection comprises about 10,000 pieces. Along with vinyl, he has cassette tapes, 8-track tapes, CDs, and reel to reel tapes. With about 500 soundtracks included, he has amassed quite a collection. But, as Winter puts it, "There's always more to find."

Directory Listings

Archangels
4629 Cass Street Suite #9
Pacific Beach, CA 92109
RHughes@Archangels.com
Archangels.com

CGC
P.O. Box 4738
Sarasota, FL 34230
PH: (877) NM-COMIC
FAX: (941) 360-2558
www.CGCcomics.com

ComicWow!
www.ComicWow.com

Ralph DeLuca
157 Park Ave.
Madison, NJ 07940
PH: 800-392-4050 toll free
PH: 973-377-1007 outside USA
FAX: 973-377-4020
ralph@ralphdeluca.com
www.ralphdeluca.com

Diamond Comic Distributors
10150 York Rd.
Suite 300
Hunt Valley, MD 21030
PH: 443-318-8001

Diamond International Galleries
1940 Greenspring Drive
Suite I
Timonium, MD 21093
GalleryQuestions@DiamondGalleries.com
www.DiamondGalleries.com

Stephen A. Geppi
10150 York Rd., Suite 300
Hunt Valley, MD 21030
PH: 443-318-8203
gsteve@diamondcomics.com

Geppi's Entertainment Museum
301 West Camden Street
Baltimore, MD 21201
PH: 410-625-7089
FAX: 410-625-7090
www.geppismuseum.com

E. Gerber Products
1720 Belmont Ave., Suite C
Baltimore, MD 21244
PH: 888-79-MYLAR

Hake's Americana
P.O. Box 12001
York, PA 17402
PH: 866-404-9800
www.hakes.com

Heritage Auctions
3500 Maple Avenue
17th Floor
Dallas, TX 75219-3941
PH: 800-872-6467
www.HA.com

Movie Poster Works
Charles R. Stevens
P.O. Box 40099
Houston, TX 77240
PH: 832-674-8124
info@movieposterworks.com

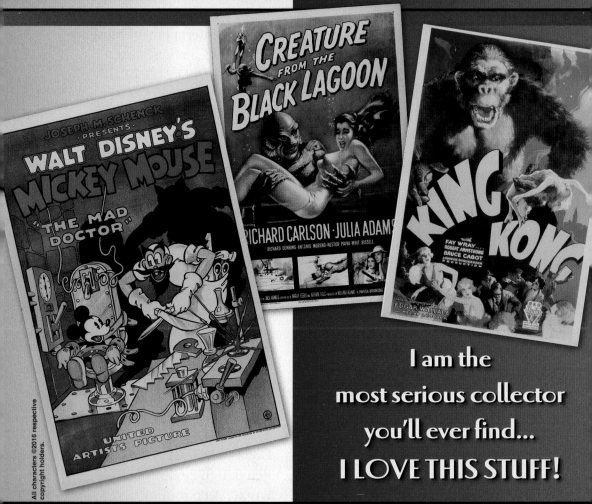